LIVING GOD'S WORD

YEAR C

DAVID KNIGHT

LIVING GOD'S WORD

Reflections on the Weekly Gospels

YEAR C

ST. ANTHONY MESSENGER PRESS

Cincinnati, Ohio

Cover design and illustrations by Karla Ann Sheppard
Book design by Mary Alfieri

ISBN 0-86716-308-9

Published by St. Anthony Messenger Press
www.AmericanCatholic.org
Printed in the U.S.A.

Contents

Lent

Easter Triduum and Easter

Ordinary Time (Ninth Sunday of the Year
Through Thirty-Fourth Sunday of the Year)

Solemnities of the Lord During the Season of the Year

Other Solemnities and Feasts Which Replace Sunday

Feasts and Saints' Days

LITURGICAL CALENDAR

Liturgical Calendar

	1999 (A)	2000 (B)	2001(C)
1st Sunday of Advent	11/29/98	11/28/99	12/3/00
2nd Sunday of Advent	12/6/98	12/5/99	12/10/00
3rd Sunday of Advent	12/13/98	12/12/99	12/17/00
4th Sunday of Advent	12/20/98	12/19/99	12/24/00
Christmas	12/25/98	12/25/99	12/25/00
Holy Family	12/27/98	12/26/99	12/31/00
Octave of Christmas	1/1/99	1/1/00	1/1/01
Epiphany	1/3/99	1/2/00	1/7/01
Baptism of the Lord	1/10/99	1/9/00	1/8/01**
2nd Sunday of the Year	1/17/99	1/16/00	1/14/01
3rd Sunday of the Year	1/24/99	1/23/00	1/21/01
4th Sunday of the Year	1/31/99	1/30/00	1/28/01
5th Sunday of the Year	2/7/99	2/6/00	2/4/01
6th Sunday of the Year	2/14/99	2/13/00	2/11/01
7th Sunday of the Year	——	2/20/00	2/18/01
8th Sunday of the Year	——	2/27/00*	2/25/01
Ash Wednesday	2/17/99	3/8/00	2/28/01
First Sunday of Lent	2/21/99	3/12/00	3/4/01
Second Sunday of Lent	2/28/99	3/19/00	3/11/01
Third Sunday of Lent	3/7/99	3/26/00	3/18/01
Fourth Sunday of Lent	3/14/99	4/2/00	3/25/01
Fifth Sunday of Lent	3/21/99	4/9/00	4/1/01
Palm/Passion Sunday	3/28/99	4/16/00	4/8/01
Easter	4/4/99	4/23/00	4/15/01
Second Sunday of Easter	4/11/99	4/30/00	4/22/01
Third Sunday of Easter	4/18/99	5/7/00	4/29/01
Fourth Sunday of Easter	4/25/99	5/14/00	5/6/01
Fifth Sunday of Easter	5/2/99	5/21/00	5/13/01
Sixth Sunday of Easter	5/9/99	5/28/00	5/20/01
Ascension (Thursday)	5/13/99	6/1/00	5/24/01
Seventh Sunday of Easter	5/16/99	6/4/00	5/27/01
Pentecost	5/23/99	6/11/00	6/3/01

2002 (A)	2003 (B)	2004 (C)	2005 (A)	2006 (B)	2007 (C)
12/2/01	12/1/02	11/30/03	11/28/04	11/27/05	12/3/06
12/9/01	12/8/02	12/7/03	12/5/04	12/4/05	12/10/06
12/16/01	12/15/02	12/14/03	12/12/04	12/11/05	12/17/06
12/23/01	12/22/02	12/21/03	12/19/04	12/18/05	12/24/06
12/25/01	12/25/02	12/25/03	12/25/04	12/25/05	12/25/06
12/30/01	12/29/02	12/28/03	12/26/04	12/30/05	12/31/06
1/1/02	1/1/03	1/1/04	1/1/05	1/1/06	1/1/07
1/6/02	1/5/03	1/4/04	1/2/05	1/8/06	1/7/07
1/13/02	1/12/03	1/11/04	1/9/05	1/9/06**	1/8/07**
1/20/02	1/19/03	1/18/04	1/16/05	1/15/06	1/14/07
1/27/02	1/26/03	1/25/04	1/23/05	1/22/06	1/21/07
2/3/02	2/2/03	2/1/04	1/30/05	1/29/06	1/28/07
2/10/02	2/9/03	2/8/04	2/6/05	2/5/06	2/4/07
——	2/16/03	2/15/04	——	2/12/06	2/11/07
——	2/23/03	2/22/04	——	2/19/06	2/18/07
——	3/2/03	——	——	2/26/06	——
2/13/02	3/5/03	2/25/04	2/9/05	3/1/06	2/21/07
2/17/02	3/9/03	2/29/04	2/13/05	3/5/06	2/25/07
2/24/02	3/16/03	3/7/04	2/20/05	3/12/06	3/4/07
3/3/02	3/23/03	3/14/04	2/27/05	3/19/06	3/11/07
3/10/02	3/30/03	3/21/04	3/6/05	3/26/06	3/18/07
3/17/02	4/6/03	3/28/04	3/13/05	4/2/06	3/25/07
3/24/02	4/13/03	4/4/04	3/20/05	4/9/06	4/1/07
3/31/02	4/20/03	4/11/04	3/27/05	4/16/06	4/8/07
4/7/02	4/27/03	4/18/04	4/3/05	4/23/06	4/15/07
4/14/02	5/4/03	4/25/04	4/10/05	4/30/06	4/22/07
4/21/02	5/11/03	5/2/04	4/17/05	5/7/06	4/29/07
4/28/02	5/18/03	5/9/04	4/24/05	5/14/06	5/6/07
5/5/02	5/25/03	5/16/04	5/1/05	5/21/06	5/13/07
5/9/02	5/29/03	5/20/04	5/5/05	5/25/06	5/17/07
5/12/02	6/1/03	5/23/04	5/8/05	5/28/06	5/20/07
5/19/02	6/8/03	5/30/04	5/15/05	6/4/06	5/27/07

Feast of the Holy Family falls on Friday, December 30, 2005.
** Baptism of the Lord moves to Monday in these years.
* 9th Week of the Year precedes Ash Wednesday in 2000.

Liturgical Calendar

	1999 (A)	2000 (B)	2001(C)
Week of the Year	8th	10th	9th
Trinity Sunday	5/30/99	6/18/00	6/10/01
Week of the Year	9th	11th	10th
Body and Blood of Christ	6/6/99	6/25/00	6/17/01
Week of the Year	10th	12th	11th
Sacred Heart (Friday)	6/11/99	6/30/00	6/22/01
9th Sunday of the Year	——	3/5/00	——
10th Sunday of the Year	——	——	——
11th Sunday of the Year	6/13/99	——	——
12th Sunday of the Year	6/20/99	——	6/24/01
13th Sunday of the Year	6/27/99	7/2/00	7/1/01
14th Sunday of the Year	7/4/99	7/9/00	7/8/01
15th Sunday of the Year	7/11/99	7/16/00	7/15/01
16th Sunday of the Year	7/18/99	7/23/00	7/22/01
17th Sunday of the Year	7/25/99	7/30/00	7/29/01
18th Sunday of the Year	8/1/99	8/6/00	8/5/01
19th Sunday of the Year	8/8/99	8/13/00	8/12/01
20th Sunday of the Year	8/15/99	8/20/00	8/19/01
21st Sunday of the Year	8/22/99	8/27/00	8/26/01
22nd Sunday of the Year	8/29/99	9/3/00	9/2/01
23rd Sunday of the Year	9/5/99	9/10/00	9/9/01
24th Sunday of the Year	9/12/99	9/17/00	9/16/01
25th Sunday of the Year	9/19/99	9/24/00	9/23/01
26th Sunday of the Year	9/26/99	10/1/00	9/30/01
27th Sunday of the Year	10/3/99	10/8/00	10/7/01
28th Sunday of the Year	10/10/99	10/15/00	10/14/01
29th Sunday of the Year	10/17/99	10/22/00	10/21/01
30th Sunday of the Year	10/24/99	10/29/00	10/28/01
31st Sunday of the Year	10/31/99	11/5/00	11/4/01
32nd Sunday of the Year	11/7/99	11/12/00	11/11/01
33rd Sunday of the Year	11/14/99	11/19/00	11/18/01
Christ the King	11/21/99	11/26/00	11/25/01

2002 (A)	2003 (B)	2004 (C)	2005 (A)	2006 (B)	2007 (C)
7th	10th	9th	7th	9th	8th
5/26/02	6/15/03	6/6/04	5/22/05	6/11/06	6/3/07
8th	11th	10th	8th	10th	9th
6/2/02	6/22/03	6/13/04	5/29/05	6/18/06	6/10/07
9th	12th	11th	9th	11th	10th
6/7/02	6/27/03	6/18/04	6/3/05	6/23/06	6/15/07
——	——	——	——	——	——
6/9/02	——	——	6/5/05	——	——
6/16/02	——	——	6/12/05	——	6/17/07
6/23/02	——	6/20/04	6/19/05	6/25/06	6/24/07
6/30/02	6/29/03	6/27/04	6/26/05	7/2/06	7/1/07
7/7/02	7/6/03	7/4/04	7/3/05	7/9/06	7/8/07
7/14/02	7/13/03	7/11/04	7/10/05	7/16/06	7/15/07
7/21/02	7/20/03	7/18/04	7/17/05	7/23/06	7/22/07
7/28/02	7/27/03	7/25/04	7/24/05	7/30/06	7/29/07
8/4/02	8/3/03	8/1/04	7/31/05	8/6/06	8/5/07
8/11/02	8/10/03	8/8/04	8/7/05	8/13/06	8/12/07
8/18/02	8/17/03	8/15/04	8/14/05	8/20/06	8/19/07
8/25/02	8/24/03	8/22/04	8/21/05	8/27/06	8/26/07
9/1/02	8/31/03	8/29/04	8/28/05	9/3/06	9/2/07
9/8/02	9/7/03	9/5/04	9/4/05	9/10/06	9/9/07
9/15/02	9/14/03	9/12/04	9/11/05	9/17/06	9/16/07
9/22/02	9/21/03	9/19/04	9/18/05	9/24/06	9/23/07
9/29/02	9/28/03	9/26/04	9/25/05	10/1/06	9/30/07
10/6/02	10/5/03	10/3/04	10/2/05	10/8/06	10/7/07
10/13/02	10/12/03	10/10/04	10/9/05	10/15/06	10/14/07
10/20/02	10/19/03	10/17/04	10/16/05	10/22/06	10/21/07
10/27/02	10/26/03	10/24/04	10/23/05	10/29/06	10/28/07
11/3/02	11/2/03	10/31/04	10/30/05	11/5/06	11/4/07
11/10/02	11/9/03	11/7/04	11/6/05	11/12/06	11/11/07
11/17/02	11/16/03	11/14/04	11/13/05	11/19/06	11/18/07
11/24/02	11/23/03	11/21/04	11/20/05	11/26/06	11/25/07

Introduction

*"By means of sacred scripture, read during the
liturgy of the word and explained during the homily,
'God speaks to his people, revealing the mystery of
their redemption and salvation and offering them
spiritual nourishment. Through his word, Christ
himself is present in the assembly of his people.'
Thus the Church at Mass 'receives the bread of life
from the table of God's word and unceasingly offers
it to the faithful.'"*[1]

There is mystery to ponder in these lines from the
Introduction to the *Lectionary for Mass.* But, in
practice, listening to the readings at Sunday Mass can
be frustrating. We frequently do not understand them. And
the more we do understand, the more we would like time to
reflect on them and absorb them—time not provided during
Mass. We are left feeling incomplete.

This is not only frustrating; it is dangerous. If our only
exposure to Scripture is at Sunday Mass and if we do not
understand what we hear, we will conclude, as many
Catholics have, that we "just don't understand" the Bible.
The obvious answer to this—"How can you understand it if
you don't read it?"—is countered by, "I hear it on Sundays,
and I don't understand it." So the danger is that we will not
ever begin reading the Bible because our experience of it at
Sunday Mass has been uninspiring or even frustrating.

This book will not change all of that, but it can help.

Typically, the liturgy includes four biblical passages
on Sunday. A Gospel passage is the centerpiece; preceding
it are a reading from the Old Testament, a psalm prayed or
sung as a response and a passage from another of the New
Testament writings.

This book will tell you what the readings are so that each

week, if you desire, you can look them over ahead of time, see the context in which they are found, call someone you know to ask about anything you don't understand, and come to Mass on Sunday prepared to sit back, enjoy and absorb what you hear.

I have been publishing weekly reflections like these in my Sunday bulletin for ten years. I began writing them because I remembered telling someone the year I graduated from high school that I could not remember one homily that had been preached in my parish church my whole life long. (In those days they were called sermons.) My experience was that, even if what was said in church inspired me momentarily, I never thought about it again once Mass was over. As a result, any seed planted in my mind died before it had a chance to root itself in my heart through decisions. The fault was not in the preacher; it was in the fact that I never took time to think about what I had heard.

I began publishing in the parish bulletin the main thoughts of my homilies in the hope that someone might read and reflect on them. And the feedback from the people was very good. Several told me they were sticking the bulletin on their refrigerator door and using it for meditation all during the week, especially the reflections on the daily readings.

All the reflections in these pages are based on the Gospel of the particular Sunday or weekday. I frequently approach the Gospel asking what light it casts on a particular question. For example, I might ask for several weeks in a row what the Gospel for the Sunday tells us about Baptism or another sacrament. When I do this, my concern is to find what there is in the reading itself, in its true meaning and interpretation, that relates to the topic at hand. The reflections are homilies; that is, reflections on the Scripture readings themselves, not sermons that develop topics for their own sake. But I have found that to approach any passage of Scripture with a question drawn from one's present concerns or experience of life is a way to discover in the text rich veins of meaning previously unmined.

How to Use This Book

I suggest that you read the reflection on the Sunday Gospel first. Ask yourself what this Gospel or this reflection says to you, what meaning it has for you. Then ask yourself what you intend to do about it.

In the section entitled "Living This Week's Gospels," I offer for each week five suggested responses you can make to the Gospel. These are based on five words which summarize our identity as Christians. Every one of us is a Christian by belief in Jesus Christ as Savior. And every one of us is called to be a disciple, which means to lead a life characterized by reflection on the teaching and example of Jesus, the Master of the Way.

In addition, at Baptism each of us was anointed with chrism and consecrated by God to continue Jesus' work as Prophet, Priest and King. These three words give us our job description as Christians.

Each week therefore offers a suggestion about how to express and live out our belief in Jesus as Savior and as Teacher (being a Christian and a disciple); how to bear witness to him in action (being a prophet); how to minister to others and nurture them (sharing in his priesthood); and how to work for the extension of his reign over every area and activity of human life (being responsible stewards of his kingship). No one could possibly live out all of these suggestions all the time, but you might try each one for a day. Or pick one and work at it all week.

For each day of the week I have chosen one line from the day's Gospel and offered one question to stimulate reflection. The ideal, of course, would be to read the whole Gospel passage for yourself—or, if your schedule permits, go to daily Mass and get it live! But in today's busy world, you may have only time to read one line and to think about one question whenever you can during the day.

Finally, there is a prayer that you can say each day all week, asking for the grace to live by the values proposed in the Sunday reflection. Repeated prayer increases desire.

Drawing People Together

Christian discipleship is both personal and communal. We grow in grace together. We nourish our hearts while we nourish the hearts of others. And so you could use this book to draw closer to others in the communion of the Holy Spirit while you yourself draw closer to God.

Invite someone to read the reflections with you and talk about them. Ask such questions as, "What does this say to you? How do you feel about it? What do you think you could do in response to it?" If you do this with family or close friends, it will raise the level of your interaction and deepen your understanding of each other. If you invite acquaintances, you will turn them into friends.

The Sunday Readings

The Sunday readings are presented in a three-year cycle (Years A, B and C). Over the course of the three years we hear the main sections of all four Gospels: Matthew in Year A, Mark in Year B, Luke in Year C (this volume). (Matthew, Mark and Luke are called the *Synoptics*, "seen as a whole," because they follow the same basic outline of Jesus' life and death. John's Gospel, written later, reflects on the *meaning* of Jesus' life and death.) In Year B, instead of Mark's version of the multiplication of the loaves, the liturgy inserts John's, along with its following teaching about the Bread of Life.

The Old Testament readings for Sundays were chosen individually because they relate in some way to the theme of the Gospel. They are presented as isolated passages, not book by book. There is no sequence or pattern in the order in which the books from the Old Testament appear. What we should be alert to, therefore, is the unity between the Old and New Testament readings, which becomes visible to us when we see how events or themes in both of them are related to each other.

The selections from other New Testament writings (Acts, the Letters and the Book of Revelation) are read "semicontinuously," that is, the main passages from one letter or book are presented sequentially. Because the readings from each book are presented as a block, it is possible to study each one as a whole during the period when selections from it are being read at Mass.

The Sunday and weekday liturgies together expose us to 128 of the 150 Psalms. The verses we use as responsorial chants are chosen to be responses to the readings they follow.

The Weekday Readings

The weekday readings are not geared to match the Sunday readings at all; they are a completely independent selection. Instead of an ABC cycle, there is a two-year cycle for the weekday readings (Year I and Year II). Only the first reading changes; the weekday Gospels are the same every year. To help us easily remember what year we are in, an odd-numbered year (like 1997, 1999) will always be Year I; Year II will always be a number divisible by two (1998, 2000).

During the Season of the Year or Ordinary Time, the weekday Gospels begin with the first one to be written, Mark (Weeks 1-9), and go straight through selected passages from Matthew (Weeks 10-21) and Luke (Weeks 22-34). Daily participation in the Eucharist gives us a tour of these three Gospels (the Synoptics) every year.

About half the selections for the first reading on weekdays come from the Old Testament. There is no precise order in the way the books are presented—Old and New Testament readings are interspersed during the year with no obvious guiding pattern—but, with a few exceptions all the readings from each book will be given consecutively. We can therefore study each book in turn while selections from it are read at Mass. In a given year, the Old Testament books are presented approximately in the order in which they were written. All of the Old Testament books except Obadiah and Judith and all of the New Testament books are represented in the readings.

During special seasons (Advent, Christmas, Lent and Easter) the themes of the season determine the choice of readings.

Special feasts and saints' days also have their own readings, which replace the weekday and sometimes the Sunday readings. Reflections for these special feasts are in a section of their own.

A liturgical calendar or church bulletin will aid tremendously in helping to match the date with the corresponding reflection. (See page x.)

"A Fountain of Renewal"

The introduction to the Roman *Lectionary for Mass* begins:

> The Church loves sacred scripture and is anxious to deepen its understanding of the truth and to nourish its own life by studying these sacred writings. The Second Vatican Council likened the bible to a fountain of renewal within the community of God's people and directed that in the revision of liturgical celebrations there should be "more abundant, varied and appropriate reading from sacred scripture." The council further directed that at Mass "the treasures of the bible should be opened up more lavishly so that richer fare might be provided for the faithful at the table of God's word. In this way a more representative portion of sacred scripture will be read to the people over a set cycle of years."[2]

That is the motive and prayer behind the writing of this book.

Notes

[1] Introduction, #1, *Lectionary for Mass*, copyright © 1970 by International Commission on English in the Liturgy. Used with permission.

[2] Ibid.

ADVENT
SEASON

Jesus Is the Way to Meaning in Life

Luke 21:25-28, 34-36; Jeremiah 33: 14-16;
1 Thessalonians 3:12—4:2

W hat is so terrifying about the second coming of Jesus? It should not be the actual fact of his coming, because this Gospel tells us to "hold our heads high" when he comes, because our "deliverance is at hand." For those who believe in him and love him, Jesus comes as the Bridegroom to the bride; as the fulfillment of all our human hopes and expectations.

The Gospel says people will "die of fright in anticipation": not of what is coming to the earth (Jesus), but of what is coming upon the earth; that is, "signs in the sun, the moon, and the stars," signs that the heavens and the earth are passing away (verse 33).

This is what is frightening to us: the prospect of everything we are used to, everything we take for granted— the very ground we walk on and the air we breathe—just ceasing to exist. It seems to take the security out of life.

It isn't just that our own lives are going to end. The end of the world has something about it that is more frightening than even our own, individual death. When we die, our time on earth is over. But when the end of the world comes, everything we lived and worked for, everything that gave meaning and value to our lives on earth, is over, just as if it had never begun. Then, not only has our time on earth come to an end, but everything we have accomplished just drops into nothingness. The very prospect of this seems to pull the rug out from under us before we even get out of bed in the morning. Unless...

Unless the coming of Jesus brings everything we have lived and worked for to fulfillment. The key question is,

"What are we working for? What is it that gives meaning and value to our lives? What are we hoping to accomplish during our time on earth?"

If we are shortsighted in our goals—that is, if we look at nothing beyond what we do to enhance human life on this planet, then the end of the world really is a canceling out of all we have accomplished. But if our goal has been to bring all people and events under the reign of God, to prepare the world to receive him as Lover and Lord, then his coming brings all our work to completion.

This Gospel presents Jesus to us, not just as the Savior of our souls, but also as the Savior of all we do on earth. He saves the meaning and value of our efforts during life by giving them significance for all eternity—provided that in everything we do we labor as true stewards of the kingship of Christ.

This is why the Gospel warns us not to let our "spirits become bloated." Our spirits are bloated when our minds and hearts (not just our bodies) are stuffed with concern for the things of this world. If we just live for ourselves ("indulgence"); or if life is so empty for us that we basically live for distractions ("drunkenness," including any escapist addiction—for example, to television); or if we are so shortsighted that we actually are excited about "worldly cares"—success, status and having sway over people and events—then the end of the world really will "close in on us like a trap." We will realize that all our lives long we had been lured by the bait of immediacy into the trap of inanity.

Jesus came to save us from this. When we recognize him as the goal of all human history, it gives us something to focus on when we seek direction in our lives and guidance in our choices. If we understand what life itself is supposed to lead to, we can make each step we take count for something. Then the end of the world will be for us a finale.

Reflecting on This Week's Gospels

First Week of Advent

Pray daily: Lord, I believe that you came to make all things count. Teach me to work for your kingdom so that everything I do and say will count forever. Lord, be the Savior of my time. Amen.

Monday: Matthew 8:5-11: The centurion said in reply, "Lord, I am not worthy to have you come under my roof; but only speak the word, and my servant will be healed." When Jesus comes into your heart in Communion, do you appreciate what he comes to do?

Tuesday: Luke 10:21-24: To his disciples Jesus said, "Blessed are the eyes that see what you see! ...[M]any prophets and kings desired to see what you see, but did not see it...." How does knowing Jesus make your life more exciting? How could knowing Jesus better make it even more exciting?

Wednesday: Matthew 15:29-37: The disciples said to Jesus, "Where are we to get enough bread in the desert to feed so great a crowd?" Jesus said to them, "How many loaves have you?" "Seven," they replied, "and a few small fish." How often do you ask Jesus what you can do to satisfy the needs of others? What do you have that he can use and multiply?

Thursday: Matthew 7:21, 24-27: "Not everyone who says to me, 'Lord, Lord,' will enter the kingdom of heaven, but only the one who does the will of my Father in heaven." When you hear or read the words of God, how much are you thinking about putting them into action? Do you give yourself any time in the day to reflect and come to some decisions about what you have heard? (For example, what have you done about what you heard last Sunday?)

Friday: Matthew 9:27-31: The blind men approached and Jesus said to them, "Do you believe that I am able to do this [heal you]?" What do you really believe Jesus can heal or change in you if you keep asking him? What do you need to do on your part?

Saturday: Matthew 9:35 to 10:1, 6-8: "The harvest is plentiful, but the laborers are few; therefore ask the Lord of the harvest to send out laborers into his harvest." What are you doing to establish the reign of God? What are you doing that means more to you than that? Are you conscious of working for Jesus in everything you do?

Living This Week's Gospels

As Christian: Write out what you would like your time on earth to contribute to life on this planet.

As Disciple: Read Ephesians, chapter 1, verses 1-14. Ask how God's plan has been realized in your life and how you are helping to bring it about.

As Prophet: For one week wear your watch on your other arm to remind you, every time you look at it, to think about the eternal significance of what you are doing.

As Priest: Each day this week, do one thing which is a conscious choice to give love for people priority over lesser things in your life.

As King: Sit down and write out an account of your stewardship. How have you worked to establish the reign of God on earth? If this were the last day of your life, how would you like to have worked?

Jesus Is the Way to Deliverance From Sin

Luke 3:1-6; Baruch 5:1-9; Philippians 1:4-6, 8-11

L uke's Gospel leaves no doubt that Jesus was a real human being born into the real world. Although as God he existed from all eternity, as a human being he was born into a particular culture at a particular time: "in the fifteenth year of the reign of Emperor Tiberius, when Pontius Pilate was governor of Judea...." Like the rest of us, Jesus was a man of his times.

Well, yes and no. Yes, the Gospel makes it clear that Jesus was born into the world as it was in the fifteenth year of the rule of Tiberius Caesar, not the fourteenth or the sixteenth, and when Pontius Pilate, not someone else, was procurator of Judea. That was the year that was. And that was the world with which Jesus began to interact the minute he was born. Like us, he was born into a particular culture and it affected him.

But there is a difference. Jesus came into the darkness of his particular culture and the darkness could not overcome him (see John 1:3). You and I are born into the light and darkness of our particular culture, and right away our attitudes and values begin to be shaped by our environment. We grow up programmed to ways of thinking both true and false. Our values and priorities, though very good in some ways, are also distorted. Before we are old enough to know what we are doing, or even to be guilty, we pick up some patterns of behavior from our culture that are destructive. The light we live by comes to us through the filter of our culture, our environment, and it is shaded with darkness.

This is a result of original sin. The first sin committed on earth put something into the environment that has never gone away, and so does every sin. Every action we commit, good or bad, does something to the human environment of this earth that affects the lives of every other person born into it. The world is like a living room: Whatever you leave there changes things for everybody else.

Like us, Jesus was affected by his environment, even formed by it in his human psychology and temperament. Any Jew of his times could have identified him as a country boy from Galilee, and anyone from Nazareth would have recognized in his personality a special way of laughing, speaking or reacting in certain situations that were the family traits of Mary and Joseph—just as people recognize our family traits in us.

The difference is that Jesus was not in any way wounded by his culture as we are. He did not absorb any false attitudes or values. The light he lived by was not just a light filtered through his environment: he was the light of the world. He came into this world to deliver it from the darkness caused by centuries of destructive behavior and distorted education. Being born into this world did not put him in need of salvation; he came to be the Savior. Although his human personality, his psychology and experience of life were greatly determined by his culture, his deepest person was not. The person of Jesus was the Second Person of the Blessed Trinity. His light, his truth, came from within, from all eternity.

The "sin" Jesus delivers us from is not just the guilt of our personal, free acts. He also delivers us from the distorted attitudes and values that set us up to sin. He frees us from the programming of our cultural conditioning. The "Baptism of repentance" John preached was not just regret for guilty acts; it was a Baptism of commitment to set our feet on a whole new path, to follow a radically new direction in life, one that leads not to destructiveness, distortion, mediocrity and meaninglessness, but to life.

Jesus came, not just to pick us up after our falls, but to give us a "straight path." If we accept him as the Savior who delivers us from sin, we need to commit ourselves to interact with him until our attitudes and values are re-formed. This takes time.

Reflecting on This Week's Gospels

Second Week of Advent

Pray daily: Lord, I believe in your power to deliver me, not just from guilt, but from all the power of sin in my environment. I want you to be my Savior. I ask you to work with me and within me to change my attitudes and values, to redirect my life.

Monday: Luke 5:17-26: "[B]ut finding no way to bring him in because of the crowd, they went up on the roof and let him down with his bed through the tiles into the middle of the crowd in front of Jesus." What obstacles are you willing to overcome in order to participate in programs, retreats and the like that allow you to enter into a deeper relationship with Jesus?

Tuesday: Matthew 18:12-14: "So it is not the will of your Father in heaven that one of these little ones should be lost." What do you see confirming people around you in false attitudes or values? Is God grateful when you make efforts to change these ways of acting or speaking?

Wednesday: Matthew 11:28-30: "Come to me, all you that are weary and are carrying heavy burdens, and I will give you rest." When you see people feeling any kind of distress, do you think about what you can do to relieve them? Do you think about what Jesus can do and wants to do for them?

Thursday: Matthew 11:11-15: "From the days of John the Baptist until now the kingdom of heaven has suffered violence, and the violent take it by force." How aware are you that Jesus and your culture are in a daily battle for control of your attitudes and values? Whose side are you on? How do you show this?

Friday: Matthew 11:16-19: "[T]o what will I compare this generation? It is like children sitting in marketplaces and calling to one another, 'We played the flute for you, and you did not dance, we wailed, and you did not mourn.'" Do you ever let the way God's grace is offered to you or the particular characteristics of the person who is ministering block you from responding to Jesus himself?

Saturday: Matthew 17:10-13: "I tell you that Elijah has already come, and they did not recognize him, but did to him whatever they pleased. So also the Son of Man is about to suffer at their hands." Would you find it easier to believe in a Savior who gave obvious signs of power and success? Why doesn't Jesus use force and fear to convert us?

Living This Week's Gospels

As Christian: Each day this week renew your Baptismal commitment by saying, "I reject Satan, and all his works, and all his empty promises."

As Disciple: Read Romans, chapter 1, verses 28 to 32. See how many of these characteristics you can find embodied in the concrete expression given to attitudes and values in your environment.

As Prophet: Change one way of thinking or acting which you take for granted. Find it by asking what in your life does not bear positive witness to the attitudes and values of Christ.

As Priest: Put the people you live or work with under one of three columns labeled: "Like," "Dislike," "Indifferent." See what you can do to express love in some concrete way for the people you dislike or feel indifferent toward.

As King: Notice what you see and hear around you: advertisements, slogans on tee shirts, comments made, music played and so on. Mark each one in your mind as scoring points for Christ's way of light or the devil's way of darkness. See if you can change anything.

December 8 • Immaculate Conception

A Sign of God's Mercy

Luke 1:26-38; Genesis 3:9-15, 20; Ephesians 1:3-6, 11-12

Mary's Immaculate Conception is a key to understanding God's mercy to us. To "have mercy" is not just to help someone; it is to come to the aid of another out of a sense of relationship. To give aid to panhandlers on the street, for example, while seeing them as "winos," or simply as "them" rather than as "us," is not mercy; it is condescension—especially if we write them off as hopeless wrecks from whom nothing can really be expected.

If a recovering alcoholic who used to beg on the street—someone who has "been there"—offers help to one who is still there, that is very different. That is to have mercy; it comes from a sense of relationship.

If God had saved us purely "from above"—without involving human nature in the work of redemption at all—that actually would have shown contempt for human nature. It would have been God's admission that the humanity he created was hopelessly flawed, and could only be saved as inert matter, by the unassisted action of God alone. And this was, as a matter of fact, an underlying theme in the Protestant reformers who taught that human nature is so corrupt that none of the good actions a person performs, even by the help of God's grace, can truly be called the work of a human being. Martin Luther taught that we are saved "by the grace of God alone and the sole working of the Holy Spirit, without any human action." This position is rooted in the belief that no good work a human being does can be attributed to that person at all; the goodness of the action is due one hundred percent to God alone. Those who think like this conclude quite naturally that to honor Mary, the saints, or any human being for good deeds performed in grace is to rob God of glory by glorifying a creature.

Catholics, on the other hand, insist on the basic goodness of human nature. A modern Protestant theologian, Karl Barth, sees devotion to Mary as the key to this Catholic belief: "It is in Marian doctrine...that the heresy of the Roman Catholic Church is apparent.... The "Mother of God" of...Catholic dogma is, quite simply, the principle, prototype and summing-up of the human creature co-operating in its own salvation.... Thus, that Church in which there is a cult of Mary must be itself understood as...that Church of man who, by virtue of grace, cooperates with grace."

Catholics would say, "Yes, what is the problem?" This is because Catholics were never taught that human beings are so incapable of anything good that they can't even cooperate with God by freely accepting the gift of grace. Catholics honor Mary for accepting to be the Mother of God, and honor the Saints and all people for accepting and using the graces they are given to do the beautiful things they do. We say that when the Saints are the glory of God, because they show the triumph of Christ's death over sin. The proof that Jesus really did win is that we are actually healed and restored, made holy by grace inside and out.

The Immaculate Conception requires us to believe that human beings have a part to play in redeeming the world. God became a man by taking real human flesh from a real human being. That is why Jesus is truly one of us. And that is the mystery of the way God "has mercy" on us: he comes to our aid as one of us. The Lord, the Christ we ask to "have mercy," comes to our aid out of a sense of relationship based on sharing our humanity.

And this is the reason why Mary, from the first instant of her conception in her mother's womb, had to be preserved from all sin: It was so that the flesh she gave to be the flesh of God, the flesh which would save the world from sin, would never itself have been under the power of sin. Because of the Immaculate Conception, God could take pure flesh from Mary and "have mercy" on us as one of our own race. Every time we pray "Lord, have mercy," we thank God for the gift of the Immaculate Conception which is a sign to us of what that mercy is.

Third Sunday of Advent

Jesus Is the Way
to the Fullness of Life

Luke 3:10-18; Zephaniah 3:14-18; Philippians 4:4-7

What John the Baptizer proclaimed about Jesus is such good news that now, two thousand years later, people are still missing the point. At least, they are missing it in practice.

We all know that John the Baptizer was just a human being, and that Jesus is God. But in practice, most of us live Christianity as if Jesus preached nothing more exalted than John did.

What John preached was pretty strong morality. He went to the heart of what keeps people in real life from obeying the law of God. To each group of people who asked him, "What should we do?" he pointed out the temptation that was, in their occupation, the hardest to overcome. He told the soldiers of an occupying army not to abuse their power: not to push people around or extort money from them by threatening arrest. He told the tax collectors who lived by graft not to take any more money than was fixed by law. And to people in general he said, "If you have two coats, give one to the poor. Do the same with food." He struck at the heart of our basic instinct to survive: We provide the maximum for ourselves before we help others find the minimum; we give from our surplus, and "surplus" means what we no longer have a use for. But John says to give right down to our basic needs. If people lived by what John says here it would transform human life on earth.

But John himself said that he was nothing in comparison with Jesus. John was just a human being; Jesus is God. John offered a Baptism that was just a human gesture of repentance; Jesus gives us a Baptism that fills us with the

Holy Spirit. And where John urged us to the highest level of human morality, Jesus tells us that we must live on the level of God.

This is what we fail to understand. We still think Jesus just came to save us from those sins that everyone recognizes as "bad." We think that we are good Christians if we do nothing "wrong": If we are honest in our business dealings and nice to everyone we meet. For an enormous number of people, to be a "good citizen" or a "good American" is the same thing as being in practice "a good Christian."

To think this is to think that Jesus just came to save us from falling "below par," below the standard level of human behavior. In reality, Jesus is a Savior who came to call us to a whole new level of life: to a whole new set of fundamental attitudes and values, to a completely different goal in life than just surviving and enjoying ourselves on earth as best we can. Jesus calls us to live our human lives on the divine level of God himself: to see and choose and act as God himself does. Jesus calls us—and enables us—to be divine: to think divinely and act divinely in everything we do.

Unless we understand this, we misunderstand Jesus as Savior and we misunderstand salvation. We are not "saved" because we have turned away from sin. We have not experienced "salvation" just because we do not sin anymore. And we do not know Jesus as Savior until we experience him as saving us from something more than sin. To really accept Jesus as Savior we have to accept him as enabling us to live on the level of God—while we are living our human lives here on this earth.

To experience concretely what this means requires a lot of thought, a lot of prayer, a lot of practice. But a good way to begin is to do to others only what you would have God do to you. Speak to others only as you would have God speak to you. Love others as you would have God love you. It's a start.

Reflecting on This Week's Gospels

Third Week of Advent

Note: Omit these readings December 17 through December 24 and use those given in the Fourth Week of Advent.

Pray daily: Lord, in Baptism I gave you my body so that you might continue to live your life in me. Give me your Spirit so that I might live my life in you.

Monday: Matthew 21:23-27: Jesus said to them in reply, "I will also ask you one question.... Did the Baptism of John come from heaven, or was it of human origin?" Can you say without hesitation that the Church is of divine origin? How does knowing this help you?

Tuesday: Matthew 21:28-32: "John came to you in the way of righteousness, and you did not believe him; but tax collectors and prostitutes believed him." Do you know people converted from deep sin or disinterest in religion who are more zealous about bringing the faith to others than you are? Why does this sometimes happen, and what does it tell you?

Wednesday: Luke 7:18-23: "John summoned two of his disciples and sent them to the Lord to ask, "Are you the one who is to come, or are we to wait for another?" What are the signs of Jesus' action on earth today that tell you he is the promised Savior?

Thursday: Luke 7:24-30: "[A]mong those born of women, no one is greater than John; yet the least in the kingdom of God is greater than he." What does Baptism give to each one of us that is better than all the impressive things John the Baptizer did?

Friday: John 5:33-36: "I have a testimony greater than John's. The works that the Father has given me to complete, the very works that I am doing, testify on my behalf that the Father has sent me." What are the works of Jesus that accredit him as not just sent from God, but as the only Son of the Father?

Saturday: *See Readings for December 17-24.*

Living This Week's Gospels

As Christian: Put a small bottle of holy water beside your bed. (If getting holy water from Church will delay you, use ordinary water.) As soon as you wake up each morning make the Sign of the Cross with the water, consciously consecrating yourself to live out your Baptism that day, trying to do everything you do as the Body of Christ.

As Disciple: Read Saint Paul's descriptions of God's purpose and plan in creating the human race. Read Ephesians 1:1-14 one day and Colossians 1:24-29 the next day. Repeat the readings each day until you feel you have understood them.

As Prophet: Go through your room or house, asking how each item you see bears witness to the ideals and values of Jesus.

As Priest: Think of the five people you love most in the world. What are you doing to help each one grow to the fullness of life both human and divine?

As King: Examine the goals you pursue in your family life, social life, professional or student life, civic life. Can you see how each goal contributes to establishing the reign of Christ over these areas of your activity?

Jesus Is the Way to Deal Humanly With God

Luke 1:39-45; Micah 5:1-4; Hebrews 10:5-10

As soon as Elizabeth heard the voice of Mary on her doorstep, the baby in her womb leapt for joy.

Ideally, or logically—which in this case means "theologically"—this is the effect we should have on everyone. As soon as we cross the threshold of anyone's consciousness, something in that person should leap up for joy at the presence of the Lord. For he is within us. Every time two people in grace encounter one another, something in each should cry out in wonder, "Who am I that the bearer of the living Body of my Lord should come to me?"

Jesus Christ, the eternal Word of God, has taken flesh in each one of us. He did not just take flesh as a baby while we were in the womb; instead he said to each one of us at our Baptism, "Give me your body. Let me join myself to you to continue my human presence, my human ministry on earth in partnership with you. I want to make your body my Body, your psychology my psychology, your character and temperament my character and temperament, your background and history my background and history. I want to be—in you and with you—what you are. And I want you to be what I am. Give me your body and be my Body, my human presence on earth." In itself, this union with Christ in grace is greater than just being physically the mother of God (see Luke 11: 27-28 and Matthew 12: 46-50).

The hardest thing to believe about the Incarnation is that it continues. God was not made flesh in Jesus for just thirty-three years, never to be humanly present in the world again. The mystery, the wonder, and the joy of God's coming to be humanly present to us is that he still is.

Jesus was not "Emmanuel—God-with-us" for just a short while in Palestine. He is still Emmanuel, still God and still humanly with us. We can meet him humanly, hear his human words, feel his human touch, deal with him as a human being, just as truly as we deal with one another. And as we do this, the grace of his human presence in the world continues for us.

But we have to believe in that presence. The infant in Elizabeth's womb leapt for joy because her faith recognized the presence of Jesus in Mary. And unless we consciously recognize in faith the presence of Jesus in the words of Scripture, in the words of the Mass, in his words of absolution spoken to us in the Sacrament of Reconciliation, in the words others speak to us as the expression of graced love, and in all the graced human words and gestures of the Church—laity and clergy alike—that are the continuing ministry of Jesus in his Body on earth, then our hearts will not leap up. We will not recognize the human presence of Jesus in our midst, and we will not find joy in God our Savior as we should.

This is the good news of Jesus the Savior: Because God took flesh in Jesus and became a human being in our midst, we can still encounter him and deal with him humanly today. In his Church, Jesus is still "Emmanuel," the saving presence of God humanly visible and active in our world.

How do we experience his human divine presence in our own lives? The first step is to believe. We have to work at being conscious that Jesus himself is speaking to us through the Scriptures, through the words of the Mass, through the Sacrament of Reconciliation, through the Anointing of the Sick, through the graced words and actions of those with which we deal. We have to believe in his human presence in order to recognize and experience it.

Secondly, we have to make a positive point of dealing humanly with Jesus ourselves. We have to spend time with him the way we do with our friends, think about his words as we think about the words of anyone who is important to us, see him in imagination doing the things he did on earth, do concrete, physical things to show him our love. In short, treat him as a human being.

Reflecting on This Week's Gospels

December 17-24

Pray daily: Lord, you took flesh so that we might see you and know you as God through your human words and actions. Teach me to be human with you and let you be human with me. Amen.

December 17: "O Wisdom": Matthew 1:1-17: "So all of the generations from Abraham to David are fourteen generations; from David to the deportation to Babylon, fourteen generations; and from the deportation to Babylon to the Messiah, fourteen generations." Jewish history peaks in David, hits its lowest point in Babylon, reaches its second peak in Jesus. How is Jesus the goal of all human history? How are you bringing Jesus to "full stature" (see Ephesians 4:13)?

December 18: "O Leader and Lord": Matthew 1:18-24: "Look, the virgin shall conceive and bear a son, and they shall name him Emmanuel," which means "God is with us." In how many ways is Jesus humanly present to us today? In how many ways do you deal with him as you deal with your other friends?

December 19: "O Sprout of Jesse": Luke 1:5-25: "He [John] will make a ready people prepared for the Lord." How does human witness and ministry help us to find and experience God in the depths of our hearts?

December 20: "O Key of David": Luke 1:26-38: "[Y]ou will conceive in your womb and bear a son, and you will name him Jesus." How does the fact that God became a visible human being in Jesus make it easier for you to know and love him?

December 21: "O Radiant Dawn": Luke 1:39-45: "For as soon as I heard the sound of your greeting, the child in my womb leaped for joy." Why should the sight of you make people feel joy? What is required in you for this to happen?

December 22: "O King of Nations": Luke 1:46-56: And Mary said: "My soul magnifies the Lord, and my spirit rejoices in God my Savior." What is the effect on others when you are conscious of God's love for you, God's presence in you, God's choice of you to serve him?

December 23: "O Emmanuel": Luke 1:57-66: "All who heard them pondered them and said, 'What, then, will this child become?'" Should there be just as much awe and wonder at the Baptism of every child as there was at the circumcision of John? Why?

December 24: Luke 1:67-79: "And you, child, will be called prophet of the Most High, for you will go before the Lord to prepare his ways." Could these words have been said to you at your Baptism? Why? What did the anointing with chrism consecrate you to be?

Living This Week's Gospels

As Christian: Make a list of everything you do for your close friends. See how many you can do for Jesus.

As Disciple: Begin reading all four Gospels the way you would read the life of a close friend.

As Prophet: Think of three things you do or values you embrace because you saw your friends doing them and realized they were good. List three things you do (or can begin to do) because of the example of Jesus.

As Priest: How do you nurture, help or show love for your friends in their need? How do you or can you do this for Jesus?

As King: How often do you help friends in their work or projects? How often can you do this for Jesus?

CHRISTMAS
SEASON

Word, Flesh and Glory

John 1:1-18; Isaiah 52:7-10; Hebrews 1:1-6

"**N**o one has ever seen God. It is God the only Son, who is close to the Father's heart, who has made him known." These words give the key to Christianity. John will write later, "For God so loved the world that he gave his only Son, so that everyone who believes in him may not perish but may have eternal life." And Jesus prayed to the Father at the Last Supper, "Now this is eternal life, that they should know you, the only true God, and the one whom you sent, Jesus Christ."

The focus of our religion is on knowing Jesus Christ so that we might know God and love him "with all our heart, with all our soul, with all our mind, and with all our strength." Jesus is "the Word become flesh." He "lived among us, and we have seen his glory." And that is the key to our religion.

John's Gospel is read on Christmas Day, the day we celebrate Jesus' birth, because it echoes and completes the words the angel said to Mary on the day he was conceived: "You will conceive in your womb and bear a son, and you will name him Jesus." Mary conceived, she gave birth and she named. "In the beginning was the Word... And the Word became flesh...and we have seen his glory."

Our religion is a process of conceiving in our hearts, of receiving the word of God through instruction and inspiration, in order to then give flesh to that word in action. For Christianity to be brought to birth in us completely, we have to go through the "labor" of discipleship and choices, actively participate in pushing out into action what is in us until it becomes visible in our life-style and behavior. And after that there is another key moment, a step we must not neglect to take: We must give a name to what we have experienced and done. We have to consciously "own" the divine life within us, recognize its fruits and be aware with wonder and awe that we have seen the glory of our religion and that its name is "Jesus—God saves."

These three steps: to let the word of God be conceived in our hearts, to give it birth by letting it take flesh in action, and then to glorify God by giving a name to what we have experienced, are the constant, continuing process of growth in the spiritual life. Each one of us can echo what Saint Paul wrote to the Galatians: "My children, for whom I am again in labor until Christ be formed in you!" We are all "building up the Body of Christ" in ourselves and in one another, "until all of us come to the unity of the faith and of the knowledge of the Son of God, to maturity, to the measure of the full stature of Christ."

To authentically celebrate Christmas, we have to rejoice in Christ's birth, not as in an event which happened once and for all two thousand years ago, but as an event that is happening, and that God is calling on us to make happen, right here and now, this day and every day of our lives. We need to rejoice as Mary did when it was first announced to her that she would be the mother of the Savior. She received that news, not as an interesting fact she could passively observe, sitting in front of a television set, but as new life conceived in her body, a new orientation given to her existence, as a call to live every moment of her life in a new way.

This is the way we celebrate the Good News at every Eucharist—not as spectators, but as players. We receive the news as something to act on. Every word spoken from the presider's chair, the pulpit, or the altar is a word to be conceived in our hearts, to be brought to birth in action by our labor, and then to be recognized and acknowledged as an experience of God. In the beginning is the word, but the word must be made flesh so that we can see its glory.

Reflecting on This Week's Gospels

December 26-31

Note: Holy Family Sunday may replace one of these days.

Pray daily: *Lord, I have seen your glory. You have cast light on my life. You have revealed to me my beginning and my end. You have given me the gift of divine life in Baptism, renewed it in Reconciliation, nurtured it in Eucharist. You have made me your co-worker in Confirmation. Now give me the love to proclaim you to the world. Amen.*

December 26: Saint Stephen: Matthew 10:17-22: "You will be dragged before governors and kings because of me, as a testimony to them...." If you were the only living witness to Jesus on earth, what is the first thing you would say about him? If you wrote a Gospel, what would be the predominant theme running through it?

December 27: Saint John: John 20:2-8: "[H]e saw and believed." What have you "seen" Jesus do in your life? What do you know about him as clearly as if you could see and hear him? What have you not seen but consciously chosen to believe?

December 28: Holy Innocents: Matthew 2:13-18: "Herod is about to search for the child, to destroy him." Who is trying to "destroy" Jesus (his influence on earth) today? How? Are you a threat to them?

December 29: Fifth Day in Octave of Christmas: Luke 2:22-35: "For my eyes have seen your salvation." Where, how do you see Jesus saving you and others today? Does he do it also through you? How? How can you cooperate with him more?

December 30: Sixth Day in Octave of Christmas: Luke 2:36-40: Anna "began to praise God and to speak about the child to all who were looking for the redemption of Jerusalem." How often do you give thanks to God for the gift of knowing Jesus Christ? How often do you speak about him to others?

December 31: Seventh Day in Octave of Christmas: John 1:1-18: "What has come into being in him was life, and the life was the light of all people." How is the life of Jesus a light for you? How has following his words or example enhanced your life?

Feast of the Holy Family (if it falls on a weekday): Luke 2:41-52: "But they did not understand what he said to them." What do you not understand of what Jesus has said? What are you doing about it? What did Mary do when she didn't understand? What, concretely, can you do to understand better the teaching of Jesus?

Living This Week's Gospels

As Christian: Make a list of all the ways you have seen the glory of God through dealing with Jesus in his Church.

As Disciple: As you read through the Gospels, notice what Jesus does that impresses people or causes them to "glorify God." Have you experienced the same thing in another way?

As Prophet: If knowing Jesus only made you different in one way, what would it be? ("Different" means from those who don't know him, from the culture, from what you were before he meant much to you.)

As Priest: How many people know what you really think and feel about Jesus? How many have you tried to share this with? Who would care to know you on this level?

As King: What are you doing to make the world different because Jesus has come? What are you trying to change in your family life, social life, school life, professional life and civic life?

Sunday After Christmas (Holy Family)

How to Be a Family

Luke 2:41-52; Sirach 3:2-6, 12-14; Colossians 3:12-21

W here do we find in our culture any explicit teaching on what a family is? Ads and commercials print images of family life on our minds that influence us probably more deeply than we know—but they are designed to sell products. Sitcoms and movies (let's don't even mention the soaps!) dramatize family life in the way they think will appeal to the largest audience. But who even tries to ask or answer authentically what family life should be?

Saint Paul does—and it is significant that he does it in the context of explaining what any Christian community should be. For Paul, a family is first of all a Christian community: a "common unity" of faith (prophets), worship (priests) and commitment (kings).

The first thing Paul says is that we should understand or think of ourselves as "chosen, holy and beloved." God loves us, and he has chosen us, "set us apart" and consecrated us for a special mission in the world.

Paul next describes the attitude or stance we should cultivate in ourselves if we know we are "chosen, holy and beloved." He says to "clothe" ourselves, to consciously put on or adopt an attitude of "mercy, kindness, humility, gentleness and patience." These are all non-aggressive attitudes. They don't aim at getting things done, at changing others, or making things just the way we like them. They are the virtues that focus us on nurturing each other, making things easier for each other, fostering an atmosphere of caring love in all our dealings with each other. This should be our first concern.

And specifically we need to "bear with" each other and

forgive. Every human community, no matter how Christian, is a community of sinners. We have to begin by consciously, deeply deciding to accept others as they are—not denying their faults, but accepting them as people we love and enjoy, even with their faults. If we insist on a perfect world, there is no place for us in this one! The same is true if we insist on a perfect family, Church or community. If God loves us as we are and is willing to accept us as we are, even with our faults, then we should accept one another.

The key to all of this is love. Love is a deliberate choice to want others to "be and become" everything they can be. It is a choice to focus our desire, not on what makes us feel good, but on seeing the goodness that already is in others and encouraging it to grow. This is a choice we have the power to make, and it transforms our own being and our lives. It is this choice that makes family life—or any Christian community—work. And it is the choice that makes us like God.

The fruit—and the sign—that we have taken the stance described above is peace. Peace is what Jesus came to bring about on earth. He came to bring everything in heaven and on earth together into unity under his headship (Ephesians 1:10). Peace is mentioned in every prayer in the Communion Service of the Mass (from the Our Father on). Peace is the Christian apostolate, and where peace exists in families they bear witness to the grace of Christ in them.

Three things will help us become the kind of community described above. First, as prophets we must fill our minds and hearts with the words of Christ, and out of the wisdom this gives, we must "instruct" one another—that is, consciously help each other to live by the teachings of Christ. Second, as priests we need to express our faith, hope and love, to celebrate it together in psalms, hymns and inspired songs. Families need to pray together. Finally, as sharers in the kingship of Christ, we need to try "in speech and action," by whatever we say or do to establish the reign of Christ's truth in every area of our activity. If we do these things our whole life will be "eucharist"—a constant experience of thanksgiving.

Note: The weekly readings for the feast of the Holy Family, if it falls on a Sunday, are the readings for the weekdays within the octave of Christmas (above), because the feast of the Holy Family is normally celebrated on the Sunday within the week that follows Christmas.

January 1 • Solemnity of Mary, Mother of God

Mother of God - Mother of Christ

Luke 2:16-21; Numbers 6:22-27; Galatians 4:4-7

T he Litany of the Blessed Virgin Mary is a series of titles which come from the heart of the Church. In this prayer we dwell on the beauty of God's grace in Mary, and of her human response to grace, by saying over and over again, in different ways, what we see in her. Like the shepherds who returned from Bethlehem, glorifying and praising God for all they had heard and seen, we look at the event of God's birth from a woman and dwell on it with wonder and awe. As Mary treasured and pondered in her heart all she heard and saw that concerned Jesus, we treasure and ponder all that the Church proclaims about Mary. This is not just to honor Mary, although we do honor her and we love her. The fact is, everything the Church proclaims about Mary, she proclaims in order to teach us something about Jesus or about the work Jesus came to accomplish in us.

We may not always be aware, however, that every title we give to Mary also says something about us. Because Mary was the Mother of the Redeemer, the first human being to give flesh to God, the one more intimately joined to Jesus in the work of salvation than any other, she was, before and above all other members of the human race, the recipient of the "blessing" Saint Paul proclaims as the fruit of our redemption: "Blessed be the God and Father of our Lord Jesus Christ, who has blessed us in Christ with every spiritual blessing in the heavenly places" (see Ephesians 1:3-6). In Mary we see realized in its perfection, as in a preview, the perfection of graced life toward which we are growing on earth.

That is why what we see in Mary is what God sees in us! Mary is an image of humanity fully redeemed, a picture of what grace is bringing about in us all. Her Immaculate Conception is a preview of that "immaculate conclusion"

Christmas / 35

which all of us will experience, the beatification and beautification for which Jesus is purifying his Bride, the Church. By the time we come to the fullness of life in heaven, we will be as totally purified of all sin, and all the consequences of sin, as if we had never been under the domination of sin at all. Mary's Assumption into heaven is a preview of our resurrection: The preservation of her body from disintegration in the grave is a sign and proof of God's power and purpose to restore our bodies to perfect wholeness after death. As we dwell on the titles of Mary, then, we dwell on the mystery of God and the mystery of the power and love of God that is "doing great things for us."

The first of Mary's titles is "Mother of God." This is the source of every other title we give her, and every other title we give her says something about Mary as Mother of God.

Speaking precisely, Mary is the Mother of God who came to earth to save us, the Mother of Jesus Christ. We make this explicit in calling her "Mother of Christ." Literally, this title means "Mother of the Anointed One." What does the Church see in Mary when she calls her this? What does this title call us to see in ourselves?

Jesus is called the Christ or Anointed One because his humanity was consecrated to carry out the mission for which the Father sent him. Consecrated means "chosen, set aside." It is the same word as *sacred* or *holy*. A sacred person or thing is one that is especially selected, set aside and dedicated by God to do some particular thing. The reverence we give to what is sacred is a recognition that this person or object is of special value to God.

What Jesus received from his mother was his humanity. She was the mother of everything he is as a person, of course—body, blood, soul and divinity—and that is why the Church calls Mary the "Mother of God." But the reason Jesus had to have a mother was so that he could redeem us as a human. What Mary first contributed was that part of her body of which the Word was made flesh. When the Church calls Mary "Mother of Christ," then, it is dwelling with love and wonder on the fact that Mary was the mother of a human being, a person of flesh and blood with a body just like ours, who was loved, selected, chosen, anointed and consecrated by God to do, not just something special on earth, but the one thing to which God himself was promised and dedicated: the salvation of the human race. That is why Jesus is the Christ— not just an anointed one, but the Anointed One. And he is this as a human being, as one like us. The body Mary gave him is anointed, holy, sacred and special. We dwell on that when we call her "Mother of Christ."

And what are we? As truly as Mary is the Mother of Christ, we are the Body of Christ. We were anointed with chrism, "Christ-ed" or "christened" at Baptism to continue his mission on earth. We, then, are consecrated, sacred, of special value to God. We are this in our bodies, in all that we are. Each of us has been specially chosen, consecrated and anointed to continue the mission of Jesus on earth as his real body. And nothing can take this away from us as long as we are united to him in grace. We may be treated with disrespect. Our bodies may be mistreated as Jesus' body was. We may even have a tendency at times to see little of value in ourselves. That is when we need to remember that Mary, our mother, is the Mother of God, the Mother of Christ. Her son was anointed, consecrated, sacred. And so are we. When we call Mary "Mother of God," we should echo, "and Mother of us, the anointed ones."

Note: *This article is rewritten and expanded from an article I published in the* Marian Helpers' Bulletin *47/4, Fall of 1992.*

Reflecting on This Week's Gospels

Week of January 2-7

> **Pray daily:** *Lord, you took flesh of Mary in order to redeem the world. And you have made me your body to continue your work of redemption in me, in my time and space. Lead me to surrender to you as Mary*

*did, so that you may do through me all that you
desire to do. Amen.*

January 2: John 1:19-28: John identified himself as "the
voice of one crying out in the desert, 'Make straight the way
of the Lord.'" Can you identify yourself in the same way? Do
you ever feel you are in a spiritual desert? What in your life
cries out, "Make straight the way of the Lord!"?

January 3: John 1:29-34: John testified, "I did not know
him, but the one who sent me to baptize with water told me,
'He on whom you see the spirit descend and remain is the
one who baptizes with the Holy Spirit.' Now I have seen and
testified that he is the Son of God." What signs have you
seen that the Holy Spirit is working within the Church? How
have you testified to this? To whom?

January 4: John 1:35-42: Andrew found his own brother
Simon and told him, "We have found the Messiah" (which is
translated "Anointed"). What does it mean to you that Jesus
is "the Anointed one"? What does it mean to you that you are?

January 5: John 1:43-51: Philip found Nathanael and told
him, "We have found the one about whom Moses wrote in
the law, and also the prophets, Jesus, son of Joseph, from
Nazareth." Have you "found" Jesus in a deep, personal,
intimate way? Whom have you told about it?

January 6: Mark 1:7-11: John said, "I have baptized you
with water; he will baptize you with the Holy Spirit." How
have you experienced the Holy Spirit in your life? How often
do you experience the gifts or fruits of the Spirit now? Do
you call them by name to give God glory?

January 7: John 2:1-12: Jesus' mother said to the servers,
"Do whatever he tells you." If Mary appeared to you tonight
and said this, what would you do? What have you done
because you believed Jesus was asking it? How do you
decide whether Jesus is speaking to you?

Living This Week's Gospels

As Christian: Look at yourself in the mirror and say, "I am the Body of Christ."

As Disciple: Read Chapter One, "Mother of God," in the book *Mary in an Adult Church* (David M. Knight, His Way Communications 1992).

As Prophet: Take olive oil, or any vegetable oil, and with it make the sign of the cross on your lips as a sign that your speech is consecrated to God. Do the same with other parts of your body.

As Priest: Try to be alert all this week to any thoughts or feelings you have to show love to another person. Ask yourself if this is the voice of Christ in you.

As King: Examine the environment where you live and work. Is there anything that indicates this is not the environment of the Body of Christ? Any objects, decorations, practices, policies or institutional structures of any sort? Do what you can to change what needs to be changed.

Epiphany

Jesus Is Universal Lord

Matthew 2:1-12; Isaiah 60:1-6; Ephesians 3:2-3, 5-6

The message of this Gospel is, "God is not limited." He can speak, not only through the words of Scripture and through angels, but even through the stars. He wants to draw the whole world to Jesus, and to do that he will speak to people of different cultures in whatever language or symbols they are able to understand.

The Magi were not Jews. They were pagans from the mysterious and faraway "east." Legend says they sought God through the study of the stars. So God spoke to them in the language of their own religion. He sent them a star.

He does the same for us. He speaks to us through whatever signs, symbols, events, persons or experiences we are able to receive. And he founded his Church to do the same.

The word "catholic" means "universal." For the Church this means that we are not the Church of one particular culture or civilization. Our religion is not identified with the particular form it takes in any particular society. As long as the content is the same, as long as Jesus Christ and his Gospel are faithfully proclaimed, it is just as "Catholic"—and even more "catholic"—that the form of celebration and the forms of observance should be different all over the world.

Actually the Catholic Church recognizes at least eighteen different groups within the Church who have their own laws, forms of celebration and spiritual traditions. These groups are called "rites," and everyone baptized into the Church is baptized both into the Catholic Church and into one particular rite of the Catholic Church. Most of us belong to the Latin rite, which is no more important than the Coptic rite, the Ethiopian rite, the Greek, Melchite, Russian, Syro-Malabar, Armenian or any other rite. All of these rites are equal. The particular rules that we Latin (or "Roman") Catholics are familiar with are not in any sense "normative" for the Catholic Church. For example, the much-discussed rule of celibacy for priests is a rule of the Latin rite that most other rites have never had. So it is false to say that Catholic priests cannot be married. It is true to say that Catholic priests of the Latin rite cannot be married, although exceptions are being made now. We have several married Catholic priests in the Latin rite who were formerly Episcopalian or Lutheran priests.

To be "Catholic" it is essential not to be narrow, and not to think there is only one way to present the faith, to celebrate it, or to practice it. That is why we cannot really understand the story of the Magi unless we also read chapters 10, 11 and 15 of the Acts of the Apostles. Those chapters tell how the Church decided to be "catholic." It was a decision not to make Gentile converts follow the rules and traditions of Judaism, which all the Jewish Christians had grown up with, and which they just assumed were inseparable from the true worship of God. This was one of the most significant decisions of the early Church, and we are not truly Catholic until we understand it and accept it.

So let your mind go some day and imagine how different (not necessarily better) your parish could be without being one bit less Catholic. How many rules and practices that we associate with being "Catholic" are just the form our religion has taken in the Latin rite, or in the last few centuries—and are not necessary to the Catholic Church at all. They are just the "stars" that speak to us. But we do not worship stars; we worship Jesus Christ to whom they lead.

And don't forget the "stars" God sends to you every day. If even the stars are his messengers, he can speak through anything he chooses. The message of the Magi is, "Look for him in everything, listen for his voice."

Reflecting on This Week's Gospels

Week After Epiphany

Pray daily: Lord, centuries of people before me have been drawn to your light. Some made tremendous sacrifices to hear you. Give me their faith, their hope, their love. Amen.

Monday: Matthew 4:12-17, 23-25: Jesus left Nazareth and went to live in Capernaum by the sea. If you had been in Nazareth, would it have made any difference to you that Jesus moved? What use do you make of his presence now—in your heart, in the Eucharist, in the other sacraments?

Tuesday: Mark 6:34-44: When Jesus saw the vast crowd, his heart was moved with pity for them, for they were like sheep without a shepherd; and he began to teach them many things. How does Jesus feel about you? Are you like a sheep without a shepherd or are you coming to him for teaching?

Wednesday: Mark 6:45-52: When the disciples saw Jesus walking on the sea, they thought it was a ghost and cried out. Through what "stars" does Jesus reveal himself, his desires, his invitations, to you? Is your first reaction to think it is "a ghost"—that is, a wild idea of your own, a crazy feeling? How can you know when you are experiencing Jesus?

Thursday: Luke 4:14-22: After Jesus had finished reading in the synagogue he rolled up the scroll, handed it back to the attendant and sat down. Then he said, "Today this scripture passage is fulfilled in your hearing." Do you believe that Jesus is present in the world now to fulfill all the promises God made in Scripture? What are you doing about it?

Friday: Luke 5:12-16: A leper fell prostrate before Jesus, pleaded with him, and said, "Lord, if you wish, you can make me clean." How often do you ask Jesus to purify your heart? Of what in particular? What helps has he made available to you? Which ones do you use? Which do you not use? Why?

Saturday: John 3:22-30: John said, "The friend of the bridegroom, who stands and hears him, rejoices greatly at the bridegroom's voice." Do you rejoice at all truth, all encouragement to do good, no matter where it comes from? Do you recognize the voice of Jesus speaking even in people you don't like? Or who are different from you?

Living This Week's Gospels

As Christian: Make a list of all the "stars" you follow looking for truth and guidance. In terms of time spent on each, compared to time given to prayer and Scripture, is Jesus first?

As Disciple: Draw up your schedule for a typical day or week. How much time do you commit to explicitly learning from Jesus? Are you, or are you not, a disciple (student) of his?

As Prophet: Ask whom you live, recreate or work with who might look to you or need you to be the star that leads them closer to Jesus. How can you do this without words?

As Priest: Decide how you can "gather around" Jesus with others to let him form you by his word. Is there a group you can join? Should you start one? Why?

As King: What effect has the light of Christ had on the world's societies and cultures? What effect is it having on your culture, your society, through you today? What effect could it have if you let the light within you shine out? Decide on one way you could you do this in your family, school, work or social life.

ORDINARY
TIME

First Sunday of
the Year
Through
Eighth Sunday of
the Year

First Sunday of the Year (Baptism of the Lord)

"The Good News of ..."

Luke 3:15-16, 21-22; Isaiah 42:1-4, 6-7; Acts 10:34-38

At the house of Cornelius Peter faced the challenge of explaining Christianity in one talk to a group of Romans who knew nothing about the Old Testament or the New. How did he begin? How would you?

The first phrase which came to Peter's lips was "the good news of peace." This is the exact phrase Paul uses to the Ephesians: "Jesus came and announced the good news of peace to you who were far off and to those who were near." His standard greeting was "grace and peace to you." To the Apostles, Jesus meant peace: peace within themselves, peace with other people, peace with God (see Ephesians 2:1-22).

This peace is a special work of God, but we have to dispose ourselves for it. Paul says, "Rejoice in the Lord... dismiss all anxiety from your minds.... Present your needs to God in prayer.... Then God's own peace, which goes beyond all understanding, will stand watch over your hearts and minds." (Philippians 4:4-7).

Alienation disturbs our peace. We are deeply uneasy if we do not feel we "belong," are accepted, are loved, are in relationship, or have secure bonds with anybody. We cannot ignore, without psychological denial, our need for relationship with other people. And we cannot ignore forever our need for relationship with God. According to the Apostles, Jesus answered both of these needs by calling us into the community of the Church.

This community is a community of witnesses (Acts 10:39). We bear witness to each other about the reality of Jesus Christ, about what we have "seen and heard and felt." Out of this comes *koinonia*—community, communion, fellowship, close relationship—both with each other and with

God (cf. 1 John 1:1-4). We do this by sharing faith with each other in communal worship. At Mass, for example, we celebrate together our common possession of and enlightenment by the word of God (Liturgy of the Word); we express our common commitment to living and offering ourselves as the Body of Christ for the life of the world—in union with Jesus who offered and offers himself for us (Liturgy of the Eucharist); we dramatize and experience our communion with one another and with God in the Sign of Peace and in receiving together the Body and Blood of Christ (Communion Service). All of these are acts that witness to the reality of Jesus Christ in our lives, and to our own grasp and experience of his Good News. They unite and strengthen us in faith.

When we have the clarity and the courage to speak the truth to one another about values—about business decisions, management policies, civic concerns, our social behavior, our prejudices, the challenge that the Good News of Jesus Christ is to the cultural assumptions of our peer group—then our lives bear witness to the present reality of what Peter said about Jesus: that "God anointed him with the Holy Spirit and power." If that Spirit and power are visibly acting in us, then Jesus is still visibly present in our world. Then we are Good News. That is what it means to be "witnesses."

Jesus went about "doing good works and healing all who were in the grip of the devil." He still does in us, if we choose to make this our concern. If we consciously go about our business looking for chances to help others—with a word, a smile, a gesture of courtesy—then we will have a healing effect all day long on all who are in the grip of sadness, affliction, alienation, prejudice or anything else that is the cumulative result of sins committed in our world. If we do this for everyone without distinction people will see what Peter saw: "How true it is that God shows no partiality."

Peter's sentence ends: "And God was with him." We constantly ask for each other, "God be with you—that you might continue the presence and mission of Jesus on earth."

Reflecting on This Week's Gospels

First Week of the Year

> *Pray daily: Lord, by accepting baptism like everyone else, you showed your desire to be identified with us, even in our sinfulness and need. Teach me to be one with you in your saving love for every person and nation in the world. Amen.*

Monday: Mark 1:14-20: Jesus came to Galilee proclaiming the Good News of God and saying, "The time is fulfilled, and the kingdom of God has come near; repent, and believe in the Good News." Is the Gospel still news to you? Good news? What changes have you made in your life recently which show that you are still responding to the Good News?

Tuesday: Mark 1:21-28: The people were astounded at Jesus' teaching, for he taught them as one having authority and not as the scribes. What "astounds" you today in Jesus' teaching? As you grow and mature, does his teaching impress you more and more? Why?

Wednesday: Mark 1:29-39: When it was evening, after sunset, they brought to Jesus all who were ill or possessed by demons. The whole town was gathered at the door. Whom have you brought to Jesus to be healed of something? To find answers or comfort? To experience his action in the life of the Church today?

Thursday: Mark 1:40-45: Moved with pity, Jesus stretched out his hand and touched the leper, and said to him, "I do choose. Be made clean!" Immediately the leprosy left him, and he was made clean. How has Jesus touched you in your life? How has he healed you? Of what?

Friday: Mark 2:1-12: Jesus asked, "Which is easier, to say to the paralytic, 'Your sins are forgiven,' or to say, 'Stand up and take your mat and walk'?" When you go to Jesus in the Sacrament of Reconciliation, do you just ask him for forgiveness, or do you ask for the grace to 'stand up and walk' in the way of God?

Saturday: Mark 2:13-17: Jesus said, "Those who are well have no need of a physician, but those who are sick; I have come to call not the righteous but sinners." In which category do you see yourself? How much need of Jesus do you think you have from day to day? What help do you seek from him? When do you seek it? How? How often?

Living This Week's Gospels

As Christian: Hear God the Father saying about each person you meet during the day, "This is my beloved son," or "my beloved daughter." Act accordingly.

As Disciple: The National Conference of Catholic Bishops' pastoral letter, "The Challenge of Peace" (May 3, 1983), said, "We urge every diocese and parish to implement balanced and objective educational programs to help people at all age levels to better understand the issues of war and peace. Development and implementation of such programs must receive a high priority during the next several years." Call the diocesan office (or your parish) to ask what is being done that is available to you.

As Prophet: Notice how often people are spoken about or treated as "them" in distinction to "us." Make a point of speaking about every person, nation, race, religion, sex and social class in a way that shows you identify with them as called into oneness by Christ.

As Priest: Reach out to someone you don't know or don't feel bonded with by culture. Make some positive gesture of recognition, acceptance or appreciation.

As King: Expand your concern to embrace in some concrete way the needs of some category of people for whose welfare you don't ordinarily take responsibility—for example, a different level of employees where you work or people of a different culture, social class or another country.

Second Sunday of the Year

Jesus: The Way to Grow

John 2:1-11; Isaiah 62:1-5; 1 Corinthians 12:4-11

Jesus changed 130 gallons of water into wine at Cana—
a little country wedding where there probably weren't
more than a hundred people. Can you imagine what this
did to that party? In Cana they are still talking about it!

The Gospel tells us that after this miracle Jesus' disciples
"believed in him." Since they were disciples, they already
believed in him. But this miracle showed them the scope of
what Jesus came to do: he came to transform human life on
this earth the way 130 gallons of wine transform a tiny
country wedding.

At Cana Jesus showed what his mission was all about.
Two clues tell us this. First, he addressed his mother as
"woman," seeing her, not just as Mary his mother, but as the
woman, the Daughter of Sion, the Spouse of God, the symbol
of his People, his Church. He didn't just hear Mary asking
about wine at a wedding; he saw the human race asking for
the true "wine of the wedding feast," the coming of the reign
of God.

That explains his answer: "My hour has not yet come." In
John's Gospel the "hour" of Jesus is always the moment of
his crucifixion and Resurrection, his defeat and his triumph.
It is the moment when Jesus pours out his blood, the true
wine of the wedding feast, to inebriate the world. And Jesus,
speaking to his mother, is in fact telling his people it is not
yet time for him to pour out his blood.

The challenge of this Gospel is to accept the scope of
what Jesus wants to do in our lives. He did not come just to
lift up our behavior a little bit, or just to heal the wounds of
sin. He came to transform human life entirely, to make it
divine. The Jesus we believe in is not just a healer or prophet
or teacher. He is God sharing the life of God with us.

The conversion to which we are called is not just a conversion from sin to good behavior. The transformation offered us is not just from defective human being to healed human being. No, we are offered the transformation of grace: the transformation from merely human life to a sharing in the life of God himself. We are the water Jesus wishes to change into wine. He wants to make the world drunk with joy.

In action, the life of God in us takes the form of lived faith, active hope, divine love. Whatever lifts us up to a higher level of faith, hope and love increases our sharing in the life of God and makes us more divine. And anything that holds us down on a merely human level of thinking, acting or loving holds us back from living the life of grace in its fullness. That is where the paradox of pain comes in.

Jesus turned water into wine; then later turned wine into his blood. Wine, the symbol of joy, becomes blood, the symbol of pain. Yet his blood is joy. Through Christ's blood we find joy. Through his death we find life. And when Jesus poured out his blood on the cross, he poured out the wine of the wedding feast. The paradox is life through death, joy through pain, wine becoming blood, blood becoming wine, and joy and pain becoming indistinguishable in the ecstasy of love.

Jesus is not a Savior who saves us from pain, any more than loving saves us from pain. In fact, Jesus often saves us through pain: ours as well as his. Anyone who has experienced love growing through pain can understand this.

The greatest pain of Christian living is the pain of going beyond ourselves, beyond our human level, to live by pure faith, pure hope, pure love—to live on the level of God. But without this pain of change and self-transcendence, we can never really know what it is to live the life of grace.

Reflecting on This Week's Gospels

Second Week of the Year

Pray daily: Lord, you came to transform life like one hundred and thirty gallons of wine transformed the wedding feast at Cana. Excite my mind and my heart. Fill me. Amen.

Monday: Mark 2:18-22: "New wine is poured into fresh wineskins." How has your faith changed, not only your behavior, but your goals in life and basic values?

Tuesday: Mark 2:23-28: "The sabbath was made for people, not people for the sabbath." How does the Sunday Eucharist serve the human race? How does your participation help you? Help others?

Wednesday: Mark 3:1-6: Jesus said to the man, "Stretch out your hand." He stretched it out and his hand was restored. When, how has Jesus said to you, "Stretch out your heart"? What have you found excitingly challenging in the Gospel?

Thursday: Mark 3:7-12: "He had cured many and, as a result, those who had diseases were pressing upon him to touch him." What is the difference between going to Jesus for healing and going because you want to grow in understanding what he teaches? When do you do each? Which do you do more?

Friday: Mark 3:13-19: "He appointed twelve that they might be with him and he might send them forth to preach." Why did the apostles have to "be with" Jesus before he could send them out to preach? How can you be with him in the same way? What is available in your parish?

Saturday: Mark 3:20-21: The crowd gathered, making it impossible for them even to eat. When his relatives heard of this they set out to seize him, for they said, "He is out of his mind." Why would Jesus' relatives have thought this? How was he acting? Has anyone ever thought this of you for the same reason?

Living This Week's Gospels

As Christian: Each day examine the goal you pursue in one area of your life—social, family, school, work, civic—asking how the "new wine" did or could transform it.

As Disciple: Each day read one of these texts, asking how this can be your goal in life: John 10:10; Ephesians 1:3-10; Ephesians 2:15-22; Ephesians 4:1-16; Philippians 2:5-11; Colossians 1:15-20.

As Prophet: Do one thing each day that visibly expresses a goal in your family or social life, school or work that is different from the goals our culture holds up to us.

As Priest: Talk to one friend, co-worker or fellow student each day, asking what is the real goal of what you do together.

As King: Select one area of your life (family, work, school, social, civic). Write down the Christian goal you pursue through it. Then examine how each policy or practice in that area does or does not contribute to that goal. See what you can change.

Third Sunday of the Year

To Grow in Faith

Luke 1:1-4; 4: 14-21; Nehemiah 8:2-4a; 5-6, 8-10;
1 Corinthians 12:12-30

Oddly enough, one of the ways Jesus saves us is by being the recurring "crisis" in our lives.

Our English word crisis comes from the Greek *krisis*, which means "judgment" or the act of coming to a decision. And Jesus "saves" us by repeatedly putting us in a position where we have to make a decision.

For Catholics, to be "saved" is to be made sharers in the life of God. And we can be more or less alive. Therefore we can be more or less "saved." To be fully saved is to share fully in the life of God—which on this earth means to live by perfect faith, hope and love. To "save" us completely, therefore, Jesus needs to keep bringing us to deepest faith, strongest hope, purest love. One way he does this is to keep calling on us to make decisions that require us to exercise more faith, more hope, more love.

He did this when he preached to the people of his hometown of Nazareth. They already believed he was something special. His reputation for preaching and miracles had "spread throughout the region," and all were "loud in his praise." And when he spoke in Nazareth his friends and neighbors "marveled at the appealing discourse which came from his lips."

Then what he said began to sink in.

He had read to them a passage from the book of Isaiah which spoke of the Messiah. When he finished reading, he said, "Today this Scripture passage is fulfilled in your hearing." He announced in his hometown that he was the Messiah.

That was too much. It is one thing to accept that a hometown boy can make good, become famous, even be chosen by God. But to believe that someone you grew up with, whose family you have seen around every day, who was always pretty much just like everyone else, can be the Messiah promised for centuries, the Savior of the world, that is something else.

It doesn't engage you personally to say, "Jesus is a great teacher, a chosen instrument of God." You can say that, admire him, and then pick and choose among his teachings. Any good teacher is a help; you can use whatever he says that you find acceptable and helpful. But to say, "Jesus is the Messiah, the promised Savior of the world," is a decision which calls you to accept everything he says, and to follow his way of life in its entirety. You can respond to a teacher more or less. But to a Savior the only response is "either/or."

Jesus' friends and neighbors could not make that response. As long as he just stood there and taught them they accepted him. But when he told them he was the Messiah they tried to throw him over a cliff.

We find the same reaction to churches. Any church which just claims to cast some light on the teachings of Jesus— which does not claim to be infallible, or to have any special place among the Christian churches—is no threat to anyone. No one is very upset, for example, if a family member transfers from one mainline Protestant church to another. All the churches are doing a good job; they are all teaching the doctrine of Jesus as best they can. They all help.

But the Catholic Church stands up and says, "We are the one Church Jesus founded for the salvation of the world. We are not just one among many. We teach with the authority of Jesus; anyone who hears the Church hears Jesus." That arouses resentment. It calls for a different act of faith. The Church that makes that claim cannot be accepted more or less, but only "either/or." That brings people into "crisis." And it leads to the fullness of faith.

Reflecting on This Week's Gospels

Third Week of the Year

Pray daily: Jesus, I believe you are God come into this world, the light and savior of the human race. I want to walk in your light. Teach me to make you a part of everything I do. Amen.

Monday: Mark 3:22-30: "Whoever blasphemes against the holy Spirit will never have forgiveness." Is there any sin you do not confess because you tell yourself it is not a sin?

Tuesday: Mark 3:31-35: "Whoever does the will of God is my brother and sister and mother." How does this make faith in Jesus different from faith in any human teacher? What difference does this make to you in daily life?

Wednesday: Mark 4:1-20: When Jesus was alone, those who were around him questioned him about the parables. And he said to them, "To you has been given the secret of the kingdom of God, but for those outside, everything comes in parables, in order that 'they may indeed look, but not perceive, and may indeed listen, but not understand.'" Do you let some of Christ's words just pass over your head, because you prefer not to be challenged? Or do you really think about what seems to be extreme?

Thursday: Mark 4:21-25: "Take care what you hear. The measure with which you measure will be measured out to you." What makes people more or less alive on earth? Can you be more or less alive by grace? How can you have divine life "to the full"?

Friday: Mark 4:26-34: "The Kingdom of God is like a mustard seed which... springs up and becomes the largest of plants." How has the faith you received as a child grown, developed and borne fruit in your life?

Saturday: Mark 4:35-41: Then he asked them, "Why are you terrified? Do you not yet have faith?" What are your greatest anxieties and fears? How can faith in Jesus relieve them?

Living This Week's Gospels

As Christian: Each time you do something bad or stupid, ask how it would have been different if you were consciously interacting with Christ at that moment.

As Disciple: Each day read one passage from the Gospel, asking what effect the words, actions and example of Jesus had on people.

As Prophet: Identify one way of acting at home, school, work, or in your social life that you think is destructive. Ask what change would embody the values Jesus taught. Make that change in your own behavior.

As Priest: Ask whether Jesus is a recognized member of the groups you belong to—family, friends, work group. Is his presence acknowledged by the group? Could it be?

As King: Ask whether the change you made as "prophet" above is something you could convince those around you to make. Would some other change be needed to make it work? What can you do to bring about that change? Who might help you?

Fourth Sunday of the Year

The Way to Hope in God

Luke 4:21-30; Jeremiah 1:4-5, 17-19;
1 Corinthians 12:31—13:13

There were two reasons why Jesus' people tried to kill him at Nazareth: first, they just couldn't believe that a hometown boy could be the Messiah. But also, Jesus dashed their hopes.

Jesus' people expected the kind of Savior all of us want: a man of power, a winner, someone who can clean up the mess this world is in and set things straight. Isn't this what most of our prayers to God are asking for? Deliverance from sickness or danger—including the moral danger of temptations or sin—help to make a living, a solution for problems that are causing us anxiety or grief; in other words, the kind of things a powerful, persuasive, all-knowing, ever-victorious rescuer could save us from?

Jesus didn't look like the kind of Messiah who could do this. Had he returned to his hometown with an entourage of rich and powerful people, at the head of an army, he probably would have been welcomed as the Messiah. He would have had the mark of victory upon him, and he would have given his people a basis for hope. A human basis.

Isn't it, after all, the visible evidence of power that gives us hope? Before we can hope, we have to see signs that the person we are counting on has the ability and the willingness to rescue us. Jesus didn't show these signs.

It is true Jesus cured a number of sick people, which at first made people think he was the answer to their problems. It soon became clear, however, that this was just about the only way he was going to use the power he had. He was a preacher and a healer. He showed no signs of being the Messiah the people expected. And, in their disappointment, they wanted to kill him.

What about us? Don't we get just as disappointed at
times with God? What about the anger we feel when a loved
one dies? What about the anger we feel toward the Church,
Christ's ministering Body on earth, when our children turn
away from the faith, or when the Sunday liturgy doesn't seem
to add anything to our lives? Haven't we all wondered at
times what Jesus is doing about war, famine, poverty, crime,
drugs, the oppression of the weak? Have we perhaps,
consciously or not, stopped trusting in Jesus to do anything
about the real problems we deal with and begun to seek our
immediate salvation from other sources? Have we lost our
hope in God?

It would be false spirituality to expect God to solve our
problems without our using every human means we can to
resolve them ourselves. But it is just as false to think that
God does not intend to help us because we see no evidence
of his power being used to do so.

Jesus is the Savior of the world. But he saves us by
empowering us to think and love as God does. If enough
people begin to do that, then the world's problems will soon
cease to exist. On the other hand, if we do not begin to think
like God and love like God, it makes no difference how often
Jesus steps in to straighten something out in our world; we
will make a mess of it again before nightfall!

It is not that Jesus does not intend to save us—even from
the problems we have in this world: in family and social life,
business and politics. It is just that he doesn't save us in the
way we expect or use the same means we would. His way of
saving us is to reveal to us the mind and heart of God. To
accept his salvation means to dedicate ourselves to receiving
what Jesus offers. This means reflecting on his words and
example, and responding to problems as he did and as he
teaches us to.

By example Jesus taught us to trust absolutely in God,
put aside our fears and give unconditional love to each other.
This is the way of salvation. We need to grow into it.

Reflecting on This Week's Gospels

Fourth Week of the Year

Pray daily: Lord, I trust in you. When I don't see you acting to help me, I will trust in you. When I don't feel your presence I will trust in you. When your words seem meaningless to me, I will trust in you. Above all, I will trust in you enough to do what you taught, always and everywhere. Amen.

Monday: Mark 5:1-20: When those who witnessed the deliverance of the possessed man explained what had happened...they began to beg him to leave their district. Is there anything you are afraid Jesus might deliver you from if you get too involved with him?

Tuesday: Mark 5:21-43: Jesus said to the synagogue official, "Do not be afraid; just have faith." What are you afraid to do—or to ask God for—because you don't have enough faith?

Wednesday: Mark 6:1-6: He was not able to perform any deed of power there, apart from curing a few sick...he was amazed at their lack of faith. What has Jesus done for you when you trusted him? Is there anything your lack of faith could be keeping him from doing for you now?

Thursday: Mark 6:7-13: Jesus instructed the disciples he sent out to take nothing for the journey but a walking stick— no food, no sack, no money in their belts. Do you hold back from doing the work of God, from following what might be his inspirations, because you don't think you have sufficient human resources to succeed? When does prudence become a lack of trust?

Friday: Mark 6:14-29: Herod swore, "I will grant you whatever you ask of me, even to half of my kingdom." She said to her mother, "What shall I ask for?" She replied, "The head of John the Baptist." If you asked Mary what you should ask Jesus for, what would she say? Would you do it?

Saturday: Mark 6:30-34: Jesus said to the Apostles, "Come away by yourselves to a deserted place and rest a while." Does Jesus invite you to do this? When? Where? Do you do it?

Living This Week's Gospels

As Christian: Try to solve some problem just by doing a loving thing. Reflect on what happens.

As Disciple: List the three people whose advice you follow most. Is Jesus one of them? Where do you find his advice?

As Prophet: Notice when you are afraid to be your real self with people. Ask yourself why and what you should do about it.

As Priest: Express yourself (your faith, your true values, your feelings about God) to someone to whom you feel afraid to reveal yourself but whom you think you can trust.

As King: Is there any change you think would be good but have been afraid to suggest—at home, at work, with your friends? Give God a chance to act through you; suggest it.

Fifth Sunday of the Year

The Way to Perfect Love

Luke 5:1-11; Isaiah 6:1-2a, 3-8; 1 Corinthians 15:1-11

T his Gospel recalls the major characteristics of Jesus as
Savior which we have seen so far: He is a Savior who
gives purpose and divine fullness to our lives ("From
now on you will be catching men"); a Savior who delivers us
from our own sins ("Leave me, Lord, I am a sinful man"); a
Savior who challenges us to grow in faith and hope ("Put out
into deep water and lower your nets for a catch"). Now this
Gospel takes us another step: Jesus is a Savior who calls forth
from us the fullness of love ("They brought their boats to
land, left everything, and became his followers").

To love is to give. The more you love, the more you give.
Giving is the measure of love.

Our Lord gives himself to us without reserve. He doesn't
say to any one of us, "I would like you to be just a casual
friend." He doesn't want to keep any one of us at a distance.
If Jesus has an "inner circle" of closest friends, it is open to
everyone who is willing to enter it. He invites each one of us
to know him deeply and intimately. He calls us to total,
passionate love.

One sign of this is that he asks each one of us to give him
everything we are. Giving is the measure of love. How much
we ask of another is the measure of the relationship we want
with that person. If we don't want to be close to another, we
ask very little. If we ask another for total gift, we are offering
total love. And Jesus asks each one of us for everything.

This is also God's way of telling us how much Jesus is
worth, and how much we can expect from friendship and
union with him. God is honest; his price tags never lie. For
the most part God just gives to us freely. But when he names
a price, he is revealing to us a value.

Jesus Christ is the pearl beyond all price. The only way we can understand what union with him is worth is to give everything we have and everything we are. We don't really know how much we want anything until we see how much we are willing to give for it. And we don't know how much we love anyone until we realize how much we are willing to sacrifice to be united to that person in mind, will and heart.

What makes a wedding ceremony so awesome? It is not the fact that two people say, "I love you." It is the fact that they are both saying, "I give up every other man or woman in the world for the sake of you. Here my quest ends. In you I will seek my joy." If the wedding vows were not a renunciation of every other possible partner in marriage, they would mean very little.

What we give is the measure of our love. If we were never asked to give, we would never realize that we can love. If we were never asked for the gift of ourselves, we would never know what it is to be loved as adults. In the act of giving ourselves we realize how much we love.

Little children are loved without being asked to give anything in return. And we can know God as our Father by just trusting in him, obeying him, and letting him give us all we need. But Jesus comes to us as Spouse. This is the relationship with him to which Baptism commits us (see Ephesians 5:22-33). And spousal love means total gift of self, total sacrifice for the sake of another. When Jesus Christ enters our lives we are no longer just little children; we are called to be adults in love.

What kind of Savior is Jesus? He is a Savior who calls us to the fullness of life—and this requires the fullness of love. He doesn't leave us infants. He won't settle for our faithful service (see John 15:15). He calls us to the length and breadth and height and depth of total, passionate love (see Ephesians 3:14-21). This means the total gift of ourselves.

Reflecting on This Week's Gospels

Fifth Week of the Year

Pray daily: Lord, you showed your love for me by coming to earth to live your whole life as one constant act of giving. Teach me to show my love for you in every word, choice and action of my life.

Monday: Mark 6:53-56: "Whatever villages he entered, they begged him that [the sick] might touch only the tassel on his cloak; and as many as touched it were healed." How can you be so loving toward everyone that anyone who is touched by you is healed in some way?

Tuesday: Mark 7:1-13: "You disregard God's commandment but cling to human tradition." Do you ever fail to do the loving thing (invite, include or defend someone) because your group would not like it?

Wednesday: Mark 7:14-23: "For it is from within people, from the heart, that evil intentions come: unchastity, theft, murder, adultery, greed, malice, deceit, loose living, envy, slander, arrogance, false values. All these evils come from within and they defile." Can you see how each and every one of these is a failure to love?

Thursday: Mark 7:24-30: "Let the children be fed first. For it is not right to take the food of the children and throw it to the dogs." Can love give its best gifts when they are not appreciated? What gifts of God do you not appreciate?

Friday: Mark 7:31-37: "The man's ears were opened, his speech impediment was removed, and he spoke plainly." Why does speaking depend on hearing? How does responding to God with love depend on hearing his word? How much do you listen to his words?

Saturday: Mark 8:1-10: Jesus said "My heart is moved with pity for the crowd, because they have been with me now for three days and have nothing to eat." How much concern do you have for all those who don't know about Communion or never receive it?

Living This Week's Gospels

As Christian: Give up one thing that is an obstacle to deeper relationship with Christ (something you spend time on instead of praying, going to daily Mass, or the like).

As Disciple: Read Matthew 13:44-45, asking how you have proved to yourself and experienced the value you place on union with Jesus Christ.

As Prophet: Examine your room, house, workplace for visible (and credible) signs of the place Jesus holds in your life.

As Priest: Each day express your love for Jesus Christ in some different, visible way.

As King: Ask yourself if there is any policy where you work, or way of acting among your friends or in your home, which uses fear instead of love to get things done. If so, see what you can do to change that.

Sixth Sunday of the Year

Guidance Systems

Luke 6:17, 20-26; Jeremiah 17: 5-8; 1 Corinthians 15:12, 16-20

There are certain basic choices everyone makes—consciously or not—which are so fundamental that they affect everything else we experience in life. They are like the choice to take one road or another: there are uphill roads, downhill roads, smooth roads, rough roads, roads that lead to interesting places, boring places, to people, to wilderness, to someplace or to nowhere. But once we have chosen a road, we have no more choice about what we are going to see and what we are going to experience. We have to make the best of whatever we meet on that particular road. Or we have to change roads.

One of these basic choices is the choice of a guidance system. What are we going to follow in making choices? Our feelings? Our reason? The guidance we get from our parents? Are we just going to follow the crowd, the culture? Do we look for guidance from God? From the Church? From a few trusted friends our own age? Or do we listen to no one but ourselves?

Most of us use all of these guidance systems at one time or another. But somewhere early in life we chose one or two of them as our primary guidance system. When we made that choice we may not have been aware we were making it. But our whole experience of life has been affected by it. The road we took has made things harder or easier for us, has shaped our lives and formed us as the persons we are.

The Scripture readings for this Sunday invite us to review that choice and decide—consciously this time—between two guidance systems that are offered to us. One is the "natural" one—which doesn't mean the one most according to the human nature God created, but the one most according to our human perceptions as they have been shaped by the world we live in. Our basic human equipment is fine; but its operation has been bent and programmed so much by the culture and by all the distorted attitudes, values and behavior we have experienced, that now all sorts of things seem "natural" to us that are not natural at all.

The guidance system Jesus offers us is the one God uses. It not only corrects the distortions of the culture; it goes beyond even what is human. By letting us share in the divine life of God, Jesus calls us and enables us to do what is natural only to God. This is what it means to live the "life of grace": to make choices in the light of faith, to put our hope in God's promises, to love like God does.

So Jesus reverses our "natural" human assumptions that it is more blessed to be rich, to have our physical desires satisfied, to be without emotional pain, and to be accepted and honored by others. He says "Blessed are you who are poor, hungry, weeping, for you will find joy and fulfillment in the Kingdom. And blessed are you who are hated, excluded, treated with contempt and lied about because of your association with me. When that happens rejoice and leap for joy, because your fulfillment will be that which continues in heaven."

Jesus is saying that we should leap for joy now, not later in heaven, because we are more blessed already here on earth when we follow his guidance system, regardless of whatever consequences we may fear. He says it clearly; the question is, do we trust him? Do we trust him enough to make his guidance system ours?

The key to it all is the Resurrection. If Jesus rose and we will rise from the dead, then "life to the full" has to be measured in terms of the kind of joy that lasts. A road that takes us through eighty or ninety years of physical and emotional satisfaction is not "life to the full" if life forever is an option. If we want our fulfillment to be like God's, we have to choose a road that takes us through the joys of truthful, loving gift of ourselves to others and to God. We have to choose his way.

Reflecting on This Week's Gospels

Sixth Week of the Year

Pray daily: Lord, you keep calling us closer to unconditional faith, to unshakable hope, to unlimited love. Don't give up on me. Teach me to respond. Amen.

Monday: Mark 8:11-13: Jesus sighed from the depth of his spirit and said, "Why does this generation seek a sign? Amen, I say to you, no sign will be given to this generation." If Jesus asked you, "Why do you believe in me?" what would you say?

Tuesday: Mark 8:14-21: Jesus said to the disciples, "Do you not remember, when I broke the five loaves for the five thousand...? Do you still not understand?" What has your experience of Eucharist revealed to you of Jesus?

Wednesday: Mark 8:22-26: "Then he laid hands on his eyes a second time and he saw clearly...." Can we "see clearly" from the beginning what the Church teaches? What are you doing to let Jesus keep touching you?

Thursday: Mark 8:27-33: Jesus asked his disciples, "Who do people say that I am?"... [Then] he asked them, "But who do you say that I am?" Who does the Church teach that Jesus is? How have you experienced him? Who is he to you?

Friday: Mark 8:34 to 9:1: "Whoever is ashamed of me and of my words in this faithless and sinful generation, the Son of Man will be ashamed of when he comes in his Father's glory." When you are around people who don't seem religious, are you ashamed to show your faith? To live your faith? To give your faith as the reason for your choices?

Saturday: Mark 9:2-13: Jesus was transfigured before them. Then Peter said, "Rabbi, it is good that we are here!" When have you said, or do you say, "Lord, it is good for you to be here!"? Why then?

Living This Week's Gospels

As Christian: Write down a list of the "guidance systems" you follow in your life. Arrange them in order of priority. Is there one to which you trust your life and well-being absolutely?

As Disciple: Write down the teachings (examples or sayings) of Jesus that you use most often or consistently as a guide for the choices you make.

As Prophet: Do one thing once or each day this week that clearly expresses to you that you are following the guidance system of Jesus and not of this world or your culture.

As Priest: Each day this week, re-read Luke 6:20-26 before you start your day. Then do something that day which shows that for you healing or ministering to others takes priority over possessions, prestige or acceptance by other people.

As King: Examine some practices, policies, structures, habits of your life-style, social life or professional work, asking what fulfillment they are designed to give: short-term or long-term (that is, eternal). Ask if any of them can be or should be changed.

The Plane of Love

Luke 6:27-38; 1 Samuel 26:2, 7-9, 12-13, 22-25;
1 Corinthians 15:45-50

The key to this Sunday's readings is "The first man, Adam, became a living being; the last Adam (Jesus) became a life-giving spirit.... Flesh and blood cannot inherit the kingdom of God." We are called to choose.

In Jesus what is "physical, from earth, made of dust" has been, not rejected, but transcended, surpassed. By grace we are an "updated version" of creation. We are in the image of Jesus who is "spiritual, from heaven." The body of Jesus, like ours, came from the dust. But it never returned to the dust; it rose uncorrupted from the dead to live forever. And we are destined to rise. Our perishable bodies will "inherit the imperishable" because we are no longer just mortal human beings, but immortal members of the Body of Christ. Our true life, true destiny, true fulfillment is not limited to the time and space of earth; it is "hidden with Christ in God." So Paul tells us, "If then you were raised with Christ, seek what is above, where Christ is seated at the right hand of God. Think of what is above, not of what is on earth. For you have died [in Baptism], and your life is hidden with Christ in God" (Colossians 3:1-4).

Only if we really accept this can the teaching of Jesus in the Gospel make sense to us. What Jesus says, in a nutshell, is, "Don't let any value on earth keep you from living the perfection of love—both for God and for other people." Nothing counts except living like Jesus Christ; and that means loving like Jesus Christ.

It means loving our enemies so much we will save their lives even if they are going to kill us. It means doing good to those who hate us instead of just avoiding or ignoring them.

It means speaking well of those who speak badly about us, and asking God to help and bless those who are trying to hurt us. It means praying for those who abuse us instead of clinging to anger and wanting them to suffer.

Jesus teaches that we should put more value on our relationship with other people than on anything else except God. We should never break up with another person over money or property (if someone takes away your coat, give your shirt also), or even over insults or rejection (offer the other cheek; stick your neck out again). This is the way God treats us.

The key to this is love. Jesus doesn't say we should just stop caring about anything in this world, as if true happiness were found in freeing ourselves from all desires through an "enlightenment" that sees all earthly values as empty. Nor does Jesus teach us to be passive in response to evil. It is not Christian just to let people abuse us, cheat us, lie to us or take advantage of us. It is Christian to respond to these things with an active, redeeming love, not only enduring whatever is necessary, but doing whatever is necessary to express to the other person the love of Christ and call that person to change, reform and to live life to the full.

When others abuse us, we have to love back, even if loving back gets us killed. When we just passively endure mistreatment, it is usually not out of love but out of fear: fear of confrontation, fear of reprisals, fear of losing a job, fear of losing the rewards we get out of a relationship. Jesus teaches us to do the most loving thing, whatever it is, without fear of anything we might lose or suffer on earth.

The first reason for this is that, no matter how much we love and value our lives on this earth, we know that nothing we enjoy here can compare with the fullness of life we possess already through union with God in grace and will experience in all its fullness in heaven.

The second is that, like Christ, and because we are united to him as "Lamb of God," we are specifically consecrated to giving and losing our lives for others. This is what we profess and celebrate in every Mass.

Reflecting on This Week's Gospels

Seventh Week of the Year

Pray daily: Lord, you accepted to take on everything human living involves for love of me. Give me the grace to take on everything divine living involves for love of you. Amen.

Monday: Mark 9:14-29: "I do believe, help my unbelief!" What do you believe and not believe at the same time? How are you asking Jesus to increase your faith?

Tuesday: Mark 9:30-37: He sat down, called the Twelve, and said to them, "Whoever wants to be first must be last of all and servant of all." Where, when do you want to be first? Why? What would it mean to be the servant of all in those situations?

Wednesday: Matthew 16:13-19: Jesus said to him in reply, "Blessed are you, Simon son of Jonah. For flesh and blood has not revealed this to you, but my heavenly Father." What do you believe about Jesus that you can only believe by the gift of faith? How do you express this belief in your life?

Thursday: Mark 9:41-50: "If any of you causes one of these little ones who believe in me to sin, it would be better for you if a great millstone were hung around your neck and you were thrown into the sea." Is this your attitude? What are you willing to lose rather than cause another person to sin or lose faith in God? Your time? Your property? Your rights?

Friday: Mark 10:1-12: The Pharisees approached and asked, "Is it lawful for a husband to divorce his wife?" How often do you ask whether something is "allowed" or "forbidden?" What should you ask?

Saturday: Mark 10:13-16: "Amen, I say to you, whoever does not accept the kingdom of God like a child will not enter it." How have you experienced being "reborn"—not emotionally, but in terms of taking on a whole new way of life?

Living This Week's Gospels

As Christian: Divide a piece of paper into two columns entitled "Human level" and "Divine level." Write each major choice of your life under the heading that expresses the level you were acting on when you made it.

As Disciple: Make a list of what in practice you consider "essentials" in your life. After each write whether this judgment comes from your gut, your culture, or from Christ's teaching. Do the same for "desirables."

As Prophet: Look at each item in your room or house. Ask yourself to what value system each one proclaims your loyalty.

As Priest: Each day this week, look ahead and choose one person to whom you will specifically minister that day. What will you do? (This is only to focus, not to limit.)

As King: Think of the people you serve—at work, at home, in your social life. To what level of needs in each do you minister? How do you, can you minister to each one's need for God?

Eighth Sunday of the Year

About Trivial Pursuits

Luke 6:39-45; Sirach 27: 4-7; 1 Corinthians 15:54-58

The blind can't guide the blind. We cannot reform others without reforming ourselves. In order to do good we have to become good. Everything we do depends on what we are in our hearts. "For it is out of the abundance of the heart that the mouth speaks."

What Jesus does in this Gospel is invite us to look into our hearts and to cooperate with him in making our hearts like his; that is, to make what we are inside match what he is in his own mind and will and heart.

And why does he do this? It is so that our lives will count for something, will "bear fruit" on this earth. It is so that when we die the world will be different for our having lived.

Everything changed with Jesus' coming. The real power is not with the powerful anymore; nor the real productivity with the most productive. We don't have to be brilliant or talented or strategically placed in order to change history or have influence on the world. In fact, those who think they are changing the world are probably having the least effect of all. For example, throughout history and to this day rulers and nations have spent enormous energy on wars to rearrange national boundaries. And we spent hours in history class learning about it! But changing frontiers and governments has about as much effect on real human history as changing the lines on notebook paper while someone else is doing the writing. The real action, the action that counts, and the actions that make people different forever take place within the human heart. The only changes that endure are the ones that take place in the heart. Everything else is ultimately trivial.

The problem with the news media is that the news they report is not really significant, but by focusing on it they make us think it is. Ten people praying can affect history more than an army invading a country. One man surrendering his whole heart to God while dying in a hospital is more important in the real history of humanity than the victory of a presidential candidate. A hundred years from now none of us now living will care who was president during this decade or see any advantage to ourselves in anything he did. We will be grateful in heaven to many people, but only for the love they gave us and for the ways they helped us to know and love God. Nothing else anyone does for us will matter then, because we will see how totally insignificant it was in terms of lasting effect.

The truth is, we can love God and other people with our whole hearts whether the government makes us rich or poor, whether the environment keeps us healthy or makes us sick, whether the military protects us or lets us be invaded, whether our houses are broken into or not, and whether we are murdered on the street or live to be a hundred. What is really important for us, what is making the only history that counts, and what we really should be following as news, is what is happening that will help us know God, love God and people, and contribute to establishing the reign of God on earth. His is the only reign, the only kingdom that lasts, and what contributes to its establishment is the only history the human race really has.

So who are our guides? To whom do we listen? To those who think that what is reported in the news really matters? Or to those whose whole focus is on the Good News that began with Jesus Christ? Where do we get if we follow guides who are so blind they can't see one step beyond the grave? Or, to say the same thing, beyond the economic and political concerns of the country? (How much time would Jesus waste worrying about the stock market?)

Why do we bother to criticize, much less to hate, politicians (or anyone) who can only affect our physical well-being? Jesus says, "Check out your own value system first. Then decide if you have anything to be concerned about."

Reflecting on This Week's Gospels

Eighth Week of the Year

Pray daily: Lord, when you came into the world you became the mainspring of human history. Join me to yourself in mind and heart, that I might continue your work on earth. Amen.

Monday: Mark 10:17-27: A man ran up, knelt down before Jesus, and asked him, "Good teacher, what must I do to inherit eternal life?" Have you ever asked this question seriously of Jesus? Recently? What did he say? What did he say to the man in the Gospel? What response have you made to that?

Tuesday: Mark 10:28-31: Peter began to say to him, "We have given up everything and followed you." Can you say this? What would you have to give up to follow Jesus totally? What is more important: to give up what you have or are doing, or to change your attitude toward it?

Wednesday: Mark 10:32-45: James and John asked Jesus, "Grant that in your glory we may sit one at your right and the other at your left." Jesus said to them, "You do not know what you are asking." Have you really thought out your goals in life? Do you think past immediate desires to ask what you are really desiring through this?

Thursday: Mark 10:46-52: Jesus said to the blind man, "What do you want me to do for you?" The blind man replied to him, "Master, I want to see." If Jesus asked you this question, what would you answer? Why?

Friday: Mark 11:11-26: Jesus was hungry. Seeing in the distance a fig tree in leaf, he went over to see whether perhaps he would find anything on it. When he came to it he found nothing but leaves, for it was not the season for figs. He said to it, "May no one ever eat fruit from you again!" What is Jesus "hungry" for today? What does he expect of you? Is there anything in your life that just gives the appearance of doing real good to others?

Saturday: Mark 11:27-33: The chief priests, the scribes, and the elders came to Jesus and said, "By what authority are you doing these things? Who gave you this authority to do them?" Every right is based on an obligation. What do you have a right to do because God requires it of you?

Living This Week's Gospels

As Christian: Look at the front page of the newspaper. Ask how much of the news there will matter to anyone after death.

As Disciple: Read a little bit of the Sermon on the Mount (Matthew, chapter 5). Ask how people living by this would change history.

As Prophet: At the end of each day this week, ask what you have done that will still matter after the end of the world.

As Priest: Each day this week, consciously do something for someone that will be of benefit to that person forever.

As King: Ask what service you are doing for people through your work or studies. Then ask how long what you do will be important for them. Then ask how you can do the same things in a way that will benefit both you and others for all eternity.

LENT

Ash Wednesday and Weekdays After Ash Wednesday

Reflecting on This Week's Gospels

Pray daily: Lord, help me believe that you want to speak to my heart, to me personally during this Lent. Give me the decisiveness to break with what I am doing and spend time with you. Call me and I will follow. Amen.

Ash Wednesday: Matthew 6:1-6, 16-18: Jesus said, "[W]henever you pray, go into your room and shut the door and pray to your Father who is in secret." Do you look forward to private times with people you love? Do you have the same feeling about being alone with God? Why?

Thursday after Ash Wednesday: Luke 9:22-25: Jesus asks, "What does it profit them if they gain the whole world, but lose or forfeit themselves?" How can you "lose yourself" in the life you are living now? Are you always conscious of your deep identity as child of God, Body of Christ, committed to spousal relationship with God? What do you lose if you lose awareness of this?

Friday after Ash Wednesday: Matthew 9:14-15: The disciples of John the Baptizer asked Jesus, "Why do we and the Pharisees fast often, but your disciples do not fast?" What do you do that shows your love for Jesus? Your desire to be more closely united to him? Your hunger to know him better?

Saturday after Ash Wednesday: Luke 5:27-32: Jesus saw a tax collector named Levi sitting at the customs post. He said to him, "Follow me." And leaving everything behind, he got up and followed him. Do you follow Jesus with passion? Leaving everything behind when he calls? What does he mean to you? How does it show?

Several Suggestions for Lent

Prayer: Choose a prayer to say every day as soon as you wake up. If necessary, put something by your bed to remind you.

Fasting: Choose something you do every day and abstain from it one day a week, just to prove to yourself you are not doing it compulsively.

Almsgiving: Make a list of what you give that can be called alms, or support to the poor.

First Sunday of Lent
Jesus Is Victory
Luke 4:1-13; Deuteronomy 26:4-10; Romans 10:8-13

In this Gospel we see Jesus overcoming the deepest temptations of the human race. We see both that he overcomes them and how he overcomes them. In this we see Jesus revealed both as Savior and Teacher.

Our first deep temptation is to material prosperity and all that it stands for: success, security and the means to comfort and enjoyment. All of this is symbolized in Jesus' temptation to turn stones into bread.

Jesus answers by teaching us something that goes contrary to most of the voices in our culture. He says that what we desire more than prosperity is to know God. He says we will find more enjoyment, happiness and fulfillment out of reading Scripture than out of having money. Let's be honest: Who can believe this? Who does believe it? (Answer: those who have dedicated their lives to it.)

A second deep temptation of the human race is to power: the power to do things, the power to accomplish things. Experience shows that once we have power we are in great danger of putting ourselves above the law when we think it is necessary in order to achieve our goals. We see this in the political scandals and cover-ups of our time. The highest powers in our country have been exposed as violating the law and the Constitution in order to achieve their goals, believing they were justified in doing it. Power corrupts. It does something to the conscience.

Jesus was tempted to make a deal with the devil in order to gain control over the sources of power in this world. It was for a good purpose, of course: to establish the reign of God. He responded by pointing out that you cannot establish the reign of God by giving the devil a place on the throne.

Nothing we can accomplish, no matter how good it seems, really helps people if it gives disobedience to God more acceptance in the world.

Jesus answers with the first commandment. The first law of our hearts must be that God is God, and nothing—nothing at all—ever justifies us in dividing our loyalty between God and any other person, authority or value.

The third temptation is to measure God by our standards: to say, for example, that a good God could not possibly ask the sacrifice of our lives—or of something really important to us. The devil tempts Jesus to run a test to see if God will preserve his life—implying that God cannot possibly let his beloved Son die. And if God does let him die (as he did later on the cross), Jesus cannot possibly be the Savior.

There is something deep in us that puts conditions on our faith, our trust in God. We will keep God's law up to the point where it seems clear we will lose our lives because of it—or lose something or someone we feel is essential to our happiness. Then we say, "A loving God could not possibly ask this of me, and if he does he cannot be a loving God." This is what it means to put God to the test.

Jesus answered that God is not to be called into question. We don't accept God because he does what we expect him to do. Rather, we observe what God does and try to learn from it.

In this Gospel Jesus is revealed as the Savior who triumphs, even though to all appearances he was defeated. The people with power in this world succeeded in killing him. And they still win out over those who live by his values. But Jesus overcame and overcomes the only real threat to our human existence: sin and the illusions that lead to sin. From the viewpoint of this world Jesus is an ineffective Savior. All the things in the environment that we want to be saved from still exist. But if we look at what Jesus actually does offer to save us from, we will understand better what salvation really is. Then we will know Jesus as Savior.

Reflecting on This Week's Gospels

First Week of Lent

> *Pray daily:* Lord Jesus, I believe that you came to triumph over sin and death, that you did triumph, and that you will come again in triumph. Help me to remember always that I am following a victorious Lord.

Monday: Matthew 25:31-46: Jesus said, "When the Son of Man comes in his glory, and all the angels with him, then he will sit on the throne of his glory. All nations will be gathered before him, and he will separate people one from another, as a shepherd separates the sheep from the goats." How much courage could you draw from remembering this when you are faced with challenges and temptations?

Tuesday: Matthew 6:7-15: Jesus said, "When you are praying, do not heap up empty phrases as the Gentiles do; for they think that they will be heard because of their many words." How can you change your prayer this Lent to make it deeper, more reflective? How much time do you give to reading prayers or to saying the same words over and over? How much to thinking about Christ's words?

Wednesday: Luke 11:29-32: Jesus said, "[J]ust as Jonah became a sign to the people of Nineveh, so the Son of Man will be to this generation." How often do you think about the Resurrection of Jesus? How does it help you? How could it?

Thursday: Matthew 7:7-12: "For everyone who asks receives, and everyone who searches finds; and for everyone who knocks, the door will be opened." Do you believe this? Do you understand it in the light of Jesus' victory on the cross? What has Jesus won the right to give us?

Friday: Matthew 5:20-26: "You have heard that it was said to those of ancient times, 'You shall not murder'; and 'whoever murders shall be liable to judgment.' But I say to you that if you are angry with a brother or sister, you will be liable to judgment." When the ideals Jesus teaches seem unrealistic and even ridiculous by the light of our cultural common sense, how can it help you to remember that he will come in triumph to judge the world on how we have accepted and followed them?

Saturday: Matthew 5:43-48: "You have heard that it was said, 'You shall love your neighbor and hate your enemy.' But I say to you, love your enemies, and pray for those who persecute you." Do you think that Jesus' way of nonviolence "works"?

Several Suggestions for Lent:

Prayer: Say the Our Father each day, conscious that you are praying with hope and confidence for the final triumph of Christ.

Fasting: For one week, give up something you don't need, just to express consciously your belief that because of the triumph of Jesus you really don't need it.

Almsgiving: Make a special contribution to your parish or to some other work of the Church, as an explicit affirmation of your belief that Christ will triumph through the efforts of his body on earth.

Jesus Is Savior

Luke 9:28-36; Genesis 15:5-12, 17-18; Philippians 3:17 to 4:1

T he Transfiguration takes place right after Jesus reveals to his disciples that he is not going to save the world in the way they expect, but by dying on the cross— and that anyone who accepts him as Savior must accept to "carry the cross," which means to accept those particular consequences of the sin of the world which happen to fall on us and to respond with love. The power Jesus uses to save the world is the power he gives us to love back, no matter what happens to us.

In this context, after Jesus has revealed the scandalous way in which he is going to save the world, the Father speaks again, as he did at the beginning of Jesus' mission (Luke 3:22, Matthew 3:17) to confirm that Jesus is truly the "Son of God," the Savior he promised to send.

The Transfiguration revealed Jesus in an extraordinary way as the promised "Son of God." His glory as God actually shone out through his human body. But Jesus is also revealed to us as Savior in a constant stream of very ordinary incidents— or which appear to be ordinary until we reflect on them.

"Son of David": Isn't it true that our whole experience of life is different because we know that Jesus has come to fulfill all God's promises to us? Through him we know the beginning and end of our existence. We know that human life and suffering are intelligible. We know that the teachings we live by are not just human speculation. We know that in the ministry of the Church Jesus Christ acts with authority and power to teach us, strengthen and heal us. We know that death itself has no real power over us. And all of this is because Jesus has come as the promised "Son of David."

"Jesus": We realize the significance for us of the name

"Jesus," "God saves," in every ordinary experience of the Sacrament of Reconciliation. This sacrament embodies the words, "You are to name him Jesus because he will save his people from their sins."

"Son of God": We don't have to see Jesus transfigured on a mountaintop to experience the presence of the divine. Every time we genuflect before the Blessed Sacrament, every time we receive Jesus in Communion, we know that we are in a live encounter with Jesus as "Son of God." Our adoration of him in faith is also our acknowledgment and our assurance of the power that is his to save us from sin and death. Jesus is a divine Savior who gives divine life and "baptizes with the Holy Spirit," giving us power to live on the level of God.

"Emmanuel": Jesus is God present to us in human ways. his human words in Scripture speak to our hearts. His human actions recorded there reveal his personality to us as truly as if we were physically present witnessing them. He teaches and ministers to us still in his human Body on earth, the Church. Every sacrament is an encounter with Jesus acting humanly to bless us, as is every experience of Jesus acting in and through another human being by grace. These are all experiences of "Emmanuel," "God-with-us."

"Universal Lord": Jesus is not restricted to one culture or language, or even to religious symbols alone. He uses a multitude of "stars" to lead us to himself as he led the Magi. Through how many signs, symbols, chance encounters and events does he inspire us, guide and enlighten us every day? If we are alert to his action in our lives, we experience him daily as the "Universal Lord" whose messenger voices, like the stars themselves, extend from one end of the universe to the other, addressing every human heart.

The Transfiguration was a mystical vision. But if we look with eyes of faith at our environment, everything is transfigured. Then we will see the glory of Jesus shining through our everyday experience, and we will know him for the Savior he is.

Reflecting on This Week's Gospels

Second Week of Lent

Pray daily: Lord, show yourself to me as you are. Enlighten my mind and win my heart. Draw me to the mountaintop this Lent, alone with you, that I might see you and hear the Father's heart.

Monday: Luke 6:36-38: Jesus said, "Be merciful, just as your Father is merciful." How often do you remember God's mercy to you when you want to hurt someone? When you are angry, do you think of how Jesus showed mercy in the Gospels?

Tuesday: Matthew 23:1-12: Jesus said, "Nor are you to be called instructors, for you have one instructor, the Messiah." On a daily basis, how much time do you give to learning from Jesus? Is it enough to prove that you really respect Jesus as the one who alone can teach you how to live?

Wednesday: Matthew 20:17-28: Jesus said, "You know that the rulers of the Gentiles lord it over them, and the great ones are tyrants over them. It will not be so among you; but whoever wishes to be great among you must be your servant." Did Jesus show himself to everyone in the glory of his transfiguration? Why not? Why do you want prestige?

Thursday: Luke 16:19-31: There was a rich man who dressed in purple garments and fine linen and dined sumptuously each day. And lying at his door was a poor man named Lazarus, covered with sores. What is your closest contact with the poor? How do you feel about those whom you see? What do you do about it?

Friday: Matthew 21:33-46: "The stone that the builders rejected has become the cornerstone." We believe that Jesus is the cornerstone of human existence; that everything good and lasting must be based on him. Can you say he is the cornerstone of your life? How does this show?

Saturday: Luke 15:11-32: When the prodigal son came to his senses he thought, "How many of my father's hired hands have bread enough and to spare, but here I am, dying of hunger!" How much spiritual nourishment does Jesus offer you through the Bible, the sacraments, the services, talks and discussions available in your parish? Are other people making use of these while you grow weak from undernourishment?

Several Suggestions for Lent

Prayer: Each day this week go "up the mountain" with Jesus, asking to see him in a new way, to understand and appreciate him more. Read a passage from Scripture to help you, but mainly just ask yourself how good he is.

Fasting: You can't enjoy what is at the top of the mountain and the foot of the mountain at the same time. What are you willing to set aside during Lent in order to have a deeper experience of Jesus?

Almsgiving: Each time you see someone who is short of a decent level of human existence, materially, morally or in any other way, try to imagine how that person will appear to you in heaven. What do you hear the Father's voice saying to you?

Seeing Jesus in Action

Luke 13:1-9; Exodus 3:1-8, 13-15; 1 Corinthians 10:1-6, 10-12

T his story shows us Jesus being our Savior in a way
we may not associate with being saved.

We think of being saved as letting the savior do something.
When we are rescued we are passive, helpless. But Jesus is a
Savior who does not just save us *from* something. He saves us
for something. He calls us to action.

Being rescued can sometimes actually keep us from the
fullness of life. By making it unnecessary for us to act, a
rescuer can prevent us from growing. Jesus does not do this.

In this Gospel story Jesus shows God as one who insists
we bear fruit. His unconditional love for us is not a write-off.
He doesn't say we are just hopelessly corrupt, incompetent
little creatures of whom nothing can be expected. On the
contrary, God's insistence that we bear fruit is God's
testimony to us that the human nature he created is able to
do great and good things, and that grace does not take the
place of nature, but rather empowers human nature to do
divine things.

The point is that by grace human nature is empowered.
Our natures are not supplanted; they are saved. Our human
actions themselves become fruitful. By grace we ourselves
become the ones who are doing good things, becoming better
persons, acting on the level of God. By grace we are not sent
to the sidelines while God takes over; we ourselves become
able to make choices that shape our own souls and give life
to the world. Grace is not just God acting within us; grace is
God acting with us.

This is such an important element of our faith that the
Church proclaims it in every Mass. At the Presentation of the
Gifts, when the priest presents the bread and wine to God he

says, "this bread...which earth has given and human hands have made.... This wine...fruit of the vine and the work of human hands." The offering we make—our own human lives and persons—is the product of God's creative act and his gift of grace, but also the product of our own choices. We had a hand in it.

The Offertory is the Catholic "altar call." The bread and wine represent us. When they are placed on the altar, we are symbolically placing ourselves on the altar again to reaffirm the gift of ourselves which we made at Baptism, when we "offered our bodies as a living sacrifice to God" (see Romans 12:1). We offered ourselves then to be transformed by grace and to become the real Body of Christ on earth. And at every Mass we offer ourselves again; we recommit ourselves to that process of total growth, that total transformation into Christ which is the goal of all human living.

There would be no point in such recommitment if we were not expected to do anything ourselves, or if our own efforts to conform our hearts to his had no effect.

The Church calls us to continual conversion and change, just as today's Gospel does. This call to conversion is at the same time a proclamation that human nature can be made perfect, and that the perfection we will enjoy forever in heaven will be both God's gift to us and "the work of human hands"—our gift of love to him. This is why Jesus as Savior is always urging us to make good choices and calling us to greater faith, hope and love.

If we are conscientious about trying to live by Christ's words and the inspirations of his Spirit, then we also experience him frequently as the "crisis" in our lives. By word and inspiration Jesus repeatedly calls upon us to take the responsibility of making decisions in faith and to live by them. Every moment of choice is a moment of "crisis," a moment in which we determine the shape of our souls, becoming either more like Jesus or less. To embrace such moments is to embrace a religion of growth.

Reflecting on This Week's Gospels

Third Week of Lent

Pray daily: Lord Jesus, you came as a human being yourself to restore our human nature wounded by sin. You have the strength to empower us to live on the level of God. Inspire me during this Lent to reach higher, relying on your grace.

Monday: Luke 4:24-30: Jesus said, "Truly I tell you, no prophet is accepted in the prophet's home town." Are you so used to being a Christian that you don't really pay much attention to Christ?

Tuesday: Matthew 18:21-35: Jesus said that we must forgive, "not seven times but seventy-seven times." How many stories in the Gospels can you name that show Jesus forgiving?

Wednesday: Matthew 5:17-19: Jesus said, "Do not think that I have come to abolish the law or the prophets. I have come not to abolish but to fulfill." What have you seen Jesus doing in the Gospels that goes beyond the teaching of the law and prophets? What do you do?

Thursday: Luke 11:14-23: Jesus said, "Whoever is not with me is against me, and whoever does not gather with me scatters." What does it mean to "gather with" Jesus? What does it mean to "scatter?" Which do you experience in your life more strongly?

Friday: Mark 12:28-34: Jesus taught that the greatest commandment is, "You shall love the Lord your God with all your heart, with all your soul, with all your mind, and with all your strength." How do you use each of your human powers to grow into greater love for God? Your memory? Your intellect? Your will? Your affectivity?

Saturday: Luke 18:9-14: Jesus said, "All who exalt themselves will be humbled, but all who humble themselves will be exalted." Is it pride to think that, by using what God has given you and asking for his grace, you can become a close friend of Jesus Christ? That you can give him great service? Do you use false humility as an excuse to be a mediocre Christian?

Several Suggestions for Lent

Prayer: Raise the level of your prayer. If you say the rosary, begin to meditate on the mysteries (if you don't know how, ask someone). If you read prayers, spend time thinking on the meaning of the words. Do the same for the prayers you hear read at Mass.

Fasting: Do something during this week that you have always given yourself an excuse not to do. For example, is it really impossible to go to daily Mass? To read Scripture each day? To have family prayer together?

Almsgiving: For this week, spend as much on the poor as you spend on pleasure for yourself (such as drinks other than water, entertainment, optional meals at restaurants, smoking if you are still addicted, and so on).

Fourth Sunday of Lent

Conversion: When Is It Real?

Luke 15:1-32; Joshua 5:9, 10-12; 2 Corinthians 5:17-21

W e live in a time of multiplied conversions. Hardly one among us does not know someone who has had a "conversion experience." Sometimes the conversion is to another religion. We see Catholics converting to fundamentalist churches or to some "non-denominational" church (no church is non-denominational; some are just undefined) in which enthusiasm replaces theology and the popularity of the preacher dispenses with any historical connection with Jesus.

Sometimes conversion is to a different way of living one's own religion, or to a significantly different level of spiritual awareness and activity. We see this happening frequently in youth who have made Search or adults who have made the Cursillo weekend. We see it in members of charismatic prayer groups.

Sometimes the conversion is away from Christianity itself, to one of the ancient "pagan" religions such as Buddhism or Hinduism. Sometimes it is away from God and religion entirely: a conversion to agnosticism or atheism.

Some conversions last a few days or weeks. Others are for a lifetime.

Whatever the conversion is to or from, we live in an age of it. And it makes us ask when a conversion or "conversion experience" is authentic. Can there be a real conversion which is nevertheless incomplete, or lacking some element which is needed for the conversion to be authentically Christian?

In the story of the Prodigal Son, Jesus himself shows us what authentic conversion involves.

Conversion is an active choice ("I will return...") which is conscious and aware ("Coming to his senses...") and expressed in action ("With that he set off..."). An authentic conversion to Christ is radical: it goes to the roots of our attitudes and values, and is, in fact, an act of emancipation from every human culture or value system ("I will break away..."). It can, however, be a gradual process ("he set off..." and "While he was still a long way off...").

Christian conversion is expressed in a confession of sin ("Father, I have sinned..."). But to be truly Christian, it must be a conversion, not just to good human behavior, but to a whole new level of life: the divine life of grace ("was dead and has come back to life").

An explicitly Christian conversion must in some way be motivated by the event of Christ's coming into this world. This is suggested in the parable by the words, "he was lost, and is found." In the story, the Prodigal was not found; he just came home. But in reality, every sinner is sought out and brought to God by Jesus, the Good Shepherd.

Likewise, a truly Christian conversion must be inspired by faith in Jesus. This can be only implicit: that is, a faith that is not conscious of Jesus as such, but which does not make sense without him. In the story, the Prodigal returns to his "Father." In reality, however, no one can legitimately believe in God as "Father" except those who know him through faith in Jesus the Son; and are "sons in the Son," made members of Jesus, the "only Son" of God, by Baptism.

Lent is a good time for us to ask about conversion—not only because the season is an invitation to "repentance"; that is, to a "change of heart," but also because during Lent the Church gives special attention to those preparing for Baptism. It is a time for all of us to reflect on the conversion which our own Baptism expressed, and to ask if we are still expressing it in action as a conscious, radical choice to live on the level of God in response to the coming of Jesus Christ into our lives.

Reflecting on This Week's Gospels

Fourth Week of Lent

Pray daily: Father, I believe that "eternal life is this, to know you, the only true God, and the one whom you sent, Jesus Christ." Give me the grace to be loyal in loving and living your word. Amen.

Monday: John 4:43-54: Jesus said, "Unless you people see signs and wonders, you will not believe." Are you conscious of believing in Jesus by a free choice? Have you given your word to him firmly? Do you need new and miraculous events to motivate you to live out what you believe?

Tuesday: John 5:1-3, 5-16: The sick man answered Jesus, "Sir, I have no one to put me into the pool when the water is stirred up; while I am on my way, someone else gets down there before me." Jesus said to him, "Rise, take up your mat, and walk." Are you lying around waiting for a miracle while Jesus is saying to you, "Get up and walk!"?

Wednesday: John 5:17-30: Jesus said, "Amen, amen, I say to you, whoever hears my word and believes in the one who sent me has eternal life and will not come to condemnation, but has passed from death to life." How often do you make a conscious act of faith in the words of Jesus that you hear? Do you do this in response to the Scripture read at Mass? To all the words of the Eucharistic liturgy? To the words of absolution in the Sacrament of Reconciliation?

Thursday: John 5:31-47: Jesus said, "The works that the Father gave me to accomplish, these works that I perform testify on my behalf that the Father has sent me. Moreover, the Father who sent me has testified on my behalf." Do you know enough about Jesus to convince you intellectually that he was sent from God? Do the works Jesus does in the Church convince you? Have you recognized the testimony to Jesus that God himself is giving you in your heart?

Friday: John 7:1-2; 10, 25-30: Jesus cried out in the temple area as he was teaching and said, "You know me and also know where I am from. I have not come on my own. But the one who sent me is true. And you do not know him." Can you truly say you know Jesus? Is it also true that you can never know him in this life as you desire? What are you doing to know him better?

Saturday: John 7:40-53: "There was division in the crowd because of Jesus. Some of them wanted to arrest him, but no one laid hands on him." Are the people you know or work with ambivalent in their attitude toward Jesus? Do they accept him and not accept him at the same time? What about you? Do you accept him absolutely and unconditionally as the only Savior of the world and only authentic Teacher of life?

Several Suggestions for Lent

Prayer: Recite the Profession of Faith or Apostles' Creed each day this week. Consciously make an act of faith in everything you say.

Fasting: Look around your house to see if anything you have, wear or use implicitly denies your faith in Jesus Christ and his values. Abstain from it during Lent—and then get rid of it.

Almsgiving: Pope John Paul II teaches that "moderation and simplicity ought to become the criteria of our daily lives" (World Day of Peace address, 1993). Take time during Lent to simplify your life-style, trim down your possessions, and give what you renounce to the poor.

Fifth Sunday of Lent

Does Baptism Forgive Sins or Take Them Away?

John 8:1-11; Isaiah 43:16-21; Philippians 3:8-14

Jesus didn't just forgive the woman caught in adultery. He said, "I do not condemn you." Does this mean she was no longer an adulteress? The answer is yes, but to understand it, we have to understand Baptism.

The earliest Christians only knew of one sacrament to take away sins: It was Baptism. Through Baptism people accepted the "grace of Our Lord Jesus Christ," came to know the "love of the Father," and entered into the "fellowship of the Holy Spirit." They received Baptism as adult converts, and by Baptism they were freed from all their sins, totally reconciled to God, made children of the Father "in Christ" and heirs of all the promises of the Good News. It all came through Baptism. Reconciliation, the confession and forgiveness of sins committed after Baptism, was only recognized as a distinct sacrament later.

This is important, because Baptism is the key to understanding all forgiveness of sin. We cannot understand what Reconciliation does except by understanding what Baptism does.

Through Baptism God does not just forgive our sins; he takes away our sins. In every eucharistic celebration we proclaim Jesus, not as the one who forgives the sins of the world, but as the Lamb of God who takes away the sins of the world. The difference is crucial.

(No play on words is intended, but "crucial," which comes from crux—"cross"—is the right word. It is because of the cross that Jesus can take away, and not just forgive, our sins.)

If God just forgave us, there would be a change in him,

but not in us. "Forgiveness" would mean that God is not angry with us, that he is not going to punish us, that he accepts us back as his children in good standing, and so forth. But we would be exactly what we were. Only God's attitude would be different.

But if Jesus takes away our sins, then we are different. We are no longer guilty. We are actually cleansed, purified, innocent again. The bad actions that were part of our history, our life story, no longer affect or determine who we are. They are no longer part of us.

This seems impossible. How can an action that is part of the history that makes us who we are cease to be part of who we are? How can we ever not be the persons we have become?

Before we give an answer, let us repeat what we believe: Jesus does not just forgive (do something on his side); he takes away the sins of the world. And what can that mean if not that our sins are no longer part of our life, no longer a real, determining element of who we are? However we explain it, the fact is that our sins no longer exist. Baptism takes them away. To see this, we need to understand Baptism.

The real nature of Baptism is best expressed through immersion. Baptism is not just a washing; it is a going down into the grave with Jesus to rise again with him. We are baptized "into Christ," into the body that hung on the cross. As members of that body on the cross, we died in him when he died. And when he rose, we rose in him to live a new and different life on earth: a life not only human but divine. We rise up from the waters of Baptism to live as the risen body of Jesus, to continue his saving presence and work on earth.

This means our past died in Jesus. Our history of sin ended when we died in him at Baptism. And our life story began anew when we rose from the grave, rose out of the waters of Baptism, as his risen body on earth. We are "a new creation." God says, "Behold, I make all things new!"

(For further reflection, read these Scripture texts: John 20:19-23; Romans 6:1-11; 2 Corinthians 5:14-21; Galatians 3:23-29; Ephesians 4:14-24; Colossians 2:9-15.)

Reflecting on This Week's Gospels

Fifth Week of Lent

Pray daily: Jesus, through your death and rising you made all things new. Through my Baptism you made me a "new creation." Help me to live out the death I accepted in Baptism and live the new life I received. Amen.

Monday: John 8:1-11: Then Jesus said, "Neither do I condemn you. Go your way, and from now on do not sin again." Are you aware that Jesus has said these same words to you through Baptism? Do you hear them again every time you receive the Sacrament of Reconciliation? What effect do they have on you? Do you truly believe God does not despise you?

Tuesday: John 8:21-30: Jesus said, "When you have lifted up the Son of Man, then you will realize that I am he, and that I do nothing on my own, but I speak these things as the Father instructed me." What actions in your life make it so obvious you have "died" to merely human goals and behavior that people recognize the divine life of grace within you?

Wednesday: John 8:31-50: Jesus said, "If you were Abraham's children, you would be doing what Abraham did." Do the things you do make you stand out as a child of God, or do you fit right in as a product of your culture? What did Abraham do? How are you doing the same thing?

Thursday: John 8:51-59: Jesus said, "Very truly, I tell you, whoever keeps my word will never see death." What do you think death will be for you? Do you believe that by dying in Christ by Baptism, you have already risen in Christ? What does that mean to you?

Friday: John 10:31-42: Jesus said, "If I am not doing the works of my Father, do not believe me. But if I do them, even though you do not believe me, believe the works, so that you may know and understand that the Father is in me and I am in the Father." Can you say this? Are you the Body of Christ by Baptism, and a temple of the Holy Spirit? How does that show in your actions?

Saturday: John 11:45-57: Caiaphas, who was high priest that year, said, "You know nothing at all! You do not understand that it is better for you to have one man die for the people than to have the whole nation destroyed." How did Jesus' death save us? Do you think it just "paid our debt," or do you understand that through Baptism "into Christ" we died in Christ on the cross and our sins were annihilated? What difference does this make in the way you feel about your past sins?

Several Suggestions for Lent

Prayer: Each day recite from memory Luke 1:28 and 42 (you know these verses; they are the first half of the Hail Mary). But hear them as said to yourself. Think of how Baptism makes you God's "highly favored one" (the biblical meaning of "full of grace"). How is the Lord "with you"? Why are you "blessed among people"? Why is the "fruit of your life" blessed? Close your refection each day with the second half of the Hail Mary.

Fasting: Abstain for a week from negative thoughts about yourself. Each time you notice a fault in yourself, think of how you have died in Christ by Baptism and risen to live a new life in him, as a "new creation." Bless yourself with water each morning as a reminder of your Baptism and to help you do this.

Almsgiving: Begin making Easter presents for people to whom you are close. Make something which will express to them that they are a new creation, filled with divine life, precious in the eyes of God.

Passion (Palm) Sunday

The Stones Would Shout

Gospel Before the Procession: Luke 19:28-40

When Jesus rode into Jerusalem to die in triumph there, the Pharisees wanted Jesus to stop his disciples from proclaiming him "the king who comes in the name of the Lord." He answered, "I tell you, if these were silent, the stones would shout out."

The words the disciples were shouting are the same ones the Church chooses to pick up and repeat in every Sunday liturgy: "Blessed is he who comes in the name of the Lord!" But where Matthew's crowd acclaims Jesus as "Son of David," and Mark turns our attention to the reign that is about to begin ("Blessed is the coming kingdom of our ancestor David"), Luke focuses on the person of Jesus as king: "Blessed is the king who comes in the name of the Lord." John does the same, but John specifies that Jesus is "the King of Israel," while Luke wants to present him from a more universal perspective as the king of the whole human race.

These differences invite us to ask how each of us would—and does—respond differently to Jesus who presents himself before the gates of our heart to enter, to dwell and to reign there. Do we accept Jesus in faith as "Son of David," the Messiah promised in prophecy and awaited as the fulfillment of all God's promises? Do we welcome him as the Lord who will bring order to our world by establishing the reign of God over every area and activity of human society? Do we open our gates in loving surrender to his person as king and commander of all that we are, desire and do? Who is Jesus for us, and what do we do to acclaim him?

When Jesus entered Jerusalem people came out to meet him carrying palm branches. Some cut branches from the trees to carpet the road before him. Others spread their cloaks on the ground, "a person's costliest piece of clothing. True to his theme of rich and poor, Luke describes people's responses to Jesus the king by means of the use of their possessions" (*The New Jerome Biblical Commentary*). All expressed their enthusiasm, each in a personal way. We will see this done very movingly on Good Friday, when every person in the Church files forward to venerate the cross. Rich and poor, old and young, reserved and spontaneous, all will express themselves by kneeling, bowing, kissing the cross, acknowledging in some individual, personal way their own indebtedness and devotion to Jesus who died for them. And this is what every liturgical celebration should be: a group of people expressing their faith, their hope, their gratitude and love communally but personally, in the same way but differently, according to the personality of each and the special meaning which each person's situation and condition gives to what is said and done. And if we are silent, "the very stones will shout out."

The passion of Jesus which we begin to relive on Passion Sunday is just that: an expression of his passion, a passionate expression of his love for the Father and for us. Nothing that we see Jesus suffering during his passion is something that he just endured passively, as something inflicted on him from outside. No, everything that his tormentors did to him, Jesus appropriated and turned into a passionate, personal expression of his own heart. In his passion he was giving expression to his feelings about the sins of his own flesh—for the body that suffered during Jesus' passion and death was a body which included all the bodies that would ever be baptized "into Christ," with all of their sins. For "God was reconciling the world to himself in Christ.... For our sake he made him to be sin who did not know sin, so that we might become the righteousness of God in him." The body that hung on the cross was guilty, not because Jesus had sinned, but because through our incorporation into Christ, all our sins were present in it. And by Jesus' death they were annihilated. This is the mystery of our redemption. And it is what we have to shout about as Holy Week begins.

Reflecting on This Week's Gospels

Holy Week

Pray daily: Lord, enter my heart and take possession of me totally. Excite in my soul the joy of my salvation, and let me cry out in acclamation of you without reserve. Blessed are you who come in the name of love. Amen.

Monday: John 12:1-11: Mary took a liter of costly perfumed oil made from genuine aromatic nard and anointed the feet of Jesus and dried them with her hair; the house was filled with the fragrance of the oil. What is the most extravagant, passionate gesture of love that you have made to Jesus Christ?

Tuesday: John 13:21-33, 36-38: Peter said to Jesus, "Lord, why can I not follow you now? I will lay down my life for you." How can you "lay down your life" for Jesus on a daily basis? Does this appeal to you?

Wednesday: Matthew 26:14-25: Jesus said, "Go into the city to a certain man and say to him, 'The teacher says, My time is near; I will keep the Passover at your house with my disciples.'" Would you have felt privileged if Jesus had asked to use your house this way? What if he asks you to let him come into your heart in Eucharist every day that it is possible for you? Is there a difference?

Holy Thursday: John 13:1-15: Jesus poured water into a basin and began to wash the disciples' feet and dry them with the towel around his waist. He came to Simon Peter, who said to him, "Lord, are you going to wash my feet?" How do you feel when you are conscious that the people serving you in restaurants and stores are the Body of Christ? Are you humbled that Jesus would "wash your feet" in them?

Good Friday: John: 18:1 to 19:42: Then the maid who was the gatekeeper said to Peter, "You are not one of this man's disciples, are you?" He said, "I am not." Can you truly say you are? How much time do you give to learning from Jesus? Are his attitudes and values visible in your behavior? Which ones? Has anyone ever accused you of being "too religious"?

Saturday: Easter Vigil: Luke 24:1-12: The women remembered his words. Then they returned from the tomb and announced all these things to the eleven and to all the others. How often do you have the experience of remembering something Jesus said and using it in conversation with others? Do you quote him as often as mothers repeat things their children have said, or readers quote from books they are reading? Are his words really important to you? How does that appear?

Several Suggestions for Lent

Prayer: Each day during Holy Week say a short prayer in front of every crucifix that is in your house. If you live with family, do this all together, going into each member's room to pray in front of the crucifix there.

Fasting: Examine your life to see if there are any parts of to which the gates are not open for Christ to enter and reign as king. Are there areas you just do not bring your religion into? Are there questions you don't want to face? Situations or conditions you prefer to ignore?

Almsgiving: Each day this week consciously "wash the feet" of someone in an act of loving, humble service.

EASTER
TRIDUUM
and
EASTER

A Conversion to Love Free of Fear

John 20:1 to 18; Acts 10:34, 37-43; Colossians 3:1-4
(or 1 Corinthians 5:6-8)

When Saint John arrived at Jesus' tomb and found the stone rolled back, the burial shroud folded and lying on the ground, and the tomb itself empty, the Gospel tells us simply, "he saw and believed."

What did John believe? What does the Resurrection of Jesus call on us to believe? It isn't just the bare fact that Jesus was raised from the dead, or that we will be raised from the dead. We have to go beyond the bare fact and accept the implications, the difference the Resurrection of Jesus makes in our way of living every day. What does the Resurrection say to us? What does it mean? How do we respond to this fact of history if we really believe it?

The key is in Hebrews (2:14-15): Jesus died and rose so that "through death he might destroy the one who has the power of death, that is, the devil, and free those who all their lives were held in slavery by the fear of death." If we believe in the Resurrection of Jesus, we must renounce all fear. Fear must never again be the motive for anything we do. The Resurrection has freed us to do only what is inspired by love.

It is fear that enslaves us. We sin because we are afraid of deprivation, boredom, loneliness, criticism, failure, physical or emotional pain. But at the root, all of these fears are fear of death. The physical act of dying may not frighten us—if our pain is great enough we may even look forward to it—but in everything we fear, including pain, it is ultimately the reality of death that we are trying to avoid.

The reality of death is not visible just in the act of dying. The reality of death seen without awareness of Resurrection is the experience of total annihilation, of absolute deprivation of everything that is the experience of being alive. Death is separation from all human contact, companionship and love. Death is total failure to function. Death is the end of all projects, all dreams and all hope. Death is worse than rejection by others; death is oblivion—an oblivion worse than that to which any human rejection can consign us. To die is to become a non-being, a nothing, a person who no longer has a place on earth or with the human race. Death in its own reality is not a peaceful sleep: only Christians can say, "Rest in peace." Death is absolute loss. But our Baptism into the death and Resurrection of Christ has made it for us absolute gain.

Our every fear is a fear of partial death. Even physical pain is the terror that it is because it screams out to us that we are dying. And in delivering us from the fear of death itself, Jesus delivered us from every fear that can enslave us.

Real belief in the Resurrection is expressed in refusal to fear—not in the refusal to feel fear or fright: our emotions are not subject to our commands; even Jesus felt terror in his agony in the garden—but in the refusal ever to act out of fear, ever to let fear be the motivation for a decision, a judgment, a choice. Because of the Resurrection, nothing can take away our life. And because of the Resurrection, nothing can take away our freedom to act purely, consistently, only out of love.

In the desert, the devil tempted Jesus to compromise, to shave something off of absolute loyalty to the Father, out of fear that in no other way could a kingdom of justice, peace and prosperity be established on earth (see Matthew 4:8-11). He offered Jesus the support of all the money and power he controlled, if only Jesus would concede in the smallest way to go against the Father's plan—a plan that left Jesus totally vulnerable to his enemies, subject to torture and death, and required him to love back in return. Jesus answered with the absoluteness of the first commandment: "Worship the Lord your God; and serve only him."

This was our Emancipation Proclamation. We are free to live totally for God, only for God, absolutely for God, without fear of any loss or deprivation, because we have a Savior who has saved us from the fear of death itself. He faced the worst this world can offer, went down into the grave and rose to live forever. If we believe, we will cancel out fear and live free.

Reflecting on This Week's Gospels

Easter Week

Pray daily: Lord, through your death and rising you have robbed death of its power and turned our greatest fear into our greatest hope. Teach me to live with the courage of those who know they can never die. Amen.

Monday: Matthew 28:8-15: The women left the tomb quickly, fearful yet overjoyed, and ran to announce this to his disciples. Suddenly Jesus met them and said, "Do not be afraid..." Does belief in your own resurrection leave you both fearful and joyful? How do you respond to Jesus' encouragement, "Do not be afraid"?

Tuesday: John 20:11-18: Mary saw two angels in white sitting in the tomb, one at the head and one at the feet where the body of Jesus had been. And they said to her, "Woman, why are you weeping?" When you mourn the death of someone you love—or think about your own death—what would you answer if an angel asked you this same question? Over what do we grieve, and over what do we not grieve?

Wednesday: Luke 24:13-35: "When he was at the table with them, he took bread, blessed and broke it, and gave it to them. Then their eyes were opened, and they recognized him." Do you consciously, actively recognize the presence of Jesus in the eucharistic sacrifice? What does this give you for the week ahead? How does it relieve your anxieties and fears?

Thursday: Luke 24:35-48: Jesus himself stood among them and said, "Peace be with you." They were startled and terrified and thought they were seeing a ghost. He said to them, "Why are you frightened? And why do doubts arise in your hearts?" What frightens you most often? Are you aware at those moments that Jesus is standing with you? What is it that you really fear? What do you doubt that you should not?

Friday: John 21:1-14: Jesus said to the disciples who had been fishing all night, "Children, you have no fish, have you?" They answered him, "No." he said to them, "Cast the net to the right side of the boat and you will find some." Have you ever experienced failure? Do you fear failure? Or that your whole life will count for too little? What is Jesus saying to you about this? Is it ever too late to make your life fruitful?

Saturday: Mark 16:9-15: When the disciples heard from Mary Magdalene that Jesus was alive and had been seen by her, they did not believe. After this he appeared in another form to two of them walking along on their way to the country. They returned and told the others; but they did not believe them either. Why are we so hesitant to believe in God's promises? Do you believe in Jesus' Resurrection, and in your own, so strongly that you don't let any fear keep you from serving him?

Living This Week's Gospels

As Christian: Get a bottle of holy water from the Church. (Or use the water blessed for Baptisms at the Easter Vigil.) Bless your house, clothes, car, everything you use, as an act of faith in the new life you are called and empowered to live.

As Disciple: Begin reading the Sermon on the Mount (Matthew, chapters 5-7)—just a tiny bit each day—and try to absorb the guidelines for living on the level of God.

As Prophet: Go through your house cleaning out the "old leaven," anything that indicates you are living for the false promises of this world. Ask what attitudes or values each thing in your house expresses.

As Priest: Each day this week decide on someone with whom you will share your own experience of encounter with the living Jesus. Even if it is someone who knows Jesus better than you do, you can help each other by sharing your experiences. (If you can't identify your own, ask others how they have experienced Jesus risen and acting on them.)

As King: Look with new eyes at your family and social life, professional and civic environment. Ask what is not appropriate for the presence of the risen Jesus. Change that if you can, or begin a movement in the direction of change.

Baptism Is a Sending

John 20: 19-31; Acts 5:12-16; Revelation 1:9-11, 12-13, 17-19

When Jesus appeared to his disciples after the Resurrection, it was not just to show them he was alive; it was also to show them they were alive with a new life—and to teach them how to live it. Now that Jesus is risen, we are his risen Body on earth. Now we are the Savior, the Messiah, because he continues his saving presence and mission in us.

The "grace of our Lord Jesus Christ" is the favor of sharing in his own divine life by being incorporated into him. It is because we are "in Christ" as members of his Body, that we live by his life, that we are identified, one with him in everything he is as the incarnate Son of God. Because we are "in Christ" we share in his divine identity, life and mission.

This means that the titles which describe Jesus in his mission now describe us. Jesus is living in us to continue carrying out his mission on earth. Everything he is as Savior he is now in us. And everything he is as Savior, we are called to be "in him." This is the logical and awesome consequence of Jesus' words, "As the Father has sent me, so I send you."

So we must be "Son of David" to the world. Jesus' first words to his disciples are "Peace be with you." He has done what the promised Messiah-King was to accomplish: He has brought God's peace to the world. It is not the kind of peace that is established through military power or which is dependent on control of the environment. It is the "peace of Christ"—that interior "tranquillity of order" which the world cannot give and the world cannot take away.

When Jesus says, with the authority of the promised Son of David, "As the Father has sent me, so I send you," he is saying that we—or rather, he in us now—must be Son of David and Messiah to our world. It is through us, through

Jesus Christ working in and through our own human actions, that all of God's promises are to be brought to fulfillment. It is we who are sent to bring the fullness of life and joy and peace to the world.

This is not the peace of the contented cow in the pasture who just rests in the satisfaction of all her felt desires. This is "God's own peace, which is beyond all understanding" (Philippians 4:7), and it is the fruit of the Holy Spirit poured out in our hearts (Galatians 5:22; Romans 14:7). What we are sent to bring to the world is not just some human contentment. Jesus was not the "Son of David" his people expected: just an earthly king bringing earthly prosperity. He was the "Son of God," bringing a divine destiny to the human race. And so we are sent, as Jesus was, to be more than human: to be the human presence of God himself in the world, and to bring the world to that divine fulfillment which is found only in union with Christ by grace. That is why Jesus breathed on his disciples and said, "Receive the Holy Spirit."

This divine fulfillment presupposes deliverance from sin. And so Jesus says, "If you forgive men's sins, they are forgiven them." This refers to more than Baptism and sacramental absolution. Each one of us is named "Jesus," "God-saves," because each one of us is sent to "save his people from their sins" (see Matthew 1:22). We do this in many and varied ways, but it is always a characteristic of our mission.

Finally, we are sent, as Jesus was, to save the world through bodily presence, through physical, human contact. Jesus was called "Emmanuel," "God-with-us," because he was on earth for people to see and touch and interact with in human ways. And he still invites people, as he invited Thomas, to see and touch his physical, risen Body. We are that Body, and it is only through experiencing Jesus made flesh in us, expressing his love in our human actions, that many people will be able to believe. As his risen Body on earth, we are "Emmanuel." We are the touchable Jesus.

Reflecting on This Week's Gospels

Second Week of Easter

Pray daily: Lord, you have made me your risen body by Baptism and sent me to make you present to the world in my flesh. Help me to believe that I am your embodied presence on earth. Strengthen me to continue your mission.

Monday: John 3:1-8: Jesus answered Nicodemus, "Very truly, I tell you, no one can see the kingdom of God without being born from above." How were you born again? When you try to be "more religious," or to help others live their religion more actively, are you conscious that you are helping yourself and them to live life more fully? On a higher plane? Do you think and speak of it this way?

Tuesday: John 3:7-15: Nicodemus asked, "How can these things be?" Jesus answered him, "Are you a teacher of Israel and yet you do not understand these things? Do you consider yourself a teacher of the faith? Were you sent to "make disciples of all nations"? What are you doing to grow in understanding of Jesus' teachings yourself so that you can speak of the good news in a way that helps others understand?

Wednesday: John 3:16-21: "And this is the judgment, that the light has come into the world, and people loved darkness rather than light, because their deeds were evil." In what ways do you make visible the light that came into the world with Christ? Does your life-style arouse controversy? Turn anyone off? Why?

Thursday: John 3:31-36: Jesus said, "He whom God has sent speaks the words of God, for he gives the Spirit without measure." When were you commissioned by God to announce the good news? When, where, to whom do you speak the words of God? Do you consciously rely on the gift of the Holy Spirit given to you?

Friday: John 6:1-15: When Jesus looked up and saw a large crowd coming toward him, he said to Philip, "Where are we to buy bread for these people to eat?" Do you see a large crowd of people who need to be fed with the word of God? Who is feeding them now? Is it enough? What can you do to feed them?

Saturday: John 6:16-21: When the disciples had rowed about three or four miles, they saw Jesus walking on the sea and coming near the boat, and they were terrified. If people saw Jesus walking toward them today, how would they react? Is Jesus in fact coming to them in you? Are they terrified? Why? Does the thought terrify you? How do you deal with it?

Living This Week's Gospels

As Christian: Kneel before Jesus and formally commit yourself to being his living, active presence in the world. Specifically, promise to give him an active part in everything you do. Think about how to do this in the concrete.

As Disciple: Before you start your day, get in your car or leave your house, think ahead to what this day is liable to be like. Then read a passage of Scripture, looking for something that will help.

As Prophet: Each day this week plan some perceptible "clue" to put into your appearance or behavior which will tell people, if they think about it, that you are trying to live on a level higher than the human.

As Priest: Go about conscious that you are sent as Jesus for the forgiveness of sins. Look for opportunities to have a healing effect on people wounded by their sins or the sins of others.

As King: Ask yourself—and perhaps a couple of other people—what changes you would most like to see take place in your family or social life, where you work or in the neighborhood where you live. Then ask if you might be able to do something to make one of them happen.

Third Sunday of Easter

Baptism Commits Us to a Reliving

John 21:1-19; Acts 5:27-32, 40-41; Revelation 5:11-14

In his Resurrection appearances, Jesus teaches his apostles—and us—how to "be Jesus": how to carry on his life and mission as his Body on earth. This means, however, that each one of us, in some way, must relive the pattern of his own life, death and resurrection.

Jesus came to be the recurring "Crisis" in people's lives. Again and again he presented people with challenging choices to make, so that they might grow. After his resurrection he continues: he comes to his disciples on a discouraging day, when the fishing is bad, and without revealing his identity, calls them to an act of faith and hope: "Cast your net on the starboard side, and you will find something."

Today it is we, as the risen Body of Christ on earth, who are sent to call people to faith and hope and growth. In reality it is Jesus doing this in us, but his identity is hidden. Like the disciples, who just saw a man standing on the shore when Jesus spoke to them, people will not see Jesus obviously visible in us. They will have to recognize his presence through what we call them to do. If we invite them to greater faith, greater hope in the fullness of life, they will know him. We have to believe, and urge others to believe, that Jesus calls every human being to the fullness of life, that everyone's net should be filled to the breaking point.

It wasn't only his own people that Jesus called into growthful crisis; that he challenged to sometimes painful but always life-giving decisions in faith and hope. We have seen how he called the pagan Magi through a star. He is the "Universal Lord," the Savior of the whole human race. To be authentically Jesus on earth, we must believe that every single human being on the face of the earth—and not just those we easily relate to—is called to and is capable of life in

Easter / 117

its fullness. To write anyone off as hopeless, or as hopelessly mediocre, is to betray our mission as Christ's Body on earth.

Life is only living when it translates itself into love. Jesus prepares breakfast on the shore for his disciples. He then says to them and to each one of us, beginning with Peter, "Feed my lambs...." To live is to be life-giving. To be life-giving is to love. And to love is to be life-giving as Jesus was: to give one's own life that others might live. Like Peter, we are all called to "stretch out our hands" in surrender, to let ourselves be led where we were not choosing to go, until the whole of our lives is consummated in love. Ultimately, it is always as the "Suffering Servant" that Jesus redeems the world and continues to redeem it in us, his offered Body on earth.

The pattern of Jesus' life led him into conflict with this world. The pattern of Christ's life in us will be the same. It will lead us into conflict: not only with the world outside of us, but with the sin and selfishness and darkness that are within us. Jesus is the crisis who leads us into conflict with ourselves—not so that we might just suffer from it, but so that we might overcome. We have to remember that this Gospel is a story of triumph. When the disciples, in faith and in hope, cast their net again at Jesus' suggestion, the net was filled to the breaking point. Jesus is the "Anointed One," the Messiah sent by God himself. He triumphs. When we live by his word, our lives become full to the breaking point.

Jesus triumphs in us. We were anointed at Baptism and sent into this world, not to be defeated by it, but to overcome. Even in the midst of trials, suffering and surrender, we are the victorious Jesus. And we are sent to proclaim his victory to the world. We are sent as the risen Jesus to be the living sign and expression of his triumph over sin and death and everything that keeps any human being from the fullness of life in grace. This is who we are. This is what Baptism sends us to do.

Reflecting on This Week's Gospels

Third Week of Easter

Pray daily: Lord, I want to be part of your mission. You came and taught and suffered and triumphed. Give me the grace to bear witness to your saving presence and power through every word and action of my life. Amen.

Monday: John 6:22-29: Jesus said, "This is the work of God, that you believe in the one he sent." How often do you actively, consciously, explicitly make an act of faith in Jesus as Savior? Teacher? Victor over sin and death?

Tuesday: John 6:30-35: Jesus said, "I am the bread of life; whoever comes to me will never hunger, and whoever believes in me will never thirst." Do you have a personal relationship with Jesus? How do you interact with him?

Wednesday: John 6:35-40: "For this is the will of my Father, that all who see the Son and believe in him may have eternal life, and I will raise them up on the last day." How frequently do you look at Jesus in your imagination, seeing him doing the things he did on earth, seeing him interacting with you today?

Thursday: John 6:44-51: "It is written in the prophets: 'They shall all be taught by God.' Everyone who listens to my Father and learns from him comes to me." What draws you to Jesus? What have you learned about him from the Father? What longing for him is in your heart?

Friday: John 6:52-59: Jesus said, "Those who eat my flesh and drink my blood abide in me and I in them. Just as the living Father sent me and I live because of the Father, so whoever eats me will live because of me." How often do you receive Jesus in Communion? How often is Eucharist available to you? How much does it mean to you? What do you think about when you are receiving Christ in Communion?

Saturday: John 6:60-69: Simon Peter answered, "Master, to whom shall we go? You have the words of eternal life. We have come to believe and are convinced that you are the Holy One of God." Can you say this? Is this why you remain in the Church? Is this why you participate in Eucharist? How do you go to Jesus to hear "the words of eternal life"?

Living This Week's Gospels

As Christian: Kneel before Jesus and formally, explicitly ask him to save your life, here and now, from veering off into destructiveness, distortion, mediocrity or meaninglessness. Decide on concrete ways to keep you conscious of consulting him before every decision.

As Disciple: Ask yourself seriously if you believe Jesus "has the words of eternal life." If you do, make a decision about how you should use the Bible.

As Prophet: Ask what your body language and other behavior during the eucharistic celebration express about your understanding of the Mass. When you enter Church, make a conscious act of acknowledging Jesus' presence in the tabernacle by bowing or genuflecting.

As Priest: Participate in the eucharistic celebration as a priest by Baptism. Remember you are a player. Participate in the liturgy fully, actively, consciously.

As King: Receive Communion at Mass with conscious faith that Jesus has overcome the world. Use the Eucharist to strengthen yourself to keep trying to change things in your environment.

Fourth Sunday of Easter

Baptism Commits Us to Discipleship

John 10:27-30; Acts 13:14, 43-52; Revelation 7:9, 14-17

J esus said, "My sheep hear my voice." So listening to Jesus goes with being one of his sheep. If we are not hearing his voice there is something wrong with our relationship.

Hearing Jesus' voice is not just a matter of receiving and recognizing his inspirations during the day, or in crucial moments of decision during our lives. Hearing the voice of Jesus can also come through systematic listening on our part. We can seek Jesus out to listen to him. And this is something that belongs to Christian life as such; it is something to which we are committed at Baptism. It is called discipleship.

Baptism is not just a washing away of sins. In fact, when Baptism is done by immersion, even the symbol of washing is swallowed up within the greater symbol of going down into the grave (under the water) and rising out of it again. Then Baptism is portrayed more clearly as a dying and rising, as a giving up of life on the level of this world's goals and guidelines in order to live life on a new level: a level of divine goals and divine guidelines.

When we see Baptism like this—as a commitment to live on a new level and walk by a new light—it is easy to understand how Baptism is a commitment to discipleship. Discipleship just means "committed learning," and for learning to be committed it has to be systematic. Unless we are listening systematically to Jesus, then, we are not his disciples. We are not sheep who listen to his voice as a regular part of life.

A "disciple" is a "student"—someone whose life is characterized by learning. We are not disciples just because we happen to learn something from the readings or homilies at Sunday Mass, anymore than we are students because we happen to pick up some information once a week from the educational channel on television. The word "disciple," like the word "student," speaks of what we are. And for discipleship or study to characterize one's life, there must be a serious commitment to it.

All human actions take place in time and space. We can only act at a particular time and in a particular place. Therefore, if we are not committed to listening to Jesus at a particular time, or in a particular place, we are not really committed. When we say to Jesus, "Lord, I would like to know you better; I would like to talk to you," he answers: "When? Where?" When are we going to talk? Where are we going to meet?" If we say, "Well, sometime, someplace," Jesus gets the message: He knows we are only pretending that we want to be his disciples—pretending to ourselves.

Discipleship is so important, so necessary for our own growth in grace, so needed in our world, that we really should stop for a moment to make sure it is a characteristic of our own lives. Each one of us needs to ask seriously, "When do I listen to Jesus each day? Where do I do this? For how long?"

If our answer is, "Well, I listen to Jesus all day long. I talk to him all day long," we are kidding ourselves. How many deep, intimate friendships are built up and maintained through nothing but casual conversation? How many marriages survive—or on what level do they survive—when spouses do not take time for deep, serious, loving communication? What can we learn from Jesus that is deep and serious if all we ever have with him is a running conversation while we are doing other things? It is true that we ought to pray always, but this does not mean that the kind of praying we are always able to do, at every moment of the day, wherever we might happen to be, is enough for serious discipleship.

Our Baptism was a physical act as well as a spiritual reality. Our discipleship, in order to be a spiritual reality, must also be a physical fact. So when, where, and for how long each day or week will we listen to the voice of Jesus?

Reflecting on This Week's Gospels

Fourth Week of Easter

Pray daily: Lord, call me to be your disciple. Give me the grace to respond to your call, and to decide here and now when I will give time to learning from you. Help me persevere in learning and believing. I ask this of you who are Christ the Lord. Amen.

Monday: John 10:1-10: Jesus said, "I came so that they may have life and have it abundantly." Do you believe this? Where do you look for this abundance of life? How consistently? Does Jesus just give it, or do you need to keep interacting with him to grow into the fullness of life?

Tuesday: John 10:22-30: Jesus said, "My sheep hear my voice; I know them, and they follow me." When do you hear Jesus' voice? Where? How often? Has Scripture reading made you familiar with his voice, his way of speaking? Does it lead you to decisions? What is the last decision you made consciously as an act of following Jesus?

Wednesday: John 12:44-50: Jesus said, "Whoever rejects me and does not receive my word has a judge: on the last day the word that I have spoken will serve as judge." Do you believe you will be judged by how well you kept the ten commandments, or by how authentically you lived by Christ's words? Are you letting his words be the "critic," the standard that determines your behavior now?

Thursday: John 13:16-20: Jesus said, "If you know these things, you are blessed if you do them." Do you know all the principles and values Jesus taught in the Gospels well enough to consciously live by them? Do you want to know everything he taught? Why?

Friday: John 14:1-6: Jesus said, "I am the way and the truth and the life. No one comes to the Father except through me." Do you believe this? Do you constantly look at Jesus' example to find your way in family and social life, business and politics? Do you keep studying his words to find the truth that casts light on your life, your problems, your decisions? Do you believe that knowing his words and following his example will enrich your life?

Saturday: John 14:7-14: Jesus said, "If you know me, you will know my Father also." Is this an incentive to read the Scripture? How else can you get to know Jesus? Do you believe that by reading Scripture you can get to know God himself? How much does this mean to you?

Living This Week's Gospels

As Christian: Kneel before Jesus and formally commit yourself to discipleship, that is, to leading a life characterized by reflection on his message. Decide when and where and for how long each day you will read Scripture.

As Disciple: Put an inexpensive copy of the Bible on your pillow. Never go to sleep without reading at least one line. Underline what strikes you.

As Prophet: In your daily reading of Scripture, pick out one teaching or example of Jesus and decide on a way to embody it in your life that day.

As Priest: As you read Scripture, pick out one truth each day that you can put into your own words and share with someone else. Ask how Jesus would explain this today to the people you live and work with.

As King: Make sure you have a copy of the Bible. Enthrone it in some visible place in your home. Give it the kind of place in your home that the Blessed Sacrament has in church.

Baptism Commits Us to Prophetic Witness

John 13:31-35; Acts 14:21-27; Revelation 21:1-5

W hy did Jesus say the Father was "glorified" in him and that he himself, through his death and resurrection, would be "glorified?"

In the early Old Testament the "glory of God" just meant his beauty and power. Later in the Bible it came to mean God's beauty and power made manifest on earth. In the New Testament God's beauty and power are made manifest in Jesus Christ, but in an unexpected way. In Jesus the power of God shows itself as a deliberate renunciation of power on this earth. In Jesus the beauty of God was revealed on the cross when, humanly speaking, there was nothing that would attract us to him (see Isaiah 53:2). Jesus on the cross was weakness and foolishness to human eyes, but in reality he was the "power of God and the wisdom of God" revealed as never before (see 1 Corinthians 1:18-25). He was the glory of God.

Jesus glorified the Father by showing what the Father really is. And now it is our mission to glorify Jesus by showing what he really was and is. Jesus prayed for his disciples at the Last Supper, saying, "It is in them that I have been glorified" (John 17:10). And Jesus is glorified in us today whenever our lives reveal the power of his grace, the truth of his identity as Savior of the world, the reality of his victory on the cross over sin and death. In other words, Jesus is glorified in us whenever our lives bear witness to the presence of his Spirit in us and to the power of his grace. We glorify Jesus, whom the world last saw defeated and dead on the cross, when our lives make it evident that we are indeed the risen Body of Jesus still present and ministering on earth.

This is a mission to which we were consecrated and committed by Baptism. By Baptism we were incorporated into Christ; we became members of his body, the body that hung and died on the cross, the body that rose again. Saint Paul teaches that through Baptism we died in Christ and rose again in Christ to live a new life, a life on his own divine level (see Romans 6:3-11; Colossians 2:12; 3:1-11). And so we are the Body of Christ on earth. We are his continuing, risen presence. We exist in this world as sent; we are sent as Jesus was sent: to be the visible manifestation of God's divine life present and acting in human flesh. By Baptism we were commissioned to be the glory of the risen Christ!

This is a consecration to Christian witness. And Christian witness, to be effective, must be prophetic. This means that what we do must express a level of insight and ideals beyond what is commonly taken for granted in our society—even beyond what is commonly and correctly identified as Christianity. Effective witness to Jesus Christ and to his Spirit dwelling within us, begins when our behavior goes beyond what is commonly expected of good human beings or even of good Christians.

The reason for this is fairly simple: if all we do is live up to what is commonly expected of Christians, there is no way for anyone to know whether we are just conforming to our religious culture out of inertia or whether we ourselves are in live, personal contact with Jesus and with his Spirit. If, on the other hand, we are "prophetic" in our behavior; that is, if we find new and creative ways to apply the teaching of Jesus to the actual circumstances of our own times, then it will be evident that Christ's words are abiding in our hearts, are part of us, and that his Spirit is guiding our response to them. We are "prophets," not when we just repeat what everybody says and accept what everybody sees (although much of our religion will obviously be this), but when we also see things nobody else has seen yet and apply the Gospel to life by doing things nobody else has ever thought to do. When we do this we glorify Jesus by showing that his defeat was in fact a victory, and that he has indeed redeemed the world. We bear witness to Jesus when our lives bear witness to his divine life working within us; that is, when our behavior is on the level of God.

Reflecting on This Week's Gospels

Fifth Week of Easter

> **Pray daily:** *Lord, fill me with desire to glorify you, to make your truth credible and your grace visible in everything I do. I want to promise you a life of continual conversion. Give me the love to keep changing things in my life-style in order to bear more authentic witness to you. Amen.*

Monday: John 14: 21-26: Jesus said, "The Advocate, the holy Spirit that the Father will send in my name.... He will teach you everything and remind you of all that I told you." What in your behavior shows that you are acting in a way that at least tries to be a response to inspirations of the Holy Spirit?

Tuesday: John 14:27-31: Jesus said, "Peace I leave with you; my peace I give to you. Not as the world gives do I give it to you. Do not let your hearts be troubled or afraid." What in your life shows that your peace, your security, are not based on money, position, power, or anything else this world can give?

Wednesday: John 15:1-8: "I am the true vine, and my Father is the vine grower. He takes away every branch in me that does not bear fruit, and everyone that does he prunes so that it bears more fruit." How has God "pruned" you most recently? What is the last thing you have changed in your life-style in order that you might bear fruit more effectively for God?

Thursday: John 15:9-11: "I have told you this so that my joy may be in you and your joy may be complete." What words of Jesus have you read recently that have increased your joy? Did the joy come from responding to them? In action? Is there a visible and growing joy in your life that bears witness to your awareness of loving him and being loved by him?

Friday: John 15:12-17: "This is my commandment, that you love one another as I have loved you." How are you loving others precisely as Jesus has loved you? What is different between the kind of love you give and the kind of love for people that any decent person respects and admires?

Saturday: John 15:18-21: Jesus said, "If you belonged to the world, the world would love its own; but because you do not belong to the world, and I have chosen you out of the world, the world hates you." What in your way of living or acting arouses hostility in people, not because it is bad, but because it is based on the values of Jesus? If everybody accepts you, is that something to worry about?

Living This Week's Gospels

As Christian: Kneel before Jesus and consciously commit yourself to living a life of prophetic witness. In practical terms, promise to keep making changes in your life-style guided by the goal of making everything you own, use, do or say bear witness to the values of Christ.

As Disciple: As you read Scripture, look for the teachings or sayings of Jesus that are so different from what "everybody" does that it is hard to take them seriously. Ask how you could take them seriously.

As Prophet: Each day this week find one thing in your environment or behavior that you can change precisely to make it bear better witness to the values of Jesus. What do people see and hear when they are around you? What values are you expressing to them?

As Priest: Each day this week, think of yourself as commissioned by God to nurture those you live and work with. See how many ways you can do this.

As King: Ask yourself—or others you know well—what the "mission" of your business is in terms of serving people or making the world a better place in which to live. Ask what needs to be changed in order to fulfill this mission more effectively. (If you are not working, ask the same question about your parish or your family life. Offer to help.)

Sixth Sunday of Easter

Baptism Commits Us to Christ's Priesthood

John 14:23-29; Acts 15:1-2, 22-29; Revelation 21:10-14, 22-23

Jesus promises that if we love him and live by his word, he and the Father will come and dwell within us. What does this mean, and what response should it evoke from us?

God obviously does not dwell within us like inert matter in a box. God inhabits our hearts to communicate himself to us deeply and intimately—more than that, to identify us with himself, to make us the visible "dwelling place of God" on earth. If we combine this with the image Jesus uses of the vine and the branches, and with Saint Paul's teaching that we are the "Body of Christ," God's indwelling is explained as a union in one shared life. For God to abide in us means that we abide in him: that we now live "in Christ"; that we live by the divine life of Jesus shared with us. Jesus has become, not only our way and our truth, but our life.

This could be for us nothing but an incomprehensible mystery lost in its own abstractness. But if we ask what this union with Christ calls us to, then it becomes a very practical reality. The mystery of God's dwelling within us gives a new direction to everything we do.

Because God dwells in us, we are mediators of his life to others. He does not dwell in us inertly; he is within us to communicate himself to us, and through us to communicate himself to others. What God's indwelling calls us to is the acceptance and exercise of the priesthood that is ours through Baptism. Because we were baptized into Christ and into his life, we share in everything he is and was sent to do. Because Jesus is the "only Son of the Father," and we are "in him," we are *filii in Filio*, "sons in the Son." In the same way we share in his priesthood as "priests in the Priest." This makes us mediators.

What is priesthood? Priests offer sacrifices. But with the sacrifice of Jesus on the cross, all other sacrifices were abolished, and all other priesthood. Now there is only one Priest offering one sacrifice: the sacrifice of himself. In the Mass Jesus still offers the sacrifice he made of himself on Calvary. But all the baptized exercise the priesthood of Jesus by offering themselves with him as the Body of Christ. Our flesh is the flesh of Christ being offered still until the end of time.

How do we do this? Not physically on a cross. The death of Jesus is the only death needed to redeem the world. But there is another way to offer ourselves: that is to "offer our bodies as a living sacrifice"—our live bodies, which means ourselves, whole and entire. In practice to be offered means that in everything we do, wherever our live bodies are, we are sacrificed to the work, to the ministry of Jesus. This means that at every moment of our lives, no matter what we are doing or with whom we are dealing, we are given to give life to the world. We live only to give his life, his light, his love to others. To live for this is to "die" to self, so that, yes, we do redeem the world as Jesus did, by dying for others, but not through physical death. It is through physical actions that express the love of Christ and which are the medium through which he gives his life to the world.

This means that priesthood is essentially mediation. It is to mediate the life of God to others by letting the God who dwells within us express himself in and through our human actions. In the priesthood of Jesus mediation and sacrifice are the same reality. The sacrifice Jesus offered was himself. And no sacrifice is redemptive unless the "self" being offered is Jesus. But when we sacrifice ourselves, putting every desire aside except the desire to mediate the life of Christ to others in love, letting Jesus express himself through us as he chooses, the body that is offered in its human, physical actions is the Body of Christ. Our priesthood is to let Christ express himself in us; to be the Body of Christ offered and offering as both Victim and Priest in every physical action of our lives. Our Baptism consecrates us to this.

Reflecting on This Week's Gospels

Sixth Week of Easter

> *Pray daily: Lord, you have made me a sharer in your
> life, your mission, your priesthood. I unite myself in
> Eucharist with your offering on the cross. Fill me
> with your desire to give myself, my flesh for the life of
> the world. Amen.*

Monday: John 15:26 to 16:4: Jesus said, "You also are to
testify, because you have been with me from the beginning."
With whom have you shared your experience of Jesus during
your life? With whom have you not shared your experience
of him? Who especially has a right to expect this of you?

Tuesday: John 16:5-11: Jesus said, "If I do not go away, the
Advocate will not come to you. But if I go, I will send him to
you. And when he comes he will prove the world wrong
about sin and righteousness and judgment." How do you let
the Holy Spirit within you give expression to the truth, the
love that Jesus died to reveal? Why do you spontaneous
expressions of faith that come from the heart have so much
impact on people?

Wednesday: John 16:12-15: "But when the Spirit of truth
comes, he will guide you into all truth; for he will not speak
on his own, but will speak whatever he hears..." What have
you heard from the Holy Spirit in your heart? How can you
recognize his voice? Do you "speak whatever you hear," or
do you keep all your thoughts about God to yourself?

Thursday: John 16:16-20: Jesus said, "A little while and
you will no longer see me, and again a little while, and you
will see me." Where is the risen Jesus seen today? How is he
recognized? How has he been able to show himself visibly in
you? To speak in you? To minister in you?

Friday: John 16:20-23: "When a woman is in labor, she has
pain because her hour has come; but when her child is born,
she no longer remembers the anguish because of the joy of

having brought a human being into the world." Do you find it difficult, even painful at times to give expression to your faith, your love? To sing at Mass? To pray out loud? To speak of your feelings about God? Have you ever experienced the joy of seeing others come to life when you share?

Saturday: John 16:23-28: Jesus said, "I came from the Father and have come into the world; again, I am leaving the world and am going to the Father." When Jesus returned to the Father, did he take his human presence completely out of the world? How is he present now? When are you most conscious of letting Jesus express himself in your human words and actions?

Living This Week's Gospels

As Christian: Kneel before Jesus and consciously, explicitly accept your Baptismal consecration as priest. Formally commit yourself to minister to others and to share the life of grace that is within you by giving expression to your faith, your hope, your love. Think of concrete ways to begin doing this.

As Disciple: Notice how many times the word "we" is used in the Mass. Be consciously aware during the Eucharist that the presiding priest is speaking in your name, and that you are praising, asking, thanking and offering together with him.

As Prophet: Ask if there is anything in your language or behavior that you would find inappropriate in an ordained priest. Is there any reason why it is not just as inappropriate in you who share in the priesthood of Jesus by Baptism?

As Priest: Ask God specifically to make you alert to the times you start to feel like expressing or sharing with others your faith or your devotion, but hold back because of embarrassment or fear. When this happens, ask yourself if you would have expected an ordained priest to express what you did not express. What is the difference?

As King: Ask your pastor how the priesthood of the baptized is expressed in your parish. Ask a few people for their reactions to lay ministers of the Eucharist and lectors. Judge whether something needs to be done to explain Baptismal priesthood to the parish.

Baptism Commits Us to Transform the World

John 17:20-26; Acts 7:55-60; Revelation 22:12-14, 16-17, 20

W hen Jesus prayed that his disciples might be "one, as you, Father, are in me, and I in you," he was speaking out of the consciousness he had of his own mission. Saint Paul tells us that the mission of Jesus, the reason why he was sent to earth by the Father, was to "gather up all things in him" (Ephesians 1:10).

Unity presupposes reconciliation and the forgiveness of sins. It also calls for union of mind and will and heart. The mission of Jesus was to bring about this unity between God and us, and between each one of us and all the rest of the human race. This was the mission of Jesus, and this is the mission of the Church, the Body of Christ on earth. No one can live authentically the life of the Church, the life of Christ on earth, without being dedicated to this task.

This means that the Sacrament of Baptism, which made us members of the Body of Christ and sharers in the life and mission of Jesus, also committed us to the work of transforming the world and all its social structures. To be a Christian means to be sent into the world to bring every area and activity of human life under the reign of Christ, under his headship.

At Baptism we were anointed with chrism to the threefold mission of Jesus as "Prophet, Priest and King." As prophets we are dedicated to bearing witness to Jesus as his Body on earth. As priests we are consecrated to mediating the life of God to others in community. And as stewards of the kingship of Christ we are mandated to go out and renew human society, to overcome all divisions and transform the world.

Baptism is not just the act that saves us; it is also the act that dedicates us to saving the world. We are consecrated to this as the Body of Christ, the extension of his presence and ministry on earth. And to "save the world" does not just mean to save people out of the world, to focus only on getting them to heaven in the end. To save the world also means to save what the world is here and now, to redeem all human institutions and activities from their bondage to darkness and sin. It means to renew family and social life, business and politics. Our mission is to bring everything in heaven and on earth together into unity under Christ's headship. And "everything" means everything.

Christians do not write off the world or anything in the world as being bad or incapable of redemption. If Christian writers, including the inspired writers of Scripture, sometimes speak of "the world" as the homeland of darkness and sin, they only mean that sin has done its work in human society, and Christians cannot follow Jesus without declaring themselves emancipated from the attitudes and values, the shortsighted goals and objectives of every human society and culture. But if Christians in a sense "leave" the world as the People of Israel left Egypt, this leaving is not a desertion or an abandonment of the world to its fate. Christians only "break" with this world in order to be free to follow Jesus, learn from him, become one with him, and then return to the world to redeem it. Christians are sent into the world as Jesus was sent: not to be enslaved by it or by human culture, but to redeem the world and all its institutions from darkness and diminishment.

What we need to fulfill this mission is unwavering faith in Jesus as the Lord who triumphed over sin and all its consequences, and unshakable hope in his power to bring everything on earth together into unity under his headship. Jesus has triumphed, and all he needs to make his victory complete is for us to persevere in working for this as the instruments of his power and the stewards of his kingship.

What Jesus asks of us is faithful stewardship. We give him this by persevering with faith in our efforts to bring every human institution and activity under his life-giving reign.

Reflecting on This Week's Gospels

Seventh Week of Easter

Pray daily: Lord, you came to transform human life on earth. You have called me, commissioned me, and sent me to bring everything I can influence under the life-giving reign of your love. Give me the courage to work for unity through peace. Amen.

Monday: John 16:29-33: Jesus said to his disciples, "In the world you face persecution. But take courage, I have conquered the world!" Do you ever experience rejection, hostility or failure because of your efforts to change things? When this happens, do you draw strength from remembering— and believing—that Jesus has overcome the powers of this world?

Tuesday: John 17:1-11: Jesus prayed to the Father, "I glorified you on earth by finishing the work that you gave me to do." Does this mean the reign of God is completely established? What did Jesus accomplish? What is left for him to accomplish through us?

Wednesday: John 17:11-19: Jesus prayed to the Father for his disciples, "I am not asking you to take them out of the world but I ask you to protect them from the evil one. They do not belong to the world, just as I do not belong to the world." In what sense do Christians belong to the world? In what sense do we not belong? How do you experience being different or emancipated from your culture and society?

Thursday: John 17:20-26: "The glory that you have given me I have given them, so that they may be one, as we are one, I in them and you in me, that they may become completely one, so that the world may know that you have sent me..." Does the obvious love and unity that people see in Christians, in our parish, draw people to the faith? Do you express or encourage any criticism that perpetuates division between people, groups, races or religions?

Friday: John 21:15-19: Jesus said to Peter, "Do you love me?" He said to him, "Yes, Lord, you know that I love you." He said to him, "Tend my sheep." What does Jesus ask you to do if you love him? What good are you in a position to do? What are you able to change in the world?

Saturday: John 17:20-25: When Peter saw John following, he said to Jesus, "Lord, what about him?" Jesus said to him, "What if I want him to remain until I come? What concern is it of yours? You follow me." Do you ever let what others are doing—or failing to do—keep you from taking responsibility for changing what you can change or doing what you can do to initiate change?

Living This Week's Gospels

As Christian: Kneel before Jesus and formally accept responsibility for extending his reign over every area and activity of human life that you can influence. Think about how you can begin: what needs changing in your family or social environment, business or civic life?

As Disciple: Read Vatican II's "Decree on the Apostolate of the Laity." This is one of the fundamental documents for Christian life in our times. If you don't have a copy of the Vatican II documents, get one from your local Catholic bookstore, or ask any priest or nun to lend you a copy.

As Prophet: Ask yourself what false attitudes or damaging ways of acting you are implicitly supporting by just "going along" with what everyone around you is doing. Stop going along, and be prepared to say why if you are questioned about it.

As Priest: Take responsibility for changing the impact of the Sunday liturgy by participating actively and fully yourself. Learn the hymns and responses. Think of yourself as a minister and player, not just as a spectator or someone being ministered to.

As King: Make a list of those policies, practices or areas over which you have actual authority or share authority with another—at home and at work. Ask whether everything you have authority over is being done according to the standards of Christ.

Pentecost (Vigil Mass)

Saved in Hope

John 7:37-39; (four options for first reading); Romans 8:22-27

Christians live in two time frames: the eternal, in which the salvation of the world has been accomplished; and the temporal, in which redemption is still taking place. From the viewpoint of eternity, we see all of time, all of human history from its beginning to the end of the world, in one glance. It is like looking at the moon: we see the whole thing at once. Then time is like a circle: we see the beginning, the end, and everything in between as present to us now.

But from the viewpoint of the time we live in on this earth, we only see as present the time we live in now. Past events are just a memory, and future events have not happened yet; they do not exist. To us who are living in it, time is like a straight line, and we only experience a little at a time. It is experienced the way someone walking on the moon would feel only the ground that is actually underfoot.

In liturgy we celebrate an eternal event that is still taking place in time. When Jesus was offered on Calvary every person who would ever be baptized "into Christ" was present in the body that died on the cross. That is why our sins are not just "forgiven" but "taken away." It is because we, with our sins, were "in Christ" when he died. We died in him, and in that death our history was over; our sins ceased to exist. And when Jesus rose, we "co-rose in him" to live as sharers in his divine life, free from sin, as his risen Body on earth. In liturgy we celebrate the eternal fact that Jesus has "overcome the world" once and for all, and by his death we are saved. (See Colossians 2:12 and 3:1; John 16:33.)

But in time Jesus is still "overcoming the world" in us. In time we are still being purified of the woundedness of sin, and we who have "died to sin" cry out with Saint Paul, "who will deliver me?" from slavery to the darkness and passions we still experience. From the viewpoint of eternity the death of Jesus has made us free, saved us and redeemed us from all darkness and sin. From the viewpoint of time, we are still being freed and purified, growing in knowledge, understanding and love. In short, we are saved—but in hope. (See Romans 6:1-11 and 7:14-25; Colossians 1:24 to 2:3; Ephesians 3:14-19.)

That is why Pentecost looks in two directions. We look backward and celebrate the gift of the Spirit poured out on the Church. But we also look forward to the work the Church is sent to do by the power of that Spirit. We celebrate the fact that the world is redeemed, that the Spirit has been given to restore order to the chaos created by sin and to bring back into unity the human race divided by sin into estranged and warring camps. At the same time we recognize that all of creation is still "groaning" with desire to be set free from the domination of sin and brought to complete fulfillment under the reign of Christ. (See Genesis 1:1-31 and compare Genesis 11:1-9 with Acts 2:1-13.)

The Spirit is given to activate the Church—and precisely to activate the Church to bring about what God has wanted from the beginning; that is, to "bring everything in heaven and on earth together into unity under Christ as head." This unity is not a uniformity that destroys all the richness of diversity; it is a unity which brings together everything and everyone that is different in a unity based precisely on the recognition of Christ in one another. It is a unity in the Spirit brought about by the Spirit of Christ. (See Ephesians and Colossians, chapters 1).

In the measure that the Spirit is active in us, we will desire to bring about unity, understanding and peace upon earth: between different races and cultural groups, different nations and social classes; between people divided by different religions and ideologies. The desire for unity is a sign of the Spirit in us; the desire to remain separate and apart is a sign that we are not moved by the Spirit of Jesus Christ.

Reflecting on This Week's Gospels

Note: Check the Liturgical calendar on page x to find out what week of the year follows Pentecost Sunday this year. Once you know which week it is, you can find the weekday Gospel reflections after that week's Sunday Gospel reflection. For example, if the week following Pentecost Sunday is the Ninth Week of the year, then locate the Ninth Sunday of the Year and the weekday reflections for the Ninth Week will follow.

ORDINARY TIME

Ninth Sunday of the Year Through Thirty-Fourth Sunday of the Year

Ninth Sunday of the Year

Focus on Love

Luke 7:1-10; 1 Kings 8:41-43; Galatians 1:1-2, 6-10

The words of the Roman centurion who did not feel worthy to have Jesus enter his house have been repeated by Christians before Communion for centuries: "Lord, I am not worthy...." And they are true. But there was a period in the Church when people focused so much on their unworthiness that they only dared to receive Communion once a year. And after that, many would not receive Eucharist unless they had received the Sacrament of Reconciliation the day before, regardless of how serious their sins were. It was a time when fear was more characteristic of our attitude toward God than love.

To overcome this, Jesus called the Church to contemplate his heart.

In the Church before Vatican II devotion to the Sacred Heart was so widespread that it was simply a part of Catholic life. Everybody knew what the "nine first Fridays" were all about, and most people knew about the twelve "promises of the Sacred Heart," even if they could not remember what they said. The image of Jesus pointing to his open heart—a heart surrounded with flames of love, pierced by thorns of ingratitude and presented under the sign of redeeming sorrow for sin, the cross—was almost as familiar to Catholics as the crucifix itself. How did this happen, and how should we think about it now?

It happened because four great revelations were given to a contemplative nun in France between December, 1673, and June, 1675, and their content spoke to the heart of the Catholic people then and ever since. The revelations made to Saint Margaret Mary were taken up by the Jesuits, preached and analyzed from a theological point of view, and, with the approval of bishops and popes, spread throughout the world.

Several religious orders were founded, both of women and of men, whose work and life-style were a response to these revelations. In 1956 Pope Pius XII wrote a letter to the whole Church in which, after a careful explanation of the content of this devotion and of its roots in Scripture and in the spiritual history of the Church, he said: "Devotion to the Sacred Heart is so important that it may be considered, so far as practice is concerned, a perfect profession of the Christian religion."

The Pope only made this statement after showing how the revelations made to Saint Margaret Mary really just focus our attention on the core of the Gospel message of God's love for us as revealed in Jesus Christ—revealed in the flesh, through the Incarnation of God the Son, who took flesh in order to give human expression on earth to the truth and love of God. "Devotion to the Sacred Heart of Jesus," he wrote, "is essentially devotion to the love with which God loved us through Jesus and is at the same time an enlivening of our love for God and others." That is why he is able to say, "If this devotion is constantly practiced with this knowledge and understanding [referring to the explanations he gave], the souls of the faithful cannot but attain to the sweet knowledge of the love of Christ which produces the height of Christian life" (see Ephesians 3:14-19).

Clearly, devotion to the Sacred Heart of Jesus is not just a focus that was appropriate for a particular time in history but which we can afford to forget about today. Devotion to the Sacred Heart is a deliberate focusing of our minds and hearts on the central mystery of our religion: the love of God made flesh for us in Jesus Christ. And we should look seriously at anything which helps us to focus on this— whether it be the image of Christ's heart as revealed to Saint Margaret Mary, or particular practices associated with devotion to the Sacred Heart.

In the first revelation to Saint Margaret Mary, Jesus simply showed her the love in his heart and asked her to dedicate herself to his love. In the second revelation he showed her the image of his heart as we know it today and asked that it be a focus of Christian devotion.

In the third revelation he asked for Communion on the first Friday of each month preceded by an hour of prayer the night before in reparation for sin. In the fourth revelation he asked that the Feast of the Sacred Heart be established and that everyone receive Communion on that day.

Four elements, then, are the inner core of devotion to the Sacred Heart: consecration, adoration, reparation and imitation. Jesus asks us to be consecrated to his love; to adore his love as made present in the Eucharist and expressed through the image of his heart; to make reparation for the sins and indifference of the world; and to love God and others in a way inspired by Christ's love for us. We will look more closely at these in the weeks to come.

Reflecting on This Week's Gospels

Ninth Week of the Year

Pray daily: Lord, you call me to contemplate your heart, to know your love. Enflame me and lead me to the deeds of love. Amen.

Monday: Mark 12:1-12: "The stone that the builders rejected has become the cornerstone; by the Lord has this been done, and it is wonderful in our eyes." Have you rejected as the cornerstone of your religion the love God showed in Jesus in order to make fear and concern over your own salvation the cornerstone instead? How often do you act out of fear of God? How often out of love?

Tuesday: Mark 12:13-17: Jesus said to the Pharisees, "Bring me a denarius to look at." They brought one to him and he said to them, "Whose image and inscription is this?" They replied to him, "The emperor's." If Jesus told you to show him your picture of God, what image would he see? Would it be a heart enflamed and burning with love for you? Why did Jesus use this image?

Wednesday: Mark 12:18-27: Jesus said, "Have you not read...how God told Moses, 'I am the God of Abraham, the God of Isaac, and the God of Jacob'?" He is not God of the dead but of the living." How has your understanding of God changed through interacting with him during your life? How has his interaction with the Church and the saints over the past two thousand years helped you understand him?

Thursday: Mark 12:28-34: Jesus said, "The first commandment is this: 'Hear, O Israel! The Lord our God is Lord alone! You shall love the Lord your God with all your heart, with all your soul, with all your mind, and with all your strength.'" Is this commandment the one you think about the most? What do you confess most often in the Sacrament of Reconciliation? What do you feel most guilty about?

Friday: Mark 12:35-37: David wrote: "The Lord said to my lord, 'Sit at my right hand until I put your enemies under your feet.'" Jesus said about this, "David himself calls the Messiah 'lord'; so how is he his son?" Do you think so much about God as your Lord that you don't relate to him as Father? Is Jesus for you more judge, or more Savior and Spouse?

Saturday: Mark 12:38-44: A poor widow came and contributed two small coins. Calling his disciples to himself, Jesus said to them, "Truly I tell you, this poor widow put in more than all the other contributors to the treasury. For she, out of her poverty, has put in everything she had, all she had to live on." Do you focus more on obligation—what you have to do for God—or on love—what you can do for God?

Living This Week's Gospels

As Christian: Somewhere in your house or workplace put an image of the Sacred Heart or some other image which speaks to you of God's love made flesh in Jesus Christ.

As Disciple: Each time you are conscious of sinning in any way, ask yourself what this has to do with loving God passionately.

As Prophet: Examine each of your religious acts. How clearly and consciously is each an expression of love in response to love?

As Priest: Consciously be the love of Christ made flesh for someone each day this week. Notice how your love increases when you express it. Reflect on how Jesus experienced his love for us in giving himself.

As King: Try to change anything in your patterns of thought or speech which does not reflect awareness of God's love. If you know anyone who seems to be motivated by fear of God, try to change that, without destroying it, to a desire to respond to his love with love.

Tenth Sunday of the Year

Love Calling Us Into Adoration

Luke 7:11-17; 1 Kings 17:17-24; Galatians 1:11-19

When Jesus raised from the dead the only son of the widow from Naim, the Gospel tells us: "Fear seized them all and they began to praise God." That is a strange expression. Fear doesn't usually lead to praise. Fear makes us want to run. What is different about the fear the Gospel talks about?

The word "fear" here doesn't mean fright. It refers to what we experience in the presence of something so far beyond our ordinary experience that it doesn't fit into any of our categories; something we cannot understand, cannot manage, cannot relate to through any ordinary human response. We call the reaction this produces in us "fear" because we are very aware of being introduced into a new and unknown dimension of existence where we do not know how to act or what to think and we know we have nothing to say.

And it makes us aware of how small we are, how insignificant in comparison. When what we see is an act of love and power combined, such as the miracle of raising a dead man to life, then even though words seem inadequate, we want to give praise and adoration to God.

Adoration, then, is an awareness of God's greatness as beyond anything human, anything created. And it is at the same time an awareness of our smallness, our dependency, our inadequacy in relationship to him. And if we add into this picture that our adoration is focused precisely on the mystery and immensity of God's love, there is an engulfing sense of unworthiness, gratitude and trust.

Devotion to the Sacred Heart invites us into a state of adoring awareness of the incomprehensible immensity of God's love—a love made flesh for us in Jesus Christ and inviting our love in return.

There is more than this. Devotion to the Sacred Heart teaches us to enter into adoration by focusing on two visible objects: the image of our Lord's heart as he showed it in a vision to Saint Margaret Mary, and the Eucharist, which is the real Body and Blood of Jesus made present on the altar. Devotion to the Sacred Heart provides us with a starter, an ignition for adoration. Our Lord proposes something concrete and down-to-earth for us to do in order to enter into contemplation of his love, which is the mystery that transcends all mysteries, the very key to the Being of God.

Devotion to the Sacred Heart of Jesus is a focus on his love. And that focus is inseparable from adoration. Devotion to the Sacred Heart, then, is something that will lead us into adoration, teach us what it is, and give us the experience of adoring God. Is that something new?

Adoration is not the same as just saying prayers. It is not the same as meditation, or thinking about the Scriptures. Reading and reflecting on the word of God is an excellent thing to do—something so necessary for the spiritual life that it would be hard to claim to be a full, authentic Christian without it. And praying over Christ's words, looking at his actions in the Gospel, can lead to adoration. But adoration is in a class by itself. It is something we need to understand and appreciate for what it is.

Adoration can only truly be understood by experiencing it. But the experience of adoration becomes understanding by passing through reflection. So we need to reflect on our experience for the sake of greater understanding and more appreciation of the place of adoration in our lives.

The first step in devotion to the Sacred Heart is just to look at the image of his heart and think about what it says, what the symbols express. Or go before the Blessed Sacrament and be aware of his presence, asking what it means that he would be there, stay there, make himself available in this way for us. Then give yourself to adoration.

Reflecting on This Week's Gospels

Tenth Week of the Year

Pray daily: Lord, the more I see your power and awesomeness, the more I wonder at your love. Teach me the mystery of this love, which is greater than your power—which is your power. Show me your heart. Amen.

Monday: Matthew 5:1-12: After Jesus had sat down, his disciples came to him. He began to teach them. Do you believe that the words of Jesus are the words of God? Do you seek them out to reflect on them as the words of God?

Tuesday: Matthew 5:13-16: Jesus said that your light must shine before others, that they may see your good deeds and glorify your heavenly Father. Is your way of living so different, so impressive, that it fills people with a sense of awe and wonder that leads to adoration of God? Is it outlandish to think that it might be? Or to aim at this?

Wednesday: Matthew 5:17-19: Jesus said, "Do not think that I have come to abolish the law or the prophets. I have come not to abolish but to fulfill." Could anyone speaking just as a human being make a statement like that? How do your actions show the difference between what the law and the prophets asked for and what Jesus asks for?

Thursday: Matthew 5:20-26: Jesus said, "I tell you, unless your righteousness surpasses that of the scribes and Pharisees, you will not enter into the kingdom of heaven." What do you do that is better than keeping all the laws of your religion? (That is what the Pharisees focused on doing.)

Friday: Matthew 5:27-32: Jesus taught, "I say to you, everyone who looks at a woman with lust has already committed adultery with her in his heart." What is the difference between looking at someone with lust or with love? How do you look at people? With desire to use them for your purposes? With an attitude of superiority? With hostility? With indifference? Are all of these as bad as looking at someone with lust?

Saturday: Matthew 5:33-37: "But I say to you, do not swear at all.... Let your 'Yes' mean 'Yes,' and your 'No' mean 'No.'" Anything more is from the evil one." Are you conscious that because you are the Body of Christ every word you speak is spoken with the lips of Christ? What effect does this have on your way of speaking?

Living This Week's Gospels

As Christian: Each morning this week, when you get out of bed, kneel and place your forehead on the floor in adoration of God.

As Disciple: Begin reading through the Sermon on the Mount, conscious that what Jesus is giving here is a set of guidelines for living on the level of God. From this perspective, do you find his instructions awesome? Inspiring? Are you more encouraged to try to live by them?

As Prophet: Each time anyone around you uses the name of God as a swear word, bow your head in adoration.

As Priest: Each morning, before leaving your bedroom, make the sign of the cross on your lips, consciously consecrating them to speak every word as a word spoken by Jesus Christ.

As King: Make yourself alert to every expression of irreverence around you: irreverence for the person and presence of God; irreverence for people who are, or whom we must presume to be, the Body of Christ; irreverence for nature, which is God's creation, to be used according to God's purpose.

Eleventh Sunday of the Year

Sin, Love, Gratitude and Reparation

Luke 7:36-50; 2 Samuel 12:7-10, 13; Galatians 2:16, 19-21

Love is a free gift, and in a sense, love demands nothing in return. We don't barter our love on a contract basis, expecting to get a certain amount back for what we give. And we don't do loving things for others expecting them to do things for us in return. Not really. Love is a free gift.

We don't even love in order to be loved back. If we give our love to another because the other is good and lovable, that gift stands of itself, whether or not the other also sees us as good and lovable. Love is a free gift, not the admission fee into a mutual admiration society.

There is one thing, however, which we can and do expect in return for our love; one thing we feel we have a right to. That is gratitude. We feel that the gift of our love should be appreciated for what it is, whether or not the other does anything after that to respond to it.

When Jesus ate in the house of Simon the Pharisee, he didn't expect Simon to leave everything and become his disciple in response—or even to accept him as Messiah and all of his teachings as the truth of God. Perhaps he saw that Simon was just too blinded by the tradition of legalism in which he grew up to convert to Jesus' message that fast. When he went to eat with Simon, Jesus showed love and acceptance for Simon as he was at that moment, loving all the good that was in him and all that could come to be in him, without rejecting Simon because of his limitations or faults. The only thing he seemed to expect in return was gratitude.

When the woman known to be a sinner came in, Simon did not accept her as Jesus had accepted him. It was then Jesus remarked to him that Simon had not shown him even the small signs of respect customarily shown to a guest. And he pointed this out—very gently—as a lack of gratitude. The woman, Jesus remarked, was more grateful to Jesus than Simon was. Although she had committed more sins, her love was great, whereas Simon's was small.

What Jesus appreciated in this woman was not just her gratitude, but her expression of it: washing his feet with her tears and drying them with her hair. Her appreciation touched Jesus especially because she did what Simon should have done and more. Her act made up for Simon's snub. Her gratitude, expressed so intensely, made up for his ingratitude.

One of the things Jesus asked for from those who would show devotion to his Sacred Heart was reparation—and specifically reparation for the rejection shown to him by those who do not appreciate his overwhelming, merciful love. When Jesus showed his heart to Saint Margaret Mary he said, "Look at this heart, which has loved people so much and received so little in return." The motive for our acts of reparation is the ingratitude shown to Jesus Christ in response to his incredible love. And the story of this woman in the Gospel is a perfect image of the reparation Jesus asked for.

We are moved to acts of reparation when we look at the sins of the world, not just as acts which are evil in themselves or destructive to people and to society, but precisely as acts of ingratitude to God. If we do this, we will not find ourselves condemning others, because even if we haven't done some of the things others have done, we also fail to give God the love and gratitude he deserves. Then if we go to the Sacred Heart to make up for others' ingratitude, we will also be making up for our own. We will not be acting as if we were a class apart, the good praying for the bad. Rather, like Jesus himself, we will be identifying ourselves with the whole human race and making reparation for the sins of the whole. And we will be seeing sin, not just as an abstract question of good or evil, but as a personal failure of response to a personal, loving God.

This puts sin, love, gratitude and reparation all in a different perspective. And it teaches love.

Reflecting on This Week's Gospels

Eleventh Week of the Year

> *Pray daily: Lord, you have loved me from the beginning of time, and you love me still. Forgive the days, the weeks, the years I have been unconscious of your love. Focus my heart on you, that I might begin now the cry of gratitude that will echo in it forever and ever. Amen.*

Monday: Matthew 5:38-42: "But I say to you, do not resist an evildoer. But if anyone strikes you on the right cheek, turn the other also." Does Jesus turn away from us when our indifference to him is like a slap in the face? Can you continue to offer friendship to those who reject you?

Tuesday: Matthew 5:43-48: "You have heard that it was said, "You shall love your neighbor and hate your enemy." But I say to you, love your enemies, and pray for those who persecute you." Are you trying to love by human standards of fairness, or by God's standards? Can you be devoted to Christ's love without trying to imitate it?

Wednesday: Matthew 6:1-6, 16-18: "When you give alms, do not let your left hand know what your right is doing, so that your almsgiving may be secret. And your Father who sees in secret will repay you." How many gifts and blessings has Jesus given to you so quietly that even you have not noticed them? Should you make a point of thanking him every day for his goodness, seen and unseen?

Thursday: Matthew 6:7-15: "When you are praying, do not heap up empty phrases as the Gentiles do; for they think that they will be heard because of their many words...." How much time do you spend just being silent before God, reflecting on the words, the love of Jesus, and letting God speak to your heart?

Friday: Matthew 6:19-23: "Where your treasure is, there also will your heart be." Where is your treasure? What do you think about most often with desire? What are you most concerned about losing? How often do you express to Jesus Christ your love and longing for him?

Saturday: Matthew 6:24-34: "No one can serve two masters. You will either hate one and love the other, or be devoted to one and despise the other. You cannot serve God and wealth." Is serving Jesus Christ the undisputed goal of all your choices and desires? Do you ever feel enslaved by other desires or goals?

Living This Week's Gospels

As Christian: Put a crucifix in a place where you will see it every day. When you look at it, consciously remember what Jesus has done for us all.

As Disciple: Each Friday read a passage from a Gospel account of the passion and death of Christ.

As Prophet: Each Friday do some small act of penance in grateful remembrance of Christ's love.

As Priest: At every Eucharist, when the Body and Blood of Christ are lifted up, offer yourself in Christ and with Christ in reparation for the sins of the world.

As King: Try to think of any damage you may be doing to someone else by your behavior or policies. Change what you are doing and try to repair the damage.

Twelfth Sunday of the Year

Consecration to the
Sacred Heart of Jesus

Luke 9:18-24; Zechariah 12:10-11; Galatians 3:26-29

Jesus asks each one of us the question he puts to his
disciples in the Gospel: "Who do you say that I am?"
The answer changes. Through various experiences, Jesus
repeatedly brings us into deeper, more intimate knowledge of
himself. And he also intervenes in history to help the whole
Church grow in understanding of who he is.

We may have grown up assuming that Jesus revealed
himself so completely during his earthly life that all we have
to do to know him perfectly is study the Scriptures. This
would narrow our focus to the past, failing to include what
Jesus is revealing of himself today.

A foundation stone of Protestant fundamentalism is the
denial of theological significance to any expression of or
about Jesus that is not already recorded in the Scriptures. In
terms of practical devotion, this means that, except in a very
secondary way, we should not look for Jesus in his Body on
earth today. We should not give faith to Jesus teaching in his
Body on earth today; or seek forgiveness from Jesus ministering
in his Body on earth today; or accept Jesus revealing himself
in his Body on earth today through the example of the saints.
Once we say that the Church has no authority to teach as
Jesus on earth, the priests have no power to minister as Jesus
on earth, and the saints have no role to play as the continuing
revelation of Jesus on earth, we have reduced our religion to
fundamentalism and reduced Jesus to history.

If we accept "devotion to the Sacred Heart," we are
taking seriously the probability that more than a thousand
years after the Scriptures were written, Jesus entrusted to a

French nun a message for the world. It is true (and significant) that there is nothing in the message to Saint Margaret Mary that is not perfectly consistent with what is in the Scriptures. But there is much in that message which corrects an impression we may have drawn from the Scriptures. If Jesus saw the need to speak to the world again at a particular time in history, it was because our understanding of him at that time was out of focus. It was his way of asking the whole Church again, "Who are you saying that I am?" And to recall us from false directions he pointed in answer to his heart and said, "Look again, and look deeply: I am love."

Devotion to the Sacred Heart is many things. It is a recognition of Jesus in the flesh, of his human heart and human-divine love. It is an acknowledgment of his continuing interaction with us in history. It leads us into adoration of his incomprehensible love and into acts of reparation for the sins and indifference of the world. And if we want to enter into it fully, it leads us to consecrate ourselves to the heart of Christ. What, precisely, does that involve?

We first have to understand clearly that all of us were consecrated to God in Christ at Baptism. There is no consecration greater than this, or that even adds to this. Any other consecration just specifies in some way what was already included in our Baptism. For example, the Sacrament of Matrimony specifies the way married couples will give themselves to God and to the world as Christ's Body on earth. Holy Orders specifies another way. So do vows in a religious order. And if we consecrate ourselves to the Sacred Heart, it simply means that we consciously, deliberately and explicitly dedicate ourselves to focusing our devotion on the love of his heart, and on trying to respond to that love with adoration, reparation, and with the gift of ourselves to be the embodied expression of his love to others.

Consecration to the Sacred Heart means that Christ's love will be our focus as we look at God, and giving expression to his love will be our focus in every interaction with others. It means giving our hearts to Jesus Christ that he might express his love through us at every moment of our lives. It means becoming love.

Reflecting on This Week's Gospels

Twelfth Week of the Year

Pray daily: Lord, you came to reveal the heart, the love of God to us. I consecrate myself to learning your love: to recalling it, pondering it, accepting it and returning it. Help me with the graces flowing in abundance through your words and sacraments. Amen.

Monday: Matthew 7:1-5: Jesus said, "For as you judge, so will you be judged, and the measure with which you measure will be measured out to you." How have you been judging God? How have you been measuring his love? When you presume that God's love for you is small, how does that limit your heart's capacity to receive it?

Tuesday: Matthew 7:6, 12-14: Jesus taught, "How narrow the gate and constricted the road that leads to life. And those who find it are few." There is nothing more narrow than a straight line. How many aim at making every action of their lives a direct response to the heart of Christ? How often do you do this?

Wednesday: Matthew 7:15-20: "By their fruits you will know them. Do people pick grapes from thorn bushes, or figs from thistles? Just so, every good tree bears good fruit, and a rotten tree bears bad fruit." Are the fruits of your religion obviously the fruits of love? Does your religion ever make you judgmental? Harsh toward others? Unmerciful? Vindictive?

Thursday: Matthew 7:21-29: "Not everyone who says to me, 'Lord, Lord,' will enter the kingdom of heaven, but only the one who does the will of my Father in heaven." What, above all, is the Father's will? What did Jesus say was the first and greatest commandment? The second? Are these the root and focus of your life?

Friday: Matthew 8:1-4: "A leper approached Jesus, did him homage, and said, 'Lord, if you wish, you can make me clean.'" With what kind of faith do you approach Jesus? Are you sure he loves you? That he wants to do for you what people do for those they love?

Saturday: Matthew 8:5-17: The centurion said to Jesus, "Lord, I am not worthy to have you enter under my roof; only say the word and my servant will be healed." Do you ever refrain from receiving Eucharist because you feel you are unworthy? Is this because you believe in your heart that you have turned away from Jesus Christ by mortal sin? Do you ever think about how much he, on his part, wants to come to you and heal you? (Note: the guideline used by confessors is that you can always receive Communion unless you are certain that you have done something so bad that it amounts to a rejection of the divine life of God given to you in Baptism, and that you did it with sufficient appreciation of how bad it was, and with the unreserved consent of your will.)

Living This Week's Gospels

As Christian: Write the word "love" somewhere where you will see it every day or all day. Live your day in response to what it says.

As Disciple: Read John's Gospel, chapter 14. If you have time, read chapter 15 also.

As Prophet: Look for something you do for some other motive than love. Change your motivation. See how that affects the way you do it.

As Priest: Find the soup kitchen nearest to where you live or work. (The diocesan office should know the Catholic ones; call a Protestant church for others.) Give a few hours of service or bring some food.

As King: Ask who you know or work with that does not feel loved. Try to identify the cause of this. See what you can do to change the cause.

Thirteenth Sunday of the Year

Spirit of Daring Freedom

Mark 5:21-43; Wisdom 1:13-15; 2:23-24;
2 Corinthians 8:7, 9, 13-15

There is a strange contrast in this Gospel: it begins with Jesus refusing to call down fire from heaven on those who did not accept him, which makes him appear very gentle, and it ends with Jesus summoning his followers to refuse even the ordinary social obligations to their families, which makes him appear very harsh. Are there any words in history harsher than, "Let the dead bury their dead!"? Of these two attitudes, which shows us the true Jesus, and which should we adopt for ourselves?

The true Jesus was not interested in projecting either gentleness or harshness as his characteristic stance toward people, because he accepted both. Jesus gave himself primarily neither to gentleness nor to harshness, but to love. Whatever love required, he was willing to do.

Jesus was more free in this than we are. How often do we fail to help someone we love because we just cannot bring ourselves to say or do something that will hurt? We fail to challenge others to live up to their potential, and we fail to live up to our own, for fear of appearing harsh—and thereby fail to contribute to the life of this world what we could contribute. And so the psychologists had to invent the phrase "tough love" to remind us that gentleness can sometimes destroy.

On the other hand, how many times do we wound and destroy because we fail to be gentle? We think that force will accomplish what love cannot, and so we raise our voices when we should lower them. We try to push our point across quickly when we should sit down and talk. Often enough, in our harshness toward those who do wrong, we are not really trying to help people; we are just trying to get out of our environment whatever evil or annoyance they are putting into it. We act, not out of love for others, but out of fear. First and foremost, we want to protect what is ours.

The second half of this Gospel addresses that. Jesus tells his followers that they must not cling to home and possessions, or to the sense of security a safe home gives. "The Son of Man has nowhere to lay his head."

He tells us we cannot put family bonds, or the sense of belonging we find in close relationships within our own circle of friends, above the gift of ourselves to the world. How often have we excluded someone who did not "fit in," or did what was not right because we wanted to fit in ourselves? Jesus says, "Come away and proclaim the kingdom of God."

There are times to be with family and friends—precious times. But there is also an acceptance of social obligation to family and friends that can be, in fact, divided loyalty. Jesus tells us that whenever we suspect that we might be hearing his call, nothing should hold us back.

The problem is our focus. When we think of what we are by Baptism—the Body of Christ, sharers in the life and mission of Jesus Christ, his embodied presence on earth—we want to give ourselves to the work of the kingdom. But then we let our minds and hearts focus on other very natural desires—desires for security, for the intimate closeness of family and friends, for acceptance by our group—and, "looking back," we take our hand from the plow and forget Christ's call to save the world with him.

The call of this Gospel is a radical call: It goes to the roots of our attitude toward life itself. And like all radical calls, it must be balanced. But before we can achieve balance between all the various attitudes and values of our life we need to give each value its full weight. Our Lord calls us to a love gentle enough to endure all things without violence, yet strong enough to stand against the whole world in loyalty to the work and ideals of the kingdom. That makes us a people of peace who accept to be at odds with the world.

Reflecting on This Week's Gospels

Thirteenth Week of the Year

> *Pray daily: Lord, you came to call us to live life and give life to the full. Teach me to love as you love, wanting only to bring all of those you love to the fullness of response to you. For this is life. Amen.*

Monday: Matthew 8:18-22: Jesus answered, "Follow me, and let the dead bury their dead." How many social obligations do you go along with that are not life-giving to you or to anyone else?

Tuesday: Matthew 8:23-27: The men were amazed and said, "What sort of man is this, whom even the winds and the sea obey?" Are you so impressed with who Jesus really is that you will do absolutely anything for him? Are you impressed enough to spend some time with him every day?

Wednesday: Matthew 8:28-34: The swineherds ran away and...reported everything, including what had happened to the demoniacs. Thereupon the whole town came out to meet Jesus, and when they saw him they begged him to leave their district. Are you afraid to let Jesus be a part of everything you do? How do you include him in your social life, your student or professional activities? Do you explicitly invite him to come with you wherever you go?

Thursday: Matthew 9:1-8: Jesus asked, "Which is easier, to say, 'Your sins are forgiven,' or to say, 'Rise and walk'?" Which do you want more: physical health or deliverance from the sins that hold you back from giving yourself to God without reserve? What do you most frequently ask Jesus to do for you?

Friday: Matthew 9:9-13: While Jesus was at table in Levi's house, many tax collectors and sinners came and sat with Jesus and his disciples. Whom do you invite to your house? If you gave a party for Jesus, would you invite the same people?

Would you be comfortable with the mix? How do you invite Jesus to be part of the dinners or parties you do give?

Saturday: Matthew 9:14-17: Jesus said, "People do not put new wine into old wineskins. Otherwise the skins burst, the wine spills out, and the skins are ruined." What are you doing to make yourself the kind of person to whom Jesus can say anything? Is he being frank with you now? What is the latest challenge he has given you? What is the last thing he has asked you to do for him?

Living This Week's Gospels

As Christian: Imagine Jesus standing in front of you saying, "Come, follow me." What is your first reaction?

As Disciple: Read the Vatican II document, "The Church in the Modern World" (*"Gaudium et Spes"*), looking for the way to harmonize radical response to the Gospel with full participation in the life of our society.

As Prophet: Ask yourself what you have been afraid to change in your family or social life, or in your student or professional activity, because of your fear of how others might react. Without being rash, weigh this in the light of Jesus' call to let nothing stand in the way of following him.

As Priest: Think of the last time you felt like "calling down fire from heaven" on someone who was wrong. Ask yourself what would be the gentle, respectful way to help that person change. Is this incompatible with "tough love"?

As King: Notice and identify the things in your environment that encourage the mediocrity of "not making waves." Call this working principle into question in conversation with others and by your own actions.

Fourteenth Sunday of the Year

Messengers of Peace;
Witnesses to Power

Luke 10:1-20; Isaiah 66:10-14; Galatians 6:14-18

The key to understanding this Gospel is believing we are sent.

Unless we really know (and we can only know it by believing it) that today we are the seventy-two who are sent, we will listen to this Gospel as if it were being spoken to someone else. We won't ask seriously what it means, because we will assume that it doesn't really apply to us. And we will miss the whole point.

The fact is, we are sent. The instructions in this Gospel are something we need to know. They tell us what we are sent to do, how we are to do it, and what we need to keep in mind in order to deal with what we will meet. But if we don't believe at the front end that we are sent, or if we haven't really accepted this mission as ours, all the instructions will be for us purely academic. And since they are given precisely to help us deal with reality, there is no way we can truly understand them unless we relate them to what is real and present and active in our lives right now. Do you live with a sense of mission? Is it your constant awareness?

The Gospel tells us we are sent "to every town and place" Jesus intends to visit. Do you really believe that Jesus is preparing to visit every single person you deal with every day? That he has sent you to prepare that person to receive his inspirations, his help, his comfort?

Do you accept the fact that you are sent precisely to those people whom you don't think of as being open to you or to what you have to say about religion? You are sent "like a lamb among wolves." Or do you wait to give your message only to those who welcome it—that is, to those who have already heard it; those who need you the least?

It is true, Jesus says not to force the message on anyone. You should not even jump right into talking about religion. The first thing to do, he says, is establish "peace" between yourself and the one to whom you are sent. How do you do this?

The answer is to respect what the person already is, what this individual person has already experienced of God. You are not to burst in, a total stranger to someone else's soul, and act as if you were the missionary sent to the heathen. How many times have you yourself been invaded by some born-again enthusiast inviting you to be "saved" as if you had never spoken to God in your life before? To approach another in "peace" is to begin by assuming and seeking to identify a common ground of experience, something in which you are already at one. And since we believe that God speaks to every human heart—and has spoken to each one long before we came on the scene, we begin by seeking with respect to stand with our brother or sister on common ground as fellow creatures, fellow children of God, fellow receivers of the love and mercy of Jesus Christ. We don't speak down to anyone like a teacher instructing the ignorant (Jesus said, "Only one is your Teacher; you are all learners"). Rather, we sit down with another human person in the darkness we all experience and gratefully share light.

We should not assume that the other does or does not identify certain experiences as experiences of "God" or of "Jesus." To come in "peace" is to come trying to communicate in the other's language, not our own. We come, first seeking to understand, then to share.

Finally, Jesus tells us not to think of our mission as something to "accomplish," as if what really mattered were the "head count" of how many people we have "saved" or converted. "Rejoice," he says, "that your names are written in heaven." Be glad you know Jesus, and be glad if you can help anyone else to know him a little better. But don't get into a power trip. The power to which we witness is God's, not ours.

Reflecting on This Week's Gospels

Fourteenth Week of the Year

Pray daily: Lord I believe you have chosen me by name and sent me to all the people with whom I live and work. Make me conscious all the time that your eyes and your hopes are resting on me. Let me love you. Amen.

Monday: Matthew 9:18-26: An official came forward, knelt down before Jesus, and said, "My daughter has just died. But come, lay your hand on her, and she will live." Do people keep asking you for favors or answers because they take for granted you want to help them? What does this say about your awareness of being "sent" by Jesus to do his work?

Tuesday: Matthew 9:32-38: Jesus said to his disciples, "The harvest is abundant but the laborers are few; so ask the master of the harvest to send out laborers for his harvest." When you hear these words, do you think Jesus is talking about the need for more priests and religious, or do you think he is talking about activating the laity? About you?

Wednesday: Matthew 10:1-7: Then Jesus summoned his twelve disciples and gave them authority over unclean spirits to drive them out and to cure every disease and every illness. What power do you think Jesus has given you over the sins and woundedness that keep people from living life to the full? Do you count on more than your human skills? Do you believe enough to try to free others?

Thursday: Matthew 10:7-15: Jesus said to those he sent, "Do not take gold or silver or copper for your belts; no sack for the journey, or a second tunic, or sandals, or walking stick." Are you afraid to take on the mission of Jesus because of a lack of human resources? Do you refuse to speak about the Gospels or to try to bring others closer to God because you are not professionally trained, don't have a degree in religious education, and have not been certified as an official minister of the Church?

Friday: Matthew 10:16-23: "Behold, I am sending you like sheep in the midst of wolves; so be shrewd as serpents and simple as doves." Do you only bear witness to the values of Christ among those who already accept his values or at least accept him as Teacher? Is there a way to bear witness that is not simplistic? That is not even overt?

Saturday: Matthew 10:24-33: Jesus said, "Everyone who acknowledges me before others I will acknowledge before my heavenly Father. But whoever denies me before others, I will deny before my heavenly Father." Do people around you—or do you yourself—proclaim belief in non-religious values more openly in the values Jesus teaches? Do you hide your personal devotion to God from others? How do you express it? When do you suppress the expression of it?

Living This Week's Gospels

As Christian: See if you think you know the religious commitment (or lack thereof) of the individuals with whom you work or go to class. What signs are you reading? Can others read the same signs in your life?

As Disciple: Write out a very simple statement of your belief as a Christian, something you could say to someone who asks you what your religious beliefs are. (Just to tell someone what religion you belong to is probably as misleading as it is enlightening.)

As Prophet: Decide on some visible sign to put or preserve in your life-style that will clearly express your relationship with Christ. Don't be simplistic. Think about it.

As Priest: Ask some people of other religions what they think is the common ground between you and them. See if you can identify with their personal experience of God. Look for "fellowship (communion) in the Holy Spirit."

As King: Ask yourself what you can do to establish or extend the reign of Christ over your work or social life without ever mentioning the name of Jesus or quoting anything he taught. What changes can you propose and defend on their own merits, using values already accepted, in principle at least, by those around you?

Fifteenth Sunday of the Year

Baptism Makes Us Family

Luke 10:25-37; Deuteronomy 30:10-14; Colossians 1:15-20

Through Baptism, Saint Paul tells us, we are "strangers and aliens no longer," but "fellow citizens of the saints and members of the household of God" (Ephesians 2:19). God has "rescued us from the power of darkness." He did it by "bringing us into the kingdom of his beloved Son" (Colossians 1:13). The sign that we have been redeemed, that we are saved, is that "there does not exist among [us] Jew or Greek, slave or freeman, male or female. All are one in Christ Jesus" (Galatians 3:28).

Baptism is not just a washing. It is above all an incorporation. The blood of Christ only washes away the sins of his own Body—and by Baptism we became the Body of Christ. We were baptized "into" the body that hung on the cross. We are saved by our union with him in one Body. It is only because we are one with Christ that, when he died, we died in him. It is only because we are his Body that when he rose, we rose in him free of sin.

Today's Gospel calls us to give external expression to the mystery of unity that is ours with Christ and with all who are "in Christ," who are members of his Body by Baptism. The fundamental commandment for those who are united to him, Jesus tells us, is love: to love God above all things; to love our neighbor as ourselves. Love is a sign of our Baptism, and love is a sign of grace, because love is a sign of unity. If we are one in Christ we don't categorize each other as being "one of us" ("Jew") or "one of them" ("Greek"—or, in today's Gospel, "Samaritan"). We don't take either a chauvinistic or a militant stance toward each other as male or female. We don't relate to people as rich or poor ("slave or free"). In the story of the Good Samaritan Jesus shows us that Baptism abolishes all these divisions. Now we are simply one people: "a 'chosen race, a royal priesthood, a holy nation, a people he claims for his own to proclaim the glorious works' of the One who called [us] from darkness into his marvelous light" (1 Peter 2:9). Our "neighbor" is anyone who is, or who is called to be, a child of God. We have no more "neighbors" and "non-neighbors." We only have brothers and sisters in Christ, actual or potential. This is what Baptism brings about.

Baptism calls us to many virtues. Saint Paul lists "heartfelt mercy," kindness, humility, meekness, patience and forgiveness. But over all of these, he says, "put on love, which binds the rest together and makes them perfect." The fruit of this is peace. "Christ's peace must reign in your hearts, since as members of the one body you have been called to that peace" (Colossians 3: 12-15).

We cannot love our neighbors "as ourselves" unless we know who we are. Before we can know what to cherish and respect in our neighbor, we have to be aware of what we should cherish and respect in ourselves. And we cannot value ourselves or anyone else as we should unless we are aware that we are the sacred Body of Christ, sanctified temples of the Holy Spirit, sharers in the life of God by grace, called to live forever in absolute beauty and lovableness in heaven. This is true of us, and this is true of every other person who has been baptized into Jesus Christ. To love our neighbors as ourselves is to be conscious that our neighbors are all of these things and relate to them accordingly.

Our neighbors don't always behave like enlightened, loving embodiments of Jesus Christ. But then, neither do we. We know from experience that it is possible to be basically redeemed and surrendered to Christ's ideals of love and goodness while still failing in many ways. That is why we need to forgive each other constantly. To do this it helps to remember that we are all one Body in Christ.

Reflecting on This Week's Gospels

Fifteenth Week of the Year

> ***Pray daily:*** *Lord, so that we all might be in communion with God and with each other you became one of us. You took on our human condition. Teach me to identify with every human being on that level where you have already made us one by creation and by grace. And teach me to grow from there into conscious communion with every person I meet. Amen.*

Monday: Matthew 10:34 to 11:1: Jesus said, "Do not think that I have come to bring peace upon the earth. I have come to bring not peace but the sword. For I have come to set a man 'against his father, a daughter against her mother, and a daughter-in-law against her mother-in-law.'" Has anyone rejected you because of the ideals you have accepted as a Christian? Because of the people you accept? If so, does this make you divisive?

Tuesday: Matthew 11:20-24: "Woe to you, Chorazin! Woe to you, Bethsaida! For if the mighty deeds done in your midst had been done in Tyre and Sidon, they would long ago have repented in sackcloth and ashes." If you reject the call to be one with all the family of God, where does that leave you?

Wednesday: Matthew 11:25-27: "No one knows the Son except the Father, and no one knows the Father except the Son and anyone to whom the Son wishes to reveal him." Do you know Jesus? Do you know the Father? Do you experience deep communion of heart with all who do?

Thursday: Matthew 11:28-30: Jesus said, "Come to me, all you who labor and are burdened, and I will give you rest." Is his voice saying this to others in you? Does your behavior toward others invite them to find comfort in you?

Friday: Matthew 12:1-8: Jesus said, "If you had known what this means, 'I desire mercy and not sacrifice,' you would not have condemned the guiltless." If you truly understand the heart of Christ, will you condemn people for doing what is right? Do you now? Do you stand by while others do?

Saturday: Matthew 12:14-21: Isaiah said of the Messiah, "He will not wrangle or cry aloud, nor will anyone hear his voice in the streets." Would Jesus shout slogans at people who are doing wrong? How would he try to convert them? What is your approach to people in error?

Living This Week's Gospels

As Christian: Sit down and face very seriously your attitude toward the rest of the human race. How has your Baptism affected it? Do you see every child of God as your brother or sister? How do you show it?

As Disciple: Read Paul's letter to the Colossians, chapter 1, verses 9 to 23.

As Prophet: Ask yourself what signs of acceptance or of fellowship you give to the people you identify with but not to others. See what happens if you make the same gesture to someone else.

As Priest: List in order of priority the people you are committed to taking care of. What seems to determine the priorities?

As King: Do the same thing with the work you take responsibility for. What goals are you most committed to accomplishing and why?

Sixteenth Sunday of the Year

Baptism Makes Us Christ

Luke 10:38-42; Genesis 18:1-10; Colossians 1:24-28

Martha and Mary show us two attitudes that people who love Jesus can choose to take.

This is not a choice between different vocations in life—life in a monastery, for example, or life in the busy marketplace of this world. Nor is it a choice between personality types: Martha, the "organizing type," or Mary, the kind of person who prefers to just rest in quiet relatedness to others. What Mary chooses is called "better," and it is a choice we are all urged by Jesus to make, regardless of our personalities or particular vocation within the Church.

What Jesus is teaching here is the attitude we should take toward himself, his Church and his religion—in other words, toward life itself.

For Martha life consists of "getting it done," and she understands the Church as the organization Jesus founded to get done the things he came to do. To be "religious" is to participate in the Church's activities in order to help accomplish her goals. Jesus is someone to work for.

Mary, on the other hand, understands life the way the catechism taught it: "We were created to know God, to love him, and to serve him"—in that order. First we need to know God, because it is the only way to love him. And the service he wants of us presupposes deep, personal knowledge and love. To serve Jesus Christ as he desires we have to be intimate with him. Christianity, then, is first and foremost a consecration to seeking knowledge and love of God through intimacy with Jesus Christ.

But intimacy with Jesus Christ is not something that can be achieved just through human efforts—because it is not just human intimacy. We believe that we are baptized into this intimacy by being baptized into union with Jesus in one shared life: his life. It is a mystical union, a mystery, the mystery of grace.

Our intimacy with Jesus is not just the fruit of reflecting on his words, his life, his example. It presupposes this, of course, and requires it; but the real source of our intimacy with him is in the fact that we have been baptized "into Christ," into his Body, into the life of grace which is a sharing in the divine life of God.

The Mass expresses this. The Mass begins with the "Liturgy of the Word," when we read the Scriptures, sing and pray together as an expression of our faith that Jesus is present among us, speaking to us now through his word, calling us to give expression to the Spirit who is rejoicing within us. We never celebrate Mass without readings from the Scriptures. Then we move into the "Liturgy of the Eucharist." This begins with the Offertory, when we offer ourselves to God under the form of bread and wine, as we offered our human lives to him at Baptism, in order to be transformed more and more into Christ as his real Body on earth. John Paul II, quoting Saint Augustine, wrote: "By the work of the Spirit, Baptism radically configures the faithful to Christ in the Paschal Mystery of death and resurrection; it 'clothes us' in Christ (cf. Galatians 3:27): 'Let us rejoice and give thanks,' exclaims Saint Augustine speaking to the baptized, 'for we have become not only Christians, but Christ.... Marvel and rejoice: we have become Christ!'" (*The Splendor of Truth*, no. 21).

As the Mass continues through the Eucharistic Prayer and the Consecration/ Elevation, we who are the Body of Christ offer ourselves "in him" as members of the body he offers on the cross. We offer ourselves as Christ to the Father for the life of the world. Finally, the Mass ends with Communion, when Jesus gives himself to us as the food and life of our souls to be one with us as we are sent out to be his presence in the world.

All of this says to us that the real goal of our lives and of our religion is to be united to Jesus Christ in the intimacy of one shared life, sharing by grace in his mind, his heart, his desires, his power, his mission on earth. Our religion is to grow into union with Jesus so that we might act in union with him, as members of his Body on earth. Baptism both enables and dedicates us to do this. Baptism gives union.

Our religion is to live out what we celebrate at Mass: to reflect on Scripture and more: to offer ourselves for continual transformation as Christ's real Body on earth. As "Mary," united with Jesus in mind and heart and will, in the intimacy of one shared life, we do all the things "Martha" is concerned about without leaving our Lord's feet, without ceasing to "listen to his words." His words are also in our hearts, and we keep listening to them there.

Reflecting on This Week's Gospels

Sixteenth Week of the Year

> ***Pray daily:*** *Lord Jesus, you loved me enough to ask me to be your own body. You have shared your heart and your Spirit with me. I want to love you so much that in every word and action of my life my body will be yours. Help me to give to you what I have received. Amen.*

Monday: Matthew 12:38-42: Jesus said, "An evil and unfaithful generation seeks a sign, but no sign will be given it except the sign of Jonah the prophet." Are you aware, on a daily basis, that Jesus counts on you to be the sign and proof of his resurrection? What is visible in your way of living that just does not make sense unless you see yourself as the risen Body of Christ?

Tuesday: Matthew 12:46-50: Stretching out his hand toward his disciples, Jesus said, "here are my mother and my brothers." Do you feel you have the same claim on Jesus that his mother and brothers had? Do you let him have the same claim on you? How does this show in your life?

Wednesday: Matthew 13:1-9: Jesus told the parable, "A sower went out to sow. And as he sowed, some seed fell on the path, and birds came and ate it up...." Do you look upon the words of Jesus as seeds growing within you? What fruit are they bearing? How do you nurture them?

Thursday: Matthew 13:10-17: Jesus said, "Blessed are your eyes, because they see, and your ears, because they hear. Amen, I say to you, many prophets and righteous people longed to see what you see but did not see it, and to hear what you hear but did not hear it." What do you see and hear that the great prophets did not? Do you try to do more than they did because of it? In what ways?

Friday: Matthew 13:18-23: Jesus said, explaining the parable of the sower, "The seed sown among thorns is the one who hears the word, but then worldly anxiety and the lure of riches choke the word and it bears no fruit. But the seed sown on rich soil is the one who hears the word and understands it, who indeed bears fruit and yields a hundred or sixty or thirtyfold." Which of these two descriptions do you relate to more? What, in the concrete, makes you feel this way?

Saturday: Matthew 13:24-30: The slaves of the householder came to him and said, "Master, did you not sow good seed in your field? Where, then did these weeds come from?" Which of your actions make it difficult for you to see yourself as Christ's embodied presence on earth? Are they so unacceptable to Jesus that he would like to root them out at any cost? How do fear and pressure inhibit growth into the fullness of free, personal, loving dedication to God?

Living This Week's Gospels

As Christian: Each day for a week, say to yourself when you wake and before every new action, "I am the embodied presence of Jesus here." Act accordingly.

As Disciple: Read just the first chapter of John Paul II's letter, *The Splendor of Truth*. It may be the shortest, deepest explanation in existence of what Jesus said it means to be a Christian.

As Prophet: Find a way to remind yourself over and over again all day that you are the embodied presence of Jesus. Try to make your every word, choice and action consistent with this truth.

As Priest: Whenever you are called upon this week to do something difficult or to sacrifice yourself for others, say with Jesus, "My flesh for the life of the world!" and give yourself to it as Jesus gave himself to the cross.

As King: Every place you go, every room you enter this week, take responsibility for what is going on there. Do what you can do to bring everything into conformity with the values of Christ. Use Jesus' means (persuasion and love, not intimidation or force).

Baptism Makes Us Co-Workers With Christ

Luke 11:1-13; Genesis 18:20-32; Colossians 2:12-14

The Jews were remarkable memorizers. If the words of the Our Father are different in Matthew (6:9-13) and Luke (11:2-4), it is not by mistake: It means that when Jesus was asked to "teach us to pray" he did not intend to give us the "right words" to say to God. Nor did he teach a method of prayer, such as meditation. What Jesus taught was the foundation of all prayer, the one thing that makes us able to grow in prayer: he taught us a set of priorities.

The secret of Jesus' own prayer was not in the words he said or the method he used. It was in the priorities of his heart. The Our Father reveals to us the priorities of Jesus' own heart, and he tells us, "If you want to pray like me, desire like me. Let my priorities be your own." What priorities does the Our Father reveal?

The very first desire Jesus expresses in this prayer was the burning desire of his life: the desire that the Father be known and loved, appreciated and enjoyed for what he really is. This is what Jesus lived and breathed for; it was the reason he came to earth. "Hallowed be thy name."

His second all-consuming desire was "Your kingdom come!" he wanted to see all of creation brought into harmony with God's will and so into harmony with itself (see Ephesians 1:9-10).

Father Raymond Brown explains the whole Our Father as a prayer for the coming of the Kingdom, a looking forward with desire to the final accomplishment of everything Christ came to do. (He says that "daily bread" is better translated as "bread of tomorrow," meaning the bread of the heavenly banquet; reference and explanation are given in my book

Make Me a Sabbath of Your Heart, p. 109.)

Do you want to know how far you have grown into identification with Christ? Into conformity with his heart? Ask yourself if now, at this stage in your life, you can say that the one thing you want more than anything else—for yourself, for your family, for the world—is just that everyone should know and love God (hallowed be...) and that his kingdom, his life-giving rule, should be established over every area and activity of human life, including your own (thy kingdom...thy will...).

Do you long for complete, irreversible union with Jesus Christ (Give us...bread)? For total reconciliation with him and with anyone else from whom you are in the slightest way estranged (forgive us...)? Is the one thing you want to avoid more than anything else separation from God through sin (and lead us not...)?

If you can identify with these desires, you are experiencing the growth that has taken place in you since your Baptism—and it is a growth into your Baptism. It is growth into that identification with Jesus Christ that was given to you in Baptism. What Baptism gives is new life (and our identification with Jesus is a sharing in his life). Therefore, like birth, Baptism is not an end but a beginning. It gives life and launches us into growth toward the fullness of life. Baptism makes us one with Jesus and launches us toward perfect union of mind and will and heart with him. The Our Father expresses what this perfect union is. When our hearts are in perfect conformity with the priority of desires expressed in this prayer, we will be able to pray like Jesus because we will be in perfect conformity with his heart.

To live our Baptism, then, is to grow into perfect conformity with the desires of Jesus Christ. And his desires are expressed in a prayer for the perfect accomplishment of his mission. We grow into our Baptism as we grow into total identification with the mission of Jesus Christ on earth. Our life is mission. His mission is our life. To be Jesus is to be Church. To be Church is to be sent. Baptism is a sending.

Reflecting on This Week's Gospels

Seventeenth Week of the Year

Pray daily: Lord Jesus, you came to earth burning with desire. You longed to bring to the world the knowledge of your Father, and to bring to your Father the love of the whole human race. Make me one with you in heart and mind and mission. Amen.

Monday: Matthew 13:31-35: Jesus said, "The kingdom of heaven is like yeast that a woman took and mixed with three measures of wheat flour until the whole batch was leavened." What effect do you have on those around you? Are you like yeast? Do you cause the ideals of all to rise?

Tuesday: Matthew 13:35-43: "He who sows good seed is the Son of Man, the field is the world, the good seed the children of the kingdom. The weeds are the children of the evil one, and the enemy who sows them is the devil." What kind of seeds do you sow in the hearts of all those you live and work with? Do you see bad seed being sown? Do you try to counteract it?

Wednesday: Matthew 13:44-46: "The kingdom of heaven is like treasure hidden in a field, which someone found and hid; then in his joy he goes and sells all that he has and buys that field." How much do you appreciate the gift of grace, of sharing in the divine life of God? Is it a constant joy to you? Are you always trying to share it with others?

Thursday: Matthew 13:47-53: "Every scribe who has been instructed in the kingdom of heaven is like the head of a household who brings from his storeroom both the new and the old." How much of your Christian inheritance are you able to share with others? How much of the classic writings of the saints and doctors of the Church have you read? How familiar are you with the Vatican II documents and the great encyclicals of recent popes (for example, John Paul's "The Splendor of Truth" and "The Gospel of Life")?

Friday: Matthew 13:54-58: Jesus came to his hometown and began to teach the people in their synagogue, so that they were astounded and said, "Where did this man get this wisdom and these deeds of power?" What do you teach those you live and work with? Would any be astounded to know you are familiar with the Bible? Or that you are a Christian? What reveals your devotion to God?

Saturday: Matthew 14:1-12: Herod had arrested John and put him in prison on account of Herodias, the wife of his brother Philip, for John had said to him, "It is not lawful for you to have her." Have you ever aroused hostility in anyone because of your efforts to extend the reign of God over every area of human life in which you are involved? Was it because you did not use the respectful, peaceful means of Jesus, or just because someone resented being faced with truth and goodness?

Living This Week's Gospels

As Christian: Each day this week pray the Our Father slowly, thinking of yourself as praying with the voice of Christ and asking how close you come to feeling about each petition as he does.

As Disciple: Read Vatican II's document on the Church (*"Lumen Gentium"*), chapter 4, on the spirituality and mission of the laity. Or read the treatment of the Lord's Prayer (Our Father) in the *Catechism of the Catholic Church*, nos. 2759 ff.

As Prophet: Each day when you dress, put on something, or put something in your pocket or purse which is one of the "tools of your trade" as a Christian. Take something that tells you that you are sent out by Jesus to do a job.

As Priest: During the eucharistic celebration, consciously unite yourself with the desires of Christ and the Church expressed in all the Mass prayers. Do it with the specific intention of growing into total conformity with the mind and heart of Christ.

As King: Wherever you are, ask yourself whether the reality of the Father is being respected and appreciated, whether the reign of Christ is being advanced, whether God's will is being done. Work toward whatever changes are called for.

Baptism Makes Us Different

Luke 12:13-21; Ecclesiastes 1:2, 2:21-23; Colossians 3:1-5, 9-11

We may not realize—or remember constantly enough—just how radically Baptism has changed our whole outlook on life. In Luke's Gospel someone asked Jesus for a favor which to us seems perfectly normal: "Teacher, tell my brother to divide the family inheritance with me." If you had been Jesus, wouldn't you have been inclined to go to the rescue and at least check out the facts? And if there was no reason not to, wouldn't you perhaps have spoken to the brother about the value of sharing wealth with one's family?

Not so Jesus. He replied, "Friend, who set me to be a judge or arbitrator over you?" Then he went on to preach to the crowd, "Take care! Be on your guard against all kinds of greed; for one's life does not consist in the abundance of possessions." What kind of answer is this? Would your lawyer say that to you if you wanted to sue someone? Would your pastor dare to answer you like that if you asked him to intercede with your family over a financial matter? Would the nuns in your local monastery tell you, if you asked for their prayers, that they didn't think money was worth praying for? (Saint Teresa of Avila said that when the would-be conquistadors setting out for the New World asked the Carmelite convent to pray that they would make a fortune, the Sisters "said yes but did no"—and for just that reason).

Once we have accepted Baptism, our focus is no longer on the benefits this world holds out to us—and that death snatches away. Baptism is not just "after-death insurance," a way to insure that we will be just as comfortable after we die as we are during life. Baptism is a change of goals, the acceptance of a new purpose for living, and it changes our whole guidance system. The baptized are not interested in acquiring wealth.

This is not my thought; it is the teaching of John Paul II, who wrote in his 1993 World Day of Peace address, "The Gospel invites believers not to accumulate the goods of this passing world: 'Do not lay up for yourselves treasures on earth...' This is a duty intrinsic to the Christian vocation, no less than the duty of working to overcome poverty."

We should not take this teaching lightly. John Paul gives it after quoting Vatican II's reversal of what was standard moral theology up to then: "We are obliged to support the poor, and not just from our surplus." But John Paul goes beyond Vatican II's teaching and concludes, "The uncontrolled search for a comfortable life risks blinding people to the needs of others.... It is therefore absolutely essential to stem the unrestrained consumption of earthly goods and to control the creation of artificial needs. Moderation and simplicity ought to become the criteria of our daily lives."

John Paul goes even farther. In the next three paragraphs he uses the term "evangelical poverty" four times, obviously speaking about the poverty all Christians are called to practice. This is the first time that I personally have ever seen this term used except to designate the poverty to which members of religious orders commit themselves by the vow of poverty. The pope is saying very strongly that everything Jesus says about poverty in the Gospels is describing a way of life all Christians are called to adopt. This is radical teaching. And when, after quoting some Scriptural passages that describe Jesus' own life, John Paul concludes, "Christ's example, no less than his words, is normative for Christians," he puts all of moral theology on a higher, more demanding, and immeasurably more inspiring plane.

It is the plane to which we are committed and consecrated by Baptism.

(See "The Links Between Poverty and Peace," World Day of Peace/1993, in *Origens*, Vol. 22, No. 28, December

29, 1992. See also John Paul's letter, *The Splendor of Truth*, August 6, 1993, Saint Paul Books, Chapter One, Nos. 12-21).

Reflecting on This Week's Gospels

Eighteenth Week of the Year

> *Pray daily: Lord, you gave me a new life, your life. Give me the faith to build a new life-style, your life-style. I believe that you are the Way, the Truth and the Life. Help me to live out my belief in action. Amen.*

Monday: Matthew 14:13-21: The disciples said to Jesus, "Five loaves and two fish are all we have here." Then he said, "Bring them here to me...." Are you willing to share whatever you have with those who are in need? When is the last time you did? How do you feel about it?

Tuesday: Matthew 14:22-36: Peter said to Jesus walking on the sea, "Lord, if it is you, command me to come to you on the water." How have you challenged Jesus to let you take seriously his promises? What risks have you taken based on faith in him?

Wednesday: Matthew 15:21-28: Jesus said to the Canaanite woman, "It is not right to take the food of the children and throw it to the dogs." She said, "Please, Lord, for even the dogs eat the scraps that fall from the table of their masters." What do you share with people with whom you have no social or cultural bonds? What kind of relationship do you have with people of other nations and economic levels? How do you express it?

Thursday: Matthew 16:13-23: Jesus turned and said to Peter, "Get behind me, Satan!" You are an obstacle to me. You are thinking not as God does, but as human beings do."

Could you be in any way an obstacle to the reign of God that Jesus is trying to establish on earth? In what specific ways do you think "as God does" rather than "as human beings do" in your family life, student or professional life, civic involvement?

Friday: Matthew 16:24-28: Jesus said that those who want to save their life will lose it, and those who lose their life for my sake will find it. For what will it profit them if they gain the whole world but forfeit their life? Or what will they give in return for their life? What effect have these words had on your way of living? Do you give them the fundamental importance Jesus gave them? Do you base all your values and priorities on them?

Saturday: Matthew 17:14-20: The disciples approached Jesus in private and said, "Why could we not drive the demon out?" He said to them, "Because of your little faith." If enough Christians had the faith to live by Jesus' values in business and politics, would the causes of poverty, ethnic division and war be exorcised from our world? What are you doing that contributes to or helps to eradicate the demons of our society?

Living This Week's Gospels

As Christian: Look seriously at whatever desire is in your heart for wealth or affluence. Reject it as a goal. Replace it with the goal of serving God and others through what you do best.

As Disciple: Read "The Links Between Poverty and Peace," John Paul II's World Day of Peace address for 1993. It is in *Origens*, Vol. 22, No. 28, for December 29, 1992. There is a good chance your pastor will have this collection. If not, the diocesan office will, and they will be glad to copy these four pages and send them to you. Or you could read my article in

Journal of Spiritual Formation, Vol. XV, No. 1 (Feb., 1994), published by Duquesne University.

As Prophet: Each day this week try to remove one status symbol from your life. Ask what in your home or office pays tribute to affluence as a value.

As Priest: Compare the way you live with the way the hardworking poor live. Look at someone in particular whom you know, who works where you do, or who goes to your Church. Surrender to compassion. See where it leads you.

As King: See what you can do on your level to work against the three causes of war John Paul II identifies: 1. The abuse of economic power—people seeking their own prosperity and security without regard for what it is doing to poorer people or nations (for example, consumerism and defense spending); 2. The abuse of political power—using positions of strength to exploit the weak, putting class or national interests above the common good of all; and 3. The pride of group superiority—thinking, even unconsciously, that the rich, respected and successful members of society are the "right kind" of people, and their life-style is the "right way" of life.

Nineteenth Sunday of the Year

Baptism Consecrates Time For Us

Luke 12:32-48; Wisdom 18:6-9; Hebrews 11:1-2, 8-19

Baptism is sometimes called "christening" or "into-Christ-ing." It is also a "chrisming." At our Baptism we were anointed on the top of the head with chrism, the word from which "Christ, the Anointed," comes. And that chrism, that anointing, marks us forever. It is a seal upon our hearts, our minds, our destiny.

Anointing gives us a destiny: something to fulfill, to await. Because we are anointed we are conscious—and we should be constantly conscious—that there is something we are destined for, something we are looking forward to. We are sealed with expectation, and we live our lives as an interim period between that sealing and its accomplishment. Because of our anointing, time for us takes on a different value.

Aristotle defined time as "the measure of motion." Time tells us how long it takes an egg to move from raw to hard-boiled and how long it takes us to get from birth to death. But the measure of motion doesn't tell us if we are going anywhere. There is no value in time as such; the value is in the movement, the activity time measures. A long life is no better than a short one if life itself has no direction or purpose. Time can be the measure of boredom, and boredom is the experience of getting nowhere at all.

Baptism anointed our time on earth. Time for us measures, not just a motion, but a motion towards. The time we spend between Baptism (our second birth) and death is consecrated to something we were anointed to do. At every moment the seal, the feel, of our anointing reminds us, binds us, summons us to something we are consecrated to accomplish.

That something is a Someone. Baptism binds us to Jesus Christ, not only with bonds of love, but with bonds of partnership. By Baptism our lives were bound up with his, our destiny identified with his. At Baptism Jesus became the whole meaning of our life, because his life, his mission, his destiny all became ours. We were baptized "into Christ" to be sharers in his life. We were consecrated, "chrismed," to his triple mission as Prophet, Priest and King. Baptism made us co-workers with Jesus (1 Corinthians 3:9), and by that fact we became co-heirs with him of the happiness of heaven and the glory of co-redeeming the world.

Baptism identified us with Jesus Christ, gave us his direction, his purpose in life, and made the destiny of Jesus our destiny. The true movement time measures for us is not the movement that appears, that is visible in what we do and accomplish on earth. The true movement going on in us is a movement toward total identification with Jesus Christ, total sharing in his life and glory. As Saint Paul puts it, "Since you have been raised up in company with Christ, set your heart on what pertains to higher realms where Christ is seated at God's right hand. Be intent on things above rather than on things of earth. After all, you have died! Your life is hidden now with Christ in God. When Christ our life appears, you shall appear with him in glory" (Colossians 3:1-4).

In a word, life for us is stewardship. We have been made one with Jesus Christ, and now the whole purpose and value of our lives is to continue his work, his mission, on earth as faithful stewards of the gifts and life that have been entrusted to us. Our lives are a period of fidelity, of faithful stewardship, until Christ comes again. Everything we have, we hold in trust from him: our lives, our talents, our energy, even our relationship with others and with the world that surrounds us. We are what we are to others because of what Baptism has made us. We are what we are to the world because of what we are by Baptism. We are what we are in our own eyes because of the transformation Baptism worked in us. The future we look forward to is what it is to us because of Baptism. Our treasure lies where it does because of Baptism, and because of Baptism our hearts are sealed in expectation.

Reflecting on This Week's Gospels

Nineteenth Week of the Year

Pray daily: Lord, you entered time from eternity in order to give our time eternal value. Teach me to seek the eternal value in everything you do. Show me how to make my time on earth count forever. Amen.

Monday: Matthew 17:22-27: Jesus said to them, "The Son of Man is going to be betrayed into human hands, and they will kill him, and on the third day he will be raised." And they were overwhelmed with grief." Do you prefer for yourself and for others a long life or a short one? Why? What gives value to our time on earth?

Tuesday: Matthew 18:1-5, 10, 12-14: Jesus said, "Whoever becomes humble like this child is the greatest in the kingdom of heaven." What gives children their value? What do you think would make you great? What is the best investment you can make of your time?

Wednesday: Matthew 18:15-20: Jesus said to his disciples, "Truly I tell you, whatever you bind on earth will be bound in heaven, and whatever you loose on earth will be loosed in heaven." How often do you think about the effect your actions are having on the way things will be in heaven? What effect could you be having through the things you do?

Thursday: Matthew 18:21 to 19:1: Jesus told about a slave who said to the master to whom he owed money, "Be patient with me, and I will pay you back in full." Moved with compassion the master of that servant let him go and forgave him the loan. Does God require you to spend your life paying off the debt you owe him because of your past sins? What does he require? How do you do this?

Friday: Matthew 19:3-12: Jesus said, "Whoever divorces his wife (unless the marriage is unlawful) and marries another commits adultery." What eternal benefits is marriage intended to give? When is a marriage failing to give those?

What means has God provided to help a couple make their marriage a school of love and holiness?

Saturday: Matthew 19:13-15: Then little children were being brought to Jesus in order that he might lay his hands on them and pray. The disciples rebuked them, but Jesus said, "Let the children come to me, and do not prevent them; for the kingdom of heaven belongs to such as these." What do you wish for the children you see? Is everything you do for your own children a blessing to them for eternity? Or do you give priority to what has value only in this life?

Living This Week's Gospels

As Christian: For a week, change the wrist you wear your watch on or the place you keep your most-used clock. Do it to remind you that your time is consecrated to bringing about the eternal happiness of people.

As Disciple: Read Vatican II's document on "The Church in the Modern World" (*"Gaudium et Spes"*), no. 39, on the value and direction Christians see in earthly progress.

As Prophet: Every time you aim at achieving something during the week, ask yourself what difference it will make to you a hundred years from now. Do the same when something angers you.

As Priest: Before each action of the day, offer what you are about to do to God to be transformed. Ask God to show you how to make it an action of divine value and eternal significance.

As King: Look carefully at your activities the way a manager would to see if they are serving the ends of the company. See if you can relate everything you do to the goal of serving God and establishing his reign on earth.

Making God Our God

Luke 12:49-53; Jeremiah 38:4-6, 8-10; Hebrews 12:1-4

In this Gospel Jesus seems to contradict the word of God! Saint Paul says Jesus came "to bring all things in the heavens and on earth into one" under his headship (Ephesians 1:10). Now Jesus says he came to bring not peace, but division! And everyone who tries to follow Jesus experiences the same thing: Our religion makes us want to be united in love with every person on earth, but in fact it breaks up families, alienates us from our friends, causes us to lose our jobs, and even becomes the banner under which nations and factions go to war. Is this what Jesus came to do?

The psychologists use the phrase "tough love," which means that sometimes the most loving thing to do for people is to make them face truth and live in reality—even if reality means suffering the very painful consequences of their own choices. Parents are sometimes urged, as a last resort, to put drug-addicted children out of the house, because in reality, in truth, anyone who chooses addiction has already rejected family life and is just refusing to face it.

Jesus tells us at the front end that anyone who chooses him is already rejecting, by that very fact, any bond with any other person which is in competition with him. This is the first commandment: "You shall not have other gods beside me." Jesus will not accept to be the person we love the most in this world, with others running a close second or third. He will not accept to be first in a field of ten, or five, or even two. If anyone else is in the field, we are not loving Jesus as God, as who he really is. The love we have for Jesus must be unique, in a class by itself. We don't love God, our family and our friends, in that order. We must love God with our whole hearts, with nothing held back, nothing kept in reserve for other people, causes or commitments. The love we give to him is not divided between him and anyone else. If we choose to love God, we are by that very fact excluding everyone else from even being in competition with him. That is reality.

Does this mean we cannot love other people? Or cannot love them deeply, passionately? No, it does not. We can love others enough to lay down our lives for them, enough to commit our whole lives to them forever. But it means that any commitment we have to any other person must be "in Christ"—must be a commitment, not alongside of our commitment to Jesus, not in addition to it, but within it. We can only commit ourselves to doing for others, and to being for others, what we can as part of our commitment to Jesus. And any act which cannot be an expression of our commitment to Jesus cannot be thought of as included in our commitment to other people.

Jesus calls us to love one another as he himself loves us (see John 15:12). Marriage, Saint Paul teaches, is an image of the relationship we have with Jesus and one way of living it out on earth. The Christian commitment to spouse and children is part of the commitment married persons have to Jesus. The same is true of the commitment friends have to each other or patriots to their country. Any commitment made and lived within one's commitment to Jesus is not in competition with him; any other commitment is. And anything we are asked to do as an act of married love, of friendship or of patriotism, if it falls outside of our commitment to Jesus, is not an authentic expression of our love, our friendship, or our loyalty to others. It is idolatry.

If we speak a truth that others find difficult to hear, we can lose our friends. If we refuse to follow a policy or conform to a way of acting that is taken for granted where we work, or by all the people we go out with, we may find that we just don't "fit in" anymore—even that we are avoided and ostracized. If we insist on doing what we really believe Jesus is calling us to do, we may find ourselves alone because no one will do it with us. Then we experience Jesus as causing division. But the truth is, there is no lasting peace or unity except under Christ's headship. Every other bond, every other experience of closeness or of unity is illusion.

Reflecting on This Week's Gospels

Twentieth Week of the Year

Pray daily: Lord, teach me to love you with my whole mind and heart and strength, and to love everything and everyone else on earth as part of my love for you. Amen.

Monday: Matthew 19:16-22: Jesus said, "If you wish to be perfect, go, sell what you have and give to the poor, and you will have treasure in heaven. Then come, follow me." What do you cling to for security, power, prestige? At what price?

Tuesday: Matthew 19:23-30: Jesus said to them, "Amen, I say to you that you who have followed me, in the new age, when the Son of Man is seated on his throne of glory, will yourselves sit on twelve thrones, judging the twelve tribes of Israel." Do you believe that true victory comes through vulnerability?

Wednesday: Matthew 20:1-6: Going out about five o'clock, he found others standing around, and said to them, "Why do you stand here idle all day?" How can you stay conscious all day that your living is working for the Kingdom?

Thursday: Matthew 22:1-14: "Go out, therefore, into the main roads and invite to the feast whomever you find." How many people are at the wedding feast because of you? Whom could you invite?

Friday: Matthew 22:34-40: "You shall love the Lord, your God, with all your heart, with all your soul, and with all your mind. This is the greatest and the first commandment." How do you show your love physically for God? How did he show his love for you?

Saturday: Matthew 23:1-12: "Call no one on earth your father; you have but one Father in heaven." Do you unthinkingly let any authority or relationship (family, friends, state) rule your life without referring everything to God?

Living This Week's Gospels

As Christian: Wear something as a sign that your body belongs to Jesus Christ.

As Disciple: Make a list of the actions of Jesus that made use of power (not counting miracles of healing) or force.

As Prophet: When, how in your life do you most display your human power to others? Ask how you could change this to rely on what Jesus relied on.

As Priest: "Offer your body as a living sacrifice to God" in some physical act that you consciously do as a sacrifice in love for someone else.

As King: In one column list the ways you or others act through power, force or rely on authority or prestige to accomplish something. In another column list alternate ways of accomplishing what you want through humility, vulnerability, persuasion, self-sacrifice, love.

Twenty-First Sunday of the Year

The Narrow Way?

Luke 13:22-30; Isaiah 66:18-21; Hebrews 12:5-7, 11-13

There is something about the word "narrow" which seems contradictory to Christianity. Jesus came that we might "have life, and have it more abundantly" (John 10:10). He came to expand our lives, not to restrict them. So when Jesus says, "Enter through the narrow gate," does something tighten up in you?

In high school geometry class we learned that the narrowest thing conceivable is a straight line. In fact, we can't draw or even imagine what the mathematicians mean by a "straight line," because it is not something drawn on paper; it is just the imaginary (but unimaginable!) line that connects two points. It is simply defined as "the shortest distance between two points." It has no breadth or thickness at all. There is nothing narrower than this: a microscopic flea walking along it drunk would not have room to weave!

When Jesus speaks of the "narrow way" we could think of a channel through the ocean, marked off by five commandments on one side and five on the other. Then if we interpret the commandments more narrowly, the channel becomes more constricted and we feel we are being hemmed in. But suppose we say that Jesus has substituted a whole new guidance system in place of the Ten Commandments? Instead of telling us to stay "within bounds" in a channel, he invites us to steer by a "fixed star," who is Jesus himself. He calls us to look to him—to his words, his example—in every decision we make, and to ask only one question: "What is more pleasing to Jesus Christ, what is more according to the desires of his heart?" To do this is to steer in a straight line. It is to do what Saint Paul exhorts each one of us to do: "Do not be conformed to this world [to the attitudes, values and goals of the culture], but be transformed by the renewing of your minds, so that you may discern what is the will of God—what is good and acceptable and perfect" (Romans 12:2). This is a whole new way of charting a course through life.

This is the narrowest way—and the least constrictive! There is nothing narrower than a straight line. To aim directly at the person of Jesus Christ in every decision we make leaves not the slightest room for deviation. And yet we do not feel restricted. We are out on the open sea, hemmed in by nothing, setting our course by a single star.

If we interpret the Gospel this way, our Lord's later words to those who have not entered by the "narrow gate" are consistent: He says to them, "I do not know where you are from." (This is the same as saying, "I do not know who you are.") Those who have never made the choice to live their whole lives in response to the person of Jesus, but who have just tried to "stay in bounds," are called strangers—because Jesus is in fact a stranger to them. He says he does not know them because they have never known him.

This presents us with a very radical choice: a religion of system or a religion of response. In a religion of system our focus is on the rules and practices—on what we do. In a religion of response our focus is on the person of Christ, on who he is and how we can show our love for him.

In a religion of response the whole focus is on knowing and pleasing God as a person, and experiencing his action in our lives. To please him we have to know him; we have to know his heart, his deepest attitudes and values, what his desires are, how he thinks. In a religion of response we don't break the law; we just seldom think about it—just as someone steering by a fixed star never gets outside the channel markers, but never looks at them either; the course is an unwavering, undeviating line toward the star. And so in a religion of response we think about what pleases our Friend, about what unites us more closely to him in mind and will and heart. Every choice is a direct response to the person we love.

Twenty-First Week of the Year

> *Pray daily: Lord, you came to be the focus and fulfillment of our lives, our fixed star, the goal of every longing and choice. Fill my horizon, fill my heart, fill my life. Amen.*

Monday: Matthew 23:13-22: Jesus said, "Woe to you, scribes and Pharisees, hypocrites. For you lock people out of the kingdom of heaven. For you do not go in yourselves, and when others are going in you stop them." How does a focus on law observance turn people away from religion? When have you felt most turned-off by what was presented to you as Christianity? What draws you most?

Tuesday: Matthew 23:23-26: "Woe to you, scribes and Pharisees, you hypocrites. For you tithe mint and dill and cumin, and have neglected the weightier matters of the law." What do you focus on most in your religion? What is the first and greatest commandment? How often do you think about that?

Wednesday: Matthew 23:27-32: "Woe to you, scribes and Pharisees... You say, 'If we had lived in the days of our ancestors, we would not have taken part with them in shedding the blood of the prophets.'" If you had lived in Jesus' time, would you have left all to follow him? If he didn't call you to do that, how would you have shown your faith in him? How do you now?

Thursday: Matthew 24:42-51: Jesus said, "Stay awake! For you do not know on which day your Lord will come." Does Jesus only come on the last day? Do you expect him to come to you repeatedly every day? How do you stay alert to his inspirations, his favors?

Friday: Matthew 25:1-13: Later the other bridesmaids came also, saying, "Lord, Lord, open to us!" But he replied, "Truly I tell you, I do not know you." Do you know Jesus? How does it affect your living? Do you long for him to open the door of his heart to you? How would you go in?

Saturday: Matthew 25:14-30: "For to all those who have, more will be given and they will have an abundance; but from those who have nothing, even what they have will be taken away." Have you experienced how loving Jesus as a person makes you grow in love? Have you seen people who just focused on obeying the rules finally stop practicing their religion altogether?

Living This Week's Gospels

As Christian: Choose some action that focuses your heart on Jesus Christ from the moment you awake. See if daily Mass is a possibility for you. (What is the closest church that has Mass when you can make it?)

As Disciple: Read the key Jesus gave to the Ten Commandments as John Paul II explains it in *The Splendor of Truth*, chapter one, nos. 12-15.

As Prophet: Each time you find yourself asking whether something is right or wrong, picture Jesus doing it instead. Do what you can easily imagine him doing.

As Priest: The next time a discussion of morality starts, see if you can turn it into a discussion of the example of Jesus Christ.

As King: Ask yourself how your neighborhood would change if Jesus lived in it. Your work site if Jesus worked there? Your school if Jesus were a student? Your home life if Jesus were a member of the family? Make the changes you can make.

The Fulfilling Life

Luke 14:1-14; Sirach 3:17-18, 20, 28-29; Hebrews 12:18-19, 22-24

Jesus came to be "good news" to us. We should expect the way of life he teaches, then, to be, not just good but new. Today's Gospel is a good example of this.

It is just natural—"normal"—for us to put ourselves first. Television commercials assume that most people want to be admired, to attract favorable attention in a crowd, to be looked up to as successful. The technique of the commercials is to keep showing us attractive, successful people using the products they are trying to sell so that we will begin to identify attractiveness and success with using their products. The commercials keep doing this, so apparently it works.

Jesus doesn't use underhanded suggestion. He tells us outright what he is proposing, so that we can freely and consciously choose. Jesus doesn't want to manipulate us. He wants us to use our intellects and our wills and respond to him as conscious, free human beings.

And so in this Gospel he tells us straightforwardly that our way of seeking admiration and satisfaction is all wrong. He does not say it is evil; he just says it won't work.

Jesus doesn't really say that we should stop seeking admiration and satisfaction. We would probably distort that to mean we should just not let people see that this is what we are seeking. We want to dress, for example, in a way that will make us look important without looking like we are trying to look important! That is the key to good dressing. We want people to think we are better than everybody else but not that we want to be thought better than anybody else. That is the key to human relations. But Jesus says these keys don't really work.

Jesus doesn't just say not to take the first place; he says to go to the last place. He doesn't just say not to give a party for our own satisfaction; he says that when we give a party we should give it for "the beggars, the crippled, the lame and the blind." He doesn't just say not to seek admiration and self-satisfaction. He says to positively seek out and do what the world thinks is humiliating and unsatisfying. And he says this is the way to be authentically admired and satisfied. This is the way that works.

It will only work, of course, if we do exactly what he says. If we only want to look like we are being humble so that we will be honored, that won't work. Jesus doesn't say to just head for the lowest place, waiting to be called back; he says to take the lowest place. Go for it. He doesn't say to put on a party for the poor and lonely in order to impress our "friends, relatives and wealthy neighbors"; he says to really serve the poor. Go to the lonely. And he insists that this is the way to be admired and satisfied.

This is a call to call the world in error. Jesus invites us to believe, and to proclaim by our actions, that what most people seem to be admired for is not really very admirable; that what most people look to for satisfaction is not really satisfying. Jesus teaches that prestige is seldom given to the people who really should be admired, and that the "successful" are very seldom satisfied by their success.

What is truly admirable is to forget all about being admired and to just serve people in their need. What is truly satisfying is to forget about one's own satisfaction and just try to make other people happy. Jesus taught this by word and he taught it by example. He taught it as the way—the only way—to fulfillment. And it is the exact opposite of what is taken for granted in the world: in our culture and in every culture.

What this really tells us is that to be a Christian does not mean just keeping a higher set of rules. It means changing our whole vision of human life. Jesus came to teach us what to desire, what to value, what to aim for in life. This is the "good news." We don't understand how good it is until we recognize that it is news.

Reflecting on This Week's Gospels

Twenty-Second Week of the Year

Note: Beginning this week, the Gospel readings are taken from Luke's Gospel.

> *Pray daily: Lord, I believe that you are the Teacher of Life—the only true teacher of what is true and good and satisfying. Give me the trust to follow what you say so that I might see where it leads. Amen.*

Monday: Luke 4:16-30: Jesus said, "The Spirit of the Lord is upon me, because he has anointed me to bring glad tidings...." Do you really believe that Jesus teaches the way to be happy on this earth as well as in heaven? How hard are you trying to learn everything you can about the way he says we should live?

Tuesday: Luke 4:31-37: Jesus taught them on the sabbath, and they were astonished at his teaching. Does Jesus still teach on the sabbath? Where? Are you astonished at his teaching? Are you listening for something new and challenging?

Wednesday: Luke 4:38-44: Jesus said to his disciples, "To the other towns also I must proclaim the good news of the kingdom of God...for I was sent for this purpose." What do you use Jesus for? Do you just interact with him when something is wrong? How much time do you spend listening to him proclaim the Good News? How can you hear him doing this?

Thursday: Luke 5:1-11: After Jesus had finished speaking, he said to Simon, "Put out into deep water and lower your nets for a catch." After you hear Jesus speaking—at Mass, or through the Scriptures, or through other people—do you "put out into deep water" to reflect on what you have heard? If not, will your nets ever be filled?

Friday: Luke 5:33-39: Jesus said, "New wine must be poured into fresh wineskins." Does Jesus' teaching excite you? Does it go to your head like wine? Could it be that you are not prepared to receive it because you need to put your whole life on a different basis?

Saturday: Luke 6:1-5: Some Pharisees said to Jesus, "Why are you doing what is unlawful on the sabbath?" He said to them in reply, "Have you not read what David did when he and those who were with him were hungry?" Have you read that story? Are you less interested in the word of God than the Pharisees were?

Living This Week's Gospels

As Christian: Make a list of your friends. How many could qualify as "the beggars, the crippled, the lame and the blind"?

As Disciple: Each time you see a commercial on television this week, try to imagine Jesus urging you to buy the same product, using the same motivation. Draw your own conclusions.

As Prophet: Try to avoid receiving any signs of special respect given, not because of what you are as a person, but because of your position or social status. Whatever signs of respect you give to others because of their position, give the same or the equivalent to the people you deal with who have the least prestige.

As Priest: Each day this week perform some gesture like that of Jesus when he washed his disciples' feet.

As King: Call into question, at least in your own mind, and if possible in conversation with others, the protocol and the hierarchy of status symbols where you work. Do the same for your school, the Church, society in general. How do they affect people? How much are you contributing to whatever damage they do?

Pricing the Kingdom: Appreciating Grace

Luke 14:25-33; Wisdom 9:13-18; Philemon 9-10, 12-17

A Lutheran minister, Dietrich Bonhoeffer, coined the phrase "cheap grace." He had the right: He gave his life under the Nazis in witness to the value he placed on grace.

"Cheap grace" is not really grace we get cheaply, because all grace is a free gift. And even if we gave everything we have for grace, it would be cheap at the price. "Cheap grace" means grace we ourselves value cheaply because we think it asks very little of us. We make grace cheap in our own eyes—and in the eyes of others—by living as if grace demanded little or no change in the way we live our lives.

Jesus never said grace was cheap in this sense. Grace is a free gift, but it calls for everything in return—or better, in response. Grace is the gift of sharing in God's own life. The only appropriate response to this gift is to "sacrifice" everything that is human in order to live on the level of God (see Romans 12:1-2).

Sacrifice is an interesting word. We think it means "to give up, to lose." Actually, the word comes from the Latin phrase *sacrum facere*, which means, "to make sacred or holy." And to be "sacred" or "holy" means to be "set apart," consecrated to some special use. Chalices, for example, are "sacred" or "holy" because they are set apart for liturgical use only; they cannot be used as wine glasses at a party.

God is the holiest of all beings, not because he is set apart, but because he is apart; he is on a totally different plane of existence. What God does is "holy" because it is on a completely different level of activity from what created beings do. And when we were made holy at Baptism, we were given a share in the life of God and consecrated to do what God does: to live and act on the level of God.

This means that every Christian is in a most radical way "set apart" from this world. We no longer "belong" to the world as we did before. We do not exist to contribute just to the goals of this world, but to bring everything on earth to that fulfillment which is found in the kingdom of God, under the headship of Jesus Christ. This means that our relationship to this world—to everything and everyone in it, to all of its goals, activities and rules—is totally different. We are a chosen race, a holy nation, a people set apart. The gift of grace consecrates us to "be holy as God is holy" (see 1 Peter 1:13 to 2:25). Not to see this is to not appreciate grace.

Jesus isn't telling us in this Gospel that the holy, the Christian thing to do is to turn our backs on our families, give up everything we own, and look for ways to turn our lives into a constant cross. He is saying that Baptism has already radically changed our relationship to our families and to every human being on earth. Because we are baptized "into Christ" to be his Body on earth, we are "holy," set apart in a special way, and every human relationship we have or form on earth is on a totally different plane from our new relationship to God and to the work of his kingdom. We don't love anyone less than before, but our love for God, our dedication to him, our consecration to him, puts even the deepest human love on a radically secondary plane. Even more so, our commitment to God and to the work of his kingdom frees us from any attachment to or concern about money and possessions. We are not dedicated to earning or to having things on earth; we are "set apart" for God and the work of God. This is the consequence of our Baptism; it is the change worked in us by grace.

We only experience the faith we express. We only experience hope and love in the measure that we express these in our choices, in our actions. We experience grace by letting grace express itself in our lives. We experience the holiness Christ gives us by being "holy," "sacrificed" to the work of God in everything we do. To accept this is to accept a new goal in life that guides every choice we make.

Reflecting on This Week's Gospels

Twenty-Third Week of the Year

> *Pray daily:* Lord, I offered my body to you at
> Baptism to be a "living sacrifice to God." Teach me
> to understand that I will experience the new life of
> Baptism in the measure I die to every goal except
> knowing you more intimately, loving you more
> passionately, and serving you more effectively. And
> give me the courage to live. Amen.

Monday: Luke 6:6-11: Jesus asked the Pharisees, "Is it
lawful to do good or to do harm on the sabbath, to save life
or to destroy it?" When do you help people by showing them
marks of respect? When do you damage them?

Tuesday: Luke 6:12-19: When day came, Jesus called his
disciples to himself, and from them he chose Twelve, whom
he also named apostles: What special marks of status did
Jesus give to his twelve apostles? Is it the same in the
Church today? How has this affected your thinking?

Wednesday: Luke 6:20-26: Raising his eyes toward his
disciples Jesus said: "Blessed are you who are poor, for the
kingdom of God is yours." Is it really possible to set your
heart on amassing riches on this earth and still have it
focused on the treasure Jesus gives? What treasure do
you think about more often?

Thursday: Luke 6:27-38: Jesus said to his disciples, "The
measure you give will be the measure you get back." How
much are you getting out of your religion? Out of Mass? Out
of Scripture reading? How much are you putting into your
religion? Into Mass? Into learning from Jesus?

Friday: Luke 6:39-42: Jesus said, "Can a blind person guide
a blind person? Will not both fall into a pit?" How much
enlightenment is your faith giving to your life? How clearly
do you see God? Whose guidance are you following from day
to day? How much time do you spend learning from Jesus?

Saturday: Luke 6:43-49: "No good tree bears bad fruit, nor again does a bad tree bear good fruit; for each tree is known by its own fruit." Is the "fruit of the Holy Spirit" evident in your life: love, joy, peace, patient endurance, kindness, fidelity, generosity, gentleness and self-control? To experience the fruit of the Spirit, what must you do to live by the Spirit?

Living This Week's Gospels

As Christian: Write out a deed, a contract, giving everything you have to Jesus Christ. Mention the main items specifically. See how you feel doing it. Ask yourself what it means in practice.

As Disciple: Read John Paul II's inspired interpretation of Jesus' command, "Go, sell your possessions and give the money to the poor." It is in *The Splendor of Truth*, chapter 1, nos. 16-19.

As Prophet: Think of what most frequently makes you impatient or angry. If possible, just give up for a week the value you are defending. Sacrifice it to love of neighbor. In your mind make a gift of it to whomever annoys you.

As Priest: Take the risk of praying out loud with someone— in your own words if you can.

As King: Ask yourself where you think you are getting off too easy—at home, at work, in your social obligations, in your parish, in your civic duty. Make the demands on yourself that you think others should make.

Twenty-Fourth Sunday of the Year

What Does It Mean to Be Alive?

Luke 15:1-32; Exodus 32:7-11, 13-24; 1 Timothy 1:12-17

T he father in this story seems to exaggerate when he says, "This brother of yours was dead and has come back to life." The younger brother had left home, but he had not died. And since we know that the younger son represents us when we sin, we have to ask: When you sin, do you see that as "dying," or just as taking a certain distance from God? Do you see sin as suicide?

There is a level of sin that is literally that. We don't commit it very often. (How "frequently" can you die and come back to life?) I think I saw this level in a friend of mine who lost the faith. She didn't just stop living the faith; she lost it—and so completely that she had no sense of loss. She didn't think she had "lost the faith"; she thought she had found truth. She pitied her friends who still believed in the myth of God. She was so blind she didn't know there was anything out there for her to see. Her faith, her power to see the truth of God, was not just on hold; it was dead. She no longer had the power to make an act of faith. She could not repent.

To know you are in the dark you have to know light exists. She could not choose anymore to turn away from darkness, because there was no way she could know anymore that light existed. She wasn't just shutting her eyes to truth; she was blind. It was the first time I had seen anyone in that condition, and I found it terrifying. Even though I knew that God had the power to restore her sight and offer her a chance to repent, I still found it terrifying. God had the power to bring her back to life, but she was visibly, frighteningly dead.

Death is the inability to act. It can be complete or partial. If a dentist kills the nerve in my tooth, the tooth is "dead." All it can do after that is fill up space in my mouth. If part of my brain dies, nothing controlled by that part of my brain works anymore. I am partially dead.

The reason we do not understand sinning as dying is that we do not understand grace as life, or being in grace as being alive. We think "being in grace" means being in God's favor, and that losing grace means losing God's favor. We think sins just make God mad at us. The truth is, every sin kills us— kills the light of God in us; kills the love of God in us; kills the life of God in us—completely or partially. Every time we choose to sin even a little bit, we choose to be a little less alive, a little less able to see, a little less able to love. And every time we repent of sin (that is, truly repent, truly "change our minds" about what we have done), God brings back to life in us what we have killed.

Take a person who consciously, deliberately chooses to sin—and who, in addition to this, denies the faith (partially, not totally) by rationalizing and saying, "I just don't believe there is anything wrong with this." That person isn't just doing something against the teaching of Jesus Christ. The person is becoming less a student (a "disciple") of Jesus Christ. Whenever we choose to reject one thing Jesus teaches, we begin to lose the ability to believe completely in Jesus as Teacher. Part of the light goes out, and our whole vision of faith becomes dimmer. That is what makes sin so terrifying: it changes us. It makes us incapable of seeing what we could see before; incapable of appreciating what we could appreciate before; incapable of relating to God as we could relate before. We aren't just "guilty"; we are different. Something in us has died.

This explanation calls for a lot of theological precision impossible to achieve in a short article like this. Every sin is an individual, personal act, and so every sin is individual, unique, in its effect on the person who commits it. But this much is clear: every time we choose to turn off a little bit of the light that has been given us, we lose some ability to see. Every time we choose to sin we give up a certain level of life. Every time we sin, to some extent we die.

Reflecting on This Week's Gospels

Twenty-Fourth Week of the Year

> **Pray daily:** Lord, you said, "Blessed are the pure of heart, for they shall see God." I want to see you so that I will be pure of heart. Open my mind to your truth and win me to follow you without reserve. Amen.

Monday: Luke 7:1-10: When the centurion heard about Jesus, he sent elders of the Jews to him, asking him to come and save the life of his slave. Do you believe anything dies in you when you sin? Do you believe Jesus can bring you back to life—and fully? How often do you ask him specifically to do this?

Tuesday: Luke 7:11-17: As Jesus drew near to the gate of the city, a man who had died was being carried out, the only son of his mother, and she was a widow.... When the Lord saw her, he was moved with pity for her. How do you think Jesus feels when an ideal dies in one of us? When someone stops coming to Mass? Stops praying as before? How does he feel about parents whose children have turned away?

Wednesday: Luke 7:31-35: "We played the flute for you, but you did not dance. We sang a dirge, but you did not weep." When does your religion make you feel like dancing? When does it make you weep? When does it leave you indifferent? Have you deadened in any way your ability to respond to the Good News?

Thursday: Luke 7:36-50: When the Pharisee who had invited Jesus saw this he said to himself, "If this man were a prophet, he would know who and what sort of woman this is who is touching him, that she is a sinner." In Jesus' eyes, was the Pharisee more of a sinner than the woman? Was the Pharisee himself aware of how little he understood about God? What had blinded him? Could the same thing be blinding you?

Friday: Luke 8:1-3: Jesus journeyed from one town and village to another, preaching and proclaiming the good news of the kingdom of God. Accompanying him were the Twelve and some women who had been cured of evil spirits and infirmities. Why did some people follow Jesus around, listening to everything he preached, while others were less interested? Is the same true today? What is the cause of the difference? Which category would you fit into? Why?

Saturday: Luke 8:4-15: Jesus said, "As for the seed that fell on rich soil, they are the ones who, when they have heard the word, embrace it with a generous and good heart, and bear fruit through perseverance." When do you hear the Good News proclaimed? Does it give you joy? Do you think deeply about what you have heard? Do you keep thinking about it until it bears fruit in your life?

Living This Week's Gospels

As Christian: Think specifically of your most frequent sins. Ask Jesus to save you from them. Ask what you have been doing to cooperate with him as Savior, what you can do.

As Disciple: See if you can find something in the Gospels or writings of the Apostles that casts light on the sins you are most inclined to commit.

As Prophet: Look at the sins you commit and change your aim. Instead of trying to avoid them as evil, try to live out positively the highest ideal they contradict. That is, instead of trying to be patient, do something extraordinarily loving for the people who make you impatient.

As Priest: Ask yourself what you can do to help heal someone whose woundedness leads to visibly destructive behavior. How can you put that person into deeper or more constant contact with the healing love of Christ?

As King: Look for destructive or distorted attitudes that are so commonplace where you live, go to school, or work that they aren't even recognized as destructive any more. Look at unquestioned competitiveness, for example, or stereotypes, or assumed goals that are not worth pursuing. Start asking "Why?" constantly. (Warning: the Surgeon General won't tell you, but this could be injurious to your health. It got Socrates killed.)

Twenty-Fifth Sunday of the Year

How a Prophet Makes a Profit

Luke 16:1-13; Amos 8:4-7; 1 Timothy 2:1-8

An enormous amount of everyone's time is taken up with managing: office work, housework, desk work, shop work, yard work, homework—these all involve the use and management of material things or of one's own skills and opportunities. This is so much a part of human life that our Lord gives us a special teaching on how to manage what is ours.

Contrary to what we might expect, Jesus doesn't urge us just to give away or forget about material things; he advises us to use them, and to use them to our own advantage! But because Jesus came to "make everything new," and because he is the Good News of human history, we expect him to say something new and radically different about how to turn to our best advantage all the money, property and talents we have. He does.

He begins with a fairly obvious but generally forgotten principle: "Look ahead." Jesus is a proponent of long-range planning. Good managers ask, "Where do you want to be and what do you want to be doing five years from now? Ten years? Twenty years?" Jesus asks, "What do you want your life to be like ninety years from now?" He suggests we think about it in detail.

His second principle is the ponder package. "What really lasts," Jesus says, "is people." When there is no more work to do, either because you are too old to do what is normally looked on as "work"—or because you are "too old" in the sense of having died and passed beyond time—there will still be people to relate to. So principle number two is: "Use money, property, and all the talents you have to build up your relationship with people." It's a long-term investment.

This is not obvious. It is not accepted as a self-evident principle in our world that the real value of having ability, money and property—even a little—is that you can use what you have to enter into lasting relationships with other persons—including the three divine Persons: Father, Son and Holy Spirit. But this is the real value, in having anything: strength, beauty, health, talent, skills, popularity, position, prestige. The only real value in any of these things is that they can all be used to build up deep, loving, lasting relationships between you and God and other people. To understand this is to know the secret of profitable ownership, profitable management of all that is yours.

The logical move at this point would be to ask, "How does one go about doing this? How can you use your talents, position, property and other advantages to help other people and to serve God?" And until we do ask this question and come to concrete answers, we have not responded to these words of God. But there is another question we need to ask first. It is the question of faith: "Do you really believe what Jesus teaches here? And do you understand how radical it is?"

Unless you understand that Jesus is inviting you to a radical change of outlook, you won't really understand what he is saying. He is not just urging us to be service-oriented people and adopt an attitude of willingness to help others in everything we do. The Boy Scouts and the Rotary Club teach this. Jesus is not just counseling unselfishness or service as the way to be happy. He is calling us to look at everything we have in a radically new way; to see our every skill, talent, opportunity and possession as something given to us to manage, to use, to invest for one single purpose: the forging of an unbreakable bond between ourselves, God and other people. What he is saying here is an echo of what he said the Sunday before last (Luke 14:25-33) and the Sunday before that (Luke 14:7-14). To be disciples of Jesus we must renounce all use of material goods that does not have God and love for others as its goal, and we must dedicate ourselves to serving others in everything we do. This is the Good News proclaimed in this reading.

Reflecting on This Week's Gospels

Twenty-Fifth Week of the Year

> *Pray daily: Lord, I believe in you as the Teacher of Life, the Master of the Way. Make my faith practical. Show me how to base my life-style on the wisdom you revealed. Amen.*

Monday: Luke 8:16-18: Jesus said, "Pay attention to how you listen; for to those who have, more will be given, and from those who do not have, even what they seem to have will be taken away." Do you really "have" Jesus as a teacher and guide for your life? How much attention do you pay to his words and example? What difference have they made in your life?

Tuesday: Luke 8:19-21: Jesus said, "My mother and my brothers are those who hear the word of God and act on it." What words of Jesus did you consciously put into practice yesterday? Which ones will you act on today? Do you feel as close to Jesus as his mother and brothers?

Wednesday: Luke 9:1-6: Jesus sent the twelve to proclaim the kingdom of God and to heal. He said to them, "Take nothing for the journey, neither walking stick, nor sack, nor food, nor money, and let no one take a second tunic." These instructions were not meant to be taken literally (see John 13:29). Does that dispense us from observing what he meant by them? What was the point Jesus was making? How do his instructions give a special tone to your life?

Thursday: Luke 9:7-9: Herod the tetrarch heard about all that was happening, and said, "Who then is this about whom I hear such things?" And he kept trying to see Jesus. Do you show as much interest in learning about Jesus as Herod did? How did Herod respond in action to what he heard about Jesus? How do I?

Friday: Luke 9:18-22: Once when Jesus was praying in solitude, and the disciples were with him, he asked them,

"Who do the crowds say that I am?... Who do you say that I am?" How would you answer this question? Could you answer it without words, just by pointing to your actions?

Saturday: Luke 9:43-45: Jesus said, "Let these words sink into your ears: The Son of Man is going to be betrayed into human hands." But they did not understand this saying; its meaning was concealed from them so that they should not perceive it. And they were afraid to ask him about this saying. Are you afraid to follow up on some of the sayings of Jesus? Which ones have you thought about until they led you to change something in your behavior or life-style?

Living This Week's Gospels

As Christian: Make a list of the things you do every day, regularly. Next to each write the value, fulfillment or satisfaction you are seeking through each one of them. Ask if you are seeking greater closeness with God in each one.

As Disciple: Use the same list, and write after each thing you do the value or teaching of Jesus Christ that inspires you to do it. Use his words if possible.

As Prophet: Put up a sign where you work: "The goal of this business is to make prophets." See how many people think it is a misspelling.

As Priest: In everything you do this week, consciously ask how this is contributing to your relationship with other people. How could it?

As King: Draw up a "personal stock portfolio." Make a list of what you are investing in what: for example, how much time and money in your house, career development, retirement, medical insurance, in maintenance of your health and appearance, your personal relationships and so on.

Include in it how much time and money you are investing in knowing Jesus more intimately, in understanding his teachings more deeply, in God's eternal retirement plan, in establishing the reign of God on earth.

Twenty-Sixth Sunday of the Year

Choices Here Are Choices Hereafter

Luke 16:19-31; Amos 6:1, 4-7; 1 Timothy 6:11-16

If there is any Gospel we can identify with today, it should be this one. Almost every time we turn on the television set we have the poor man of this story lying, not at our doorstep, but in our living room. How many times in the past few years have we literally had starving adults and children from the famine-ridden countries of Africa and Asia presented to us in living color as we watched the news? And how often in a single week does the television screen bring to within a few feet of our eyes the vivid physical and spiritual needs of the people in our own country, our own city? And what do we do about it? Realistically, what can we do about it? How can we take seriously the point of this Gospel without just feeling uselessly, ineffectively guilty?

First, what is the point of the Gospel? The rich man is not condemned for being rich. He is condemned for not sharing—and ultimately for not caring. When Abraham says to him, "Between you and us there is fixed a great abyss," he is giving the key to the whole story. That same abyss existed on earth between the rich man and the poor man. The rich man wanted it that way. He saw the difference between his way of life and the poor man's, between his abundance and the poor man's need, and he did nothing to bridge the gap. The rule was already established on earth by the rich man himself: "Those who might wish to cross from here to you cannot do so, nor can anyone cross from your side to us." Americans could write these words on a billboard and plant it on the Mexican border!

The point of the Gospel is that the choices we make here are the choices we make for hereafter. If we choose for ourselves isolation from other people on this earth, insulation from the poor and the needy, then we are choosing this for the next life also. If we choose to be one with other people, to be concerned about others as we are about ourselves, and to enter into a community of sharing with everyone God made, then we will be one with others in the next life, sharing in the celebration that God has prepared for all his children.

This Gospel is not just a call to give alms to the poor. It is a call to accept what Jesus Christ came to do. It is a call to surrender in faith to the wisdom of the mystery, the plan God was pleased to decree in Christ, to be carried out in the fullness of time: namely, to bring all things in the heavens and on earth into one under Christ's headship (see Ephesians 1:9-10). To accept this Gospel means we accept this plan, agree with its wisdom, see it as good, embrace it for ourselves, and work with Jesus to bring about this oneness, this community on earth.

We don't respond to this Gospel just by helping the poor. We could do that and still live with a mental abyss between them and us, just as the poor could accept help from the rich without accepting the rich themselves. What Jesus is condemning is the attitude itself of division, of self-enclosedness, of separate worlds to live in. He accepts no distinctions between rich and poor, educated and uneducated, between one race and another, between one nationality and another. For Jesus there are not blacks and whites, Vietnamese and Cambodians, North Americans and Latin Americans, college graduates and illiterates, members of our particular club and non-members. There are only people created in love by the Father and called to be one in Christ as members of the same Body, children of God the Father, sharers in the same Holy Spirit; people called to be one with God and with each other and to celebrate this oneness forever together in heaven. To reject this oneness on earth is to reject it in heaven. And not to express it on earth is to reject it.

Before we ask "What can I share and with whom?" perhaps we should ask, "Do I accept God's basic plan? Do I see Christian living as sharing? Am I willing to be one community with others and to share what I have and am?"

Reflecting on This Week's Gospels

Twenty-Sixth Week of the Year

> **Pray daily:** *Lord, you love every member of the human race and you want us to love one another. You want us all to be one family, brothers and sisters to each other. Show me how I am blocking what you desire. Show me how to help you make it happen. Amen.*

Monday: Luke 9:46-50: Jesus took a little child and put it by his side, and said, "Whoever welcomes this child in my name welcomes me, and whoever welcomes me welcomes the one who sent me. For the least among all of you is the greatest." Would you welcome a renowned research scientist who wanted to emigrate from Mexico? Would you welcome just as much an unskilled laborer? What is your basis for accepting or not accepting immigrants? Is it the same as Christ's?

Tuesday: Luke 9:51-56: Jesus sent messengers ahead of him. On the way they entered a Samaritan village to prepare for his reception there, but they would not welcome him because the destination of his journey was Jerusalem. Have you ever failed to welcome people because of where they come from? (Country? Ethnic group? Part of town?) Do you refuse to give people a hearing because of where you think they are headed?

Wednesday: Luke 9:57-62: Someone said to Jesus, "I will follow you wherever you go." Jesus answered him, "Foxes have dens and birds of the sky have nests, but the Son of Man has nowhere to rest his head." Why could Jesus not have found lodging in any house he came to? Under what conditions could any member of the Body of Christ find lodging in your house?

Thursday: Luke 10:1-12: Jesus said to those he sent on mission, "Whatever town you enter and they do not receive you, go out into the streets and say, 'The dust of your town that clings to our feet, even that we shake off against you.'" What kind of reception do guest preachers or speakers get in your parish? Do you welcome them in the only way that is real, by going to hear them? Do you take part in everything your parish offers to help you grow in understanding and response to the Gospel?

Friday: Luke 10:13-16: Jesus said, "Woe to you, Chorazin! Woe to you, Bethsaida! For if the mighty deeds done in your midst had been done in Tyre and Sidon, they would long ago have repented, sitting in sackcloth and ashes. But it will be more tolerable for Tyre and Sidon at the judgment than for you." How many people would be at Mass every morning if they knew and believed that the real body and blood of Jesus Christ were offered to them there? Do you have any faults for which the Lord will condemn you, not because you had them, but because you didn't use the means he offered you to overcome them?

Saturday: Luke 10:17-24: Jesus rejoiced in the Holy Spirit and said, "I thank you, Father, Lord of heaven and earth, because you have hidden these things from the wise and the intelligent and have revealed them to infants." Do you assume that the educated, successful people in our society are the ones who know how to live? Do you accept their values in your life-style? Do you believe they are the ones who know God best?

Living This Week's Gospels

As Christian: Write on a piece of paper, "I consider my family on this earth to be..." and complete the sentence.

As Disciple: Read Vatican II's decree on the missionary activity of the Church (*"Ad Gentes"*). Use it to deepen your spirit of openness to all the needs of all people, at home and abroad.

As Prophet: For just this week, in some place where you have a picture of a family member, put next to it a picture of a starving child or adult from a developing country.

As Priest: Each day this week give comfort, help, or a friendly gesture to someone you normally don't think of being in relationship with.

As King: Think seriously about how your buying habits encourage or discourage exploitation of the poor, unhealthy products on the market, environmental devastation.

Servants or Lovers?
Obligation or Passionate Gift?

Luke 17:5-10; Habakkuk 1:2-3 and 2:2-4; 2 Timothy 1:6-8, 13-14

What disappoints Jesus Christ the most? Judging from the Gospel, it is not "sin" as we think of sin. Jesus understands sin; he showed in his life that he knew how to talk to sinners, understood what they were going through, and believed in the greatness to which they could be led through conversion. Jesus seems to have had more trouble with mediocrity than with sin.

Jesus was compassionate toward the adulteress and the serial wife (John 8:3; 4:18), and patient with the wild kid (Luke 15:11). He could respect the cleverness of the embezzler (Luke 16:1) and even reach out to oppressive military and defrauders of the poor (Matthew 8:5; Luke 3:14, Matthew 9:9, Luke 19:1). The straight-out sinners he was comfortable with. But self-righteous mediocrity seems to have been something he just could not deal with.

Ultimately, Jesus can deal with anybody, heal anything, save us from any kind of sin. But it seems that in order to deal with self-righteousness or with complacent mediocrity he first has to convert us either to a sense of sin or to an understanding of what love is all about. And if it seems odd that "sin" and "love" should be linked together in the same sentence, the answer may be that, in dealing with Jesus Christ, the greatest sin of all is simply not to love.

People who are committing obvious sins, sins they recognize as such, know that they are failing in some way. It may even be that the perceived absence of love is already a preliminary understanding of what love is. The dimensions of emptiness can reveal the shape of fulfillment. But the people least able to respond to love are those who spoil their appetite for loving through constant, compulsive nibbling at righteousness. They are so used to being petty they don't know what it is to respond to another in love with a reckless, passionate heart. Like the Pharisees Jesus condemned, they are so preoccupied straining at gnats that they swallow the camel whole—their attention is so focused on not breaking little rules that they break the greatest rule of all, which is to love with one's whole heart, whole strength, whole mind.

Rabbi Heschel said it all in one phrase: "To respond moderately to God is a desecration."

This Gospel does not say we should disregard the rules or the law of God, whether in big things or in little things. What it says is that when we have kept all the rules and done everything that is required of us—everything that is of "obligation"—we should say that we are only on the threshold of being Christians. We are "useless servants" in the sense that we have not yet begun to give Jesus Christ the service he asks of us; we are only on the brink of love.

For example, to come to Sunday Mass out of obligation is good—but it is not an authentic participation in the Mass. The youth who went to Mass dutifully all the time they lived in their parents' house, and then just stopped because, as they say, "It never meant anything to me; I never got anything out of it," were not authentically participating in the Mass. They were there, but they were not participating. They were fulfilling their obligation, but they were not expressing together with the rest of the community what the Mass expresses. They were not there to give themselves passionately, wholeheartedly, to the Father and to the human race in love, in union with Jesus Christ given on the cross. The Mass was meaningless to them because they were speaking the language of mediocrity in a service that speaks the language of passionate, total love.

If we as a community are going to give valid expression to our faith, and be authentic, effective witnesses to others, we have to go beyond what is of "obligation" and start responding passionately, generously, to him. In everything we do. Only then can we experience authentically the religion of Jesus Christ. And only then can we share his religion, his life, with others.

Reflecting on This Week's Gospels

Twenty-Seventh Week of the Year

Pray daily: Lord, if you did for us as God only what you are obliged in fairness to do, you would not be the God we know. And if I do for you only what I am commanded to do, I will never know what it is to be a Christian. Teach me the way of personal, passionate love. Teach me your heart. Amen.

Monday: Luke 10:25-37: "You shall love the Lord, your God, with all your heart, with all your being, with all your strength, and with all your mind, and your neighbor as yourself." Jesus said, "...Do this and you will live." Are you constantly looking for ways to love God more? What is the primary focus of your religion? Of your life?

Tuesday: Luke 10:38-42: Jesus said, "Martha, Martha, you are anxious and worried about many things. There is need of only one thing. Mary has chosen the better part and it will not be taken from her." What concerns and worries keep you from taking time to spend just in communion with God every day?

Wednesday: Luke 11:1-4: Jesus was praying in a certain place, and when he had finished, one of his disciples said to him, "Lord, teach us to pray just as John taught his disciples." Have you ever asked Jesus to teach you how to pray? Have you ever asked anyone else? How many methods of praying do you know?

Thursday: Luke 11:5-13: Jesus said, "I tell you, ask and you will receive; seek and you will find; knock and the door will be opened to you." What do you ask Jesus for? Is it to know him better, give him more? In how much of your prayer are you seeking? What have you found in prayer? When is your prayer a knocking, asking entry? Entry to what?

Friday: Luke 11:15-26: Jesus said, "Whoever is not with me is against me, and whoever does not gather with me scatters." To be "with" Jesus, is it enough just to "keep in bounds" by not sinning? What does it mean to "gather" with him?

Saturday: Luke 11:27-28: A woman from the crowd called out, "Blessed is the womb that bore you and the breasts that nursed you." Jesus replied, "Blessed rather, are those who hear the word of God and obey it." Is Jesus talking here just about people who keep the ten commandments? Do you believe that a greater blessing is offered to you than that of being the mother of the Messiah? Does this motivate you to live a life characterized by reflection on the words of Jesus?

Living This Week's Gospels

As Christian: See if it is possible to participate in the daily celebration of Christ's redemption of the world. If daily Mass is impossible, what is possible?

As Disciple: Read the Bible daily, as faithfully as if it were as much an obligation as Sunday Mass.

As Prophet: Each day this week consciously do more than you are commanded to do. Be a little more friendly, give a little more service.

As Priest: Go the "extra mile" with someone who takes up your time. Look beyond what you have to do for people; look instead at what you can do—and do it willingly.

As King: Help someone with a job that is not your specific responsibility. Think about everything that is done on earth as being the service of God to which you are committed.

Twenty-Eighth Sunday of the Year

Gratitude: A Foundation for Love

Luke 17:11-19; 2 Kings 5:14-17; 2 Timothy 2:8-13

The Mass is called "Eucharist," which means "thanksgiving." This Gospel invites us to take a long, deep look at what we have to be thankful to Jesus Christ for.

The list could be interminable. But, fortunately, this Gospel focuses our attention on just one out of the many things for which we need to be consciously grateful to Jesus: we are grateful to him for forgiveness and healing.

Actually, we have experienced what it is like to be a leper—not the physical affliction of Hansen's disease, which is a sickness like any other, but the "leprosy" which the storytellers have made grotesque and terrifying to the popular imagination. This is the leprosy which makes us feel "unclean," ugly, and outcast from human society. This is the experience of sin.

This "leprosy" (like the real Hansen's disease), is not immediately perceptible. Its first effect on us is just numbness. It doesn't become terrifying until we know we have it. Sin is the same. While we are committing sin we blind ourselves to its evil. The first effect of sin, too, is numbness: numbness to God, numbness to justice, to love, to the effect of our behavior on others and on ourselves. But when the reality of what we have done, and of what we have become through that, becomes evident to us, then we feel "unclean," ugly and outcast.

If this is not immediately evident, reflect on the sins you have recognized as such. Did you ever consciously, deliberately cheat someone? Lie to a friend? Take out your feelings on someone weaker than yourself? Stand by and let someone else suffer because you were afraid? Have sex without the total and permanent commitment sex expresses?

You may have been numb to the evil at the time you did any of these things, but when you realized what you were making of yourself, how did you feel? Unclean? Ugly? Alienated from people and from God? When we felt this way, weren't we unable to reach out for love and acceptance?

When we felt most deeply, most painfully, that no one else would want to have anything to do with us, that is when Jesus sought us out. His love for us is not conditional on how good we are, how attractive. He came to save us—and "saving" includes salvaging what is wrecked.

"Jesus" is the name God chose for himself when he came among us as a human being. It means "God saves." We appreciate its significance more when we think of all the other names God could have chosen to express what he intended to be for us. God could have called himself "Justice," for example, or "Avenging Sword." He could have named himself "Collector" and called in all our debts. He could have come just as "Advisor," pointing out the way for those who were ready to take it. Or as "Leader," calling to himself all who were strong enough to follow. But he chose to come as "Jesus," a name which means "God saves." And this is what he does for us: He saves us.

We have to respond, of course. We can't just go limp and wait for him to carry us off to heaven. But as long as we are willing to cry out for help and do the little we can do, his relationship to us is not "God advises," or "God points the way," or even "God helps," but "God saves."

The point of this Gospel is gratitude. Jesus is saying we need to be thankful for salvation. Why is that?

The reason is that gratitude makes our relationship with Jesus a constant, abiding reality. Without gratitude, we may be glad or relieved that we have been healed or forgiven, but we do not remain in contact with the one who saved us. Relief focuses on a past affliction; joy on a present state of well-being. But gratitude focuses on a person. Gratitude is the basis for an abiding relationship of love for Jesus Christ. And it is this relationship that saves us.

Reflecting on This Week's Gospels

Twenty-Eighth Week of the Year

Pray daily: Lord, thank you. Amen.

Monday: Luke 11:29-32: Jesus claimed, "Something greater than Solomon is here. Something greater than Jonah is here." Are you thankful for the gift of Jesus? How do you show it?

Tuesday: Luke 11:37-41: The Lord said, "Oh you Pharisees! Although you cleanse the outside of the cup and the dish, inside you are filled with plunder and evil. Do you know from experience what it is to go through religious gestures without really making them inside of your heart? How can you make every Mass, every use of the Sacrament of Reconciliation an encounter with Jesus that leaves you glad and grateful?

Wednesday: Luke 11:42-46: Jesus said, "Woe to you Pharisees! You pay tithes of mint and of rue and of every garden herb, but you pay no attention to judgment and to love for God. These you should have done, without overlooking the others." What religious acts do you do which are just acts of love and gratitude to God? Do you do anything conscious only that it is your duty?

Thursday: Luke 11:47-54: Jesus said, "Woe to you, scholars of the law! You have taken away the key of knowledge. You yourselves did not enter and you stopped those trying to enter." When you were younger, were you taught so much about avoiding sin that you did not really think about how to enter into personal relationship with Jesus? What is your focus now?

Friday: Luke 12:1-7: Jesus said, "I tell you, my friends.... Even the hairs of your head have all been counted. Do not be afraid. You are worth more than many sparrows." Are you aware of being loved by God? Are you grateful for his love? For the security he promises you? Do you thank him for placing so much value on you?

Saturday: Luke 12:8-12: Jesus said, "I tell you, everyone who acknowledges me before others the Son of Man will acknowledge before the angels of God. But whoever denies me before others will be denied before the angels of God." How do you acknowledge Jesus before others? Is it obvious you believe all your gifts and talents come from God? Do you ever pray publicly in thanksgiving when something good happens to you? Are you ashamed to?

Living This Week's Gospels

As Christian: At every Eucharist give thanks to God consciously for "the grace of our Lord Jesus Christ, the love of God, and communion in the Holy Spirit."

As Disciple: Be grateful for the word of God. It is given to help us know God and know how to live on earth. Show your gratitude by reading from the Bible every day.

As Prophet: Say grace after every meal, whether in public or in private.

As Priest: Make the Eucharist your personal act of thanksgiving to God by participating in every Mass fully, actively, consciously.

As King: Look around you at people who seem to have little to be thankful for, at least in some areas of their lives. See if you can change this.

Twenty-Ninth Sunday of the Year

Why Keep Asking?

Luke 18:1-8; Exodus 17:8-13; 2 Timothy 3:14 to 4:2

Nobody likes to be nagged or hounded. Parents get annoyed with a child who won't take no for an answer but keeps begging over and over for the same thing. But in this Gospel our Lord encourages us to do just that with the Father. "Keep asking," he says, "Bug him to death!" Why is that?

It could be that God invented the answering machine before we did, and he just filters out unwanted calls! But a better answer is that there are reasons why God sometimes delays answering prayers. And the first of these reasons is that we ourselves need to persevere in prayer.

A first principle in understanding God is that God always desires what is for our good—and not only for our good, but for our greatest good. He is a loving Father, not just an indulgent Father. And even when he gives us what we ask for, he does it in the way that will let us get the most good out of it.

A second principle is that what God responds to in prayer is faith. The more faith we bring to our prayer, the more God is liable to answer it. And the reason for this is already given in the first principle above: the best thing we can get out of our prayer, out of any prayer, is an increase in faith—and hope, and love. Nothing we ask for will benefit us as much, or for as long, as an increased sharing in God's divine life, which is grace, and which is measured on earth by faith, hope and love. Whatever increases faith, hope and love within us increases our sharing in God's divine life. Nothing we can ask for is better for us than this. And, as we will see below, persevering in prayer increases our faith.

Even when our prayer is that grace be given to another, the most loving way God can answer us is to let our prayer bring us to greater growth in grace at the same time it brings grace to the other. Of course, when we pray for someone else, another factor enters in: God won't force grace on anyone, and the other may not be ready to accept the grace we are asking God to give. Then we have to keep praying, not until God is ready to give, but until the other is ready to receive.

This last reason applies also to the prayer we make for ourselves: sometimes we ask God for graces we are not yet ready to receive. When that happens, God may make us wait, so that, by persevering in prayer, we will get more in touch with our own hearts, come to realize more clearly just what it is we want and how much we want it, and grow to a deeper faith and trust in God.

This brings us to our third principle: we grow in grace by letting grace express itself in our human acts. We grow in faith by expressing faith in action—and praying is one of those actions. We grow in hope by making choices based on trust in God's promises, choices which make clear that the good which God holds out to us is the good that we are most deeply hoping for in life. And we grow in love by giving expression to our love in deeds. Whatever moves us, then, to give expression to our faith, our hope, our love, is what helps us to grow in grace.

Among the things that move us most frequently to express our faith, our hope, our love, are our desires—those desires that drive us to go to God in prayer. If we are honest, we have to admit that without these desires we might hardly speak to God at all! The old saying, "If you want to learn to pray, go to sea" applies to more than sailors. We pray when we are in need, when we want something. And these needs, these desires push us to our initial contact with God. Later, when we have come to appreciate God more, we might seek him out just to read and reflect on his words, just to get to know him better. But this is a different level of prayer. The prayer Jesus talks about in this Gospel, however, is the prayer of petition. And persevering in the prayer of petition is a way to grow in grace: in faith, in hope and in love.

Reflecting on This Week's Gospels

Twenty-Ninth Week of the Year

> *Pray daily:* Lord, I know your love. I know you desire nothing more than to help me in every way I will accept. Teach me to trust you, and to grow in trust by praying to you constantly for everything I desire. I know that your answers will form your desires. Thank you. Amen.

Monday: Luke 12:13-21: Someone in the crowd said to Jesus, "Teacher, tell my brother to share the inheritance with me." He replied to him, "Friend, who appointed me as your judge and arbitrator?" Why did Jesus not answer this person's prayer? Do you ever feel in your prayer that you are asking for the wrong thing?

Tuesday: Luke 12:35-38: Jesus said, "Where your treasure is, there your heart will be also. Be dressed for action and have your lamps lit; be like those who are waiting for their master to return from the wedding banquet, so that they may open the door for him as soon as he comes and knocks." If this is the attitude and stance of your heart, what will you be praying for most of the time?

Wednesday: Luke 12:39-48: Jesus said, "From everyone to whom much has been given, much will be required; and from the one to whom much has been entrusted, even more will be demanded." How much knowledge of God's revelation have you been given, compared to the rest of the human race? How many do not know the Bible at all? How many have lost part of Christ's teaching by breaking off from the Church? How many have received only the barest religious instruction? Because of what you have known, what would God expect you to pray for?

Thursday: Luke 12:49-53: Jesus said, "I have come to set the earth on fire, and how I wish it were already blazing!" Do you share Jesus' desire? Do you feel it when you pray, "Thy kingdom come!'"? How much do you pray that the people in your family, your parish, where you work, where you live, will grow in knowledge and love of God?

Friday: Luke 12:54-59: Jesus also said to the crowds, "When you see a cloud rising in the west you immediately say, 'It is going to rain'; and so it happens.... You hypocrites! You know how to interpret the appearance of the earth and the sky; but why do you not know how to interpret the present time?" How much time do you spend listening to weather reports each day? How much do you spend reading the words of Christ which teach you to recognize what is going on in your world? Is it more useful to you to know about approaching storms or to understand the winds that are blowing across the Church in the wake of Vatican II?

Saturday: Luke 13:1-9: A man had a fig tree planted in his vineyard, and he came looking for fruit on it and found none. So he said to the gardener, "Cut it down." The gardener replied, "Sir, let it alone for one more year, until I dig around it and put manure on it." What fruit is our Lord receiving from you? Is it proportionate to the gifts of knowledge and grace he has given you? What could you do this year to increase your fruitfulness?

Living This Week's Gospels

As Christian: Each day this week say the Our Father, conscious that each petition echoes a desire of Christ's heart. Unite your desires to his.

As Disciple: Begin reading the *Catechism of the Catholic Church*, Part Four, entitled "Christian Prayer."

As Prophet: When you are with a group of people who profess to be religious, suggest you begin what you are doing with a prayer. Use only a prayer that is acceptable to all; for example, do not pray to Jesus with non-Christians present.

As Priest: Consciously offer up Jesus on the cross in Eucharist for the needs of your time, your circle of friends and acquaintances.

As King: Make prayer together a part of your family life. If you are not living in family, think about joining or forming a group that prays together.

Thirtieth Sunday of the Year

"At Least I'm Not a Hypocrite!" (Said the Pharisee)

Luke 18:9-14; Sirach 35:12-14, 16-18

W hen I was first ordained I was in a country where many people would come to confession only once a year, at Easter time, and they had no sins! They probably had not been to Mass since the previous Easter, but they didn't bother to mention that. If asked, they would say, "I don't go to Mass, but I'm not a hypocrite! The people who go to Mass, they talk about their neighbors, they lie, they cheat. I wouldn't do business with them. Mass I don't need, but I am a good Christian. I am faithful to my wife, I don't talk bad about anybody, and I am honest in my business. I am just not a hypocrite."

The strange thing is, they really didn't have any of the sins they saw as sin. I used to go through the ten commandments with them, and except for "keeping holy the Sabbath day" with Mass, they came up clean on every one. It puzzled me.

I am a slow learner. It took me two years to realize that I was seeing today's Gospel lived out in action. Only now the Pharisee is standing outside the Church saying, "Thank God I'm not like most people who call themselves Christian—grasping, crooked, adulterous—or like those hypocrites in there at Mass. I'm no Pharisee: I don't lie or cheat; I'm faithful to my wife. The last place I need to be is in there with them!"

And the people inside the Church, the ones who are supposed to be the Pharisees, what are they doing? They are lined up outside the confessional, saying, "God, be merciful to me, a sinner!"

The real Pharisees are the people who have only one sin: They don't love God. And they have never really experienced or accepted Jesus Christ as Savior, because they feel no need of him. They are upright, moral people who are satisfied they are doing perfectly well on their own. They feel no need for anything more.

Let's get a little closer to home. What of the people who do go to Mass every Sunday, because they know this is a law, but who feel no need for anything else? They don't come to adult religious formation sessions; they don't take part in programs for spiritual growth; they don't belong to any prayer group or study Scripture with anyone; they don't really take part in parish life except to do what is of obligation. And they are living upright, moral lives. They are not big sinners. But they get along without thinking too much about Jesus in their family, social, and professional lives. They have no sense of failing as Christians, and they feel no need for any more contact with Jesus Christ than they get at Sunday Mass. What about them?

Do you feel like you're being talked about? Can you identify with the kind of person described above? If so, think about this Gospel.

Keeping the law, keeping out of sin, is not what Christianity is all about. Christianity is a religion of intimate, loving relationship with God. Unless we are growing in understanding of the Father's mind, growing in loving intimacy with Jesus Christ as a person, becoming more like him in mind and heart and desire, becoming more and more committed to carrying out his mission on earth, we are not really living the Christian life. We are just law keepers. And we may be Pharisees. We should think about it.

The paradox is that the more we come to know Jesus Christ, and the more we draw near to him in understanding and in love, the more unworthy we feel! We feel loved, yes. Accepted, yes. Secure, yes. But the more we experience Christ's love, the less we feel we are returning it. The more we give ourselves to continuing his work on earth, the less we feel we are doing for him. Oddly enough, the closer we are to him, the more distant we sometimes feel, and the more need we feel for deeper, more frequent contact with him. That is when we stop being Pharisees, and when our Christianity comes alive.

Reflecting on This Week's Gospels

Thirtieth Week of the Year

Pray daily: Lord, speak to my heart of love. Teach me to show my love for you the way you showed your love for me: seeking me out, inviting me to intimate communion of mind and will and heart with you. Draw me to experience you in knowing you, and to know you in experiencing you. Amen.

Monday: Luke 13:10-17: "A woman was in the synagogue who for eighteen years had been...bent over, completely incapable of standing erect. When Jesus saw her, he...laid his hands on her, and she at once stood up straight and glorified God." Although you too are in church, are you in any way bent over, incapable of standing up straight in vigor and joy? Is it because you focus on laws more than on growing in love?

Tuesday: Luke 10:18-21: Jesus said, "To what shall I compare the kingdom of God? It is like yeast that a woman took and mixed in with three measures of wheat flour until the whole batch of dough was leavened." What is causing the level of your spiritual life to rise? What is the "yeast" that is working in you? What keeps you growing?

Wednesday: Luke 13:22-30: "Then you will begin to say, 'We ate and drank with you, and you taught in our streets.' But he will say, 'I do not know where you come from. Go away from me, all you evildoers!'" If Jesus were your pastor, how would he know you by name? Where would he see you and get to know you? When he teaches in the parish, are you there?

Thursday: Luke 13:31-35: "Jerusalem, Jerusalem, you who kill the prophets and stone those sent to you, how many times I yearned to gather your children together as a hen gathers her brood under her wings, but you were unwilling!" Could Jesus make this lament over you? When do you experience him "gathering you together" with others to nourish you? Is Sunday Mass sufficient for this?

Friday: Luke 14:1-6: Jesus said to them, "If one of you has a child or an ox that has fallen into a well, will you not immediately pull it out on the sabbath day?" When you examine your conscience or evaluate your religious observance, do you stop short after asking whether you are keeping all the laws? Or do you ask whether your way of keeping the laws is healing and nourishing people? Who is growing spiritually because of your help?

Saturday: Luke 14:1, 7-11: Jesus said, "When you are invited by someone to a wedding banquet, do not sit down at the place of honor...." What marks of prestige do you accept without thinking about it? Do you have a reserved parking place where you work? Do people address you by a title of honor? Do you accept service in shops and restaurants as if Jesus were serving you, washing your feet? How do you positively express your belief that affluence and position do not make you superior to anyone?

Living This Week's Gospels

As Christian: Begin each morning with conscious awareness of your need for Jesus as Savior. What will you need him for today at work, in your family and social life? How will you make him part of everything you do?

As Disciple: Decide when and how often you will use the Sacrament of Reconciliation, not just for forgiveness, but as a regular "progress report" and evaluation of your response to

God. Be as systematic about this as you are about business appointments: put it on your agenda, prioritize it, and assign a date and time.

As Prophet: During the Penitential Rite of the Mass, consciously identify with the tax collector Jesus spoke about: bow your head or strike your breast as a sign that you are present as a sinner in need of grace to change things in your life.

As Priest: As you start your activities each morning, recall the words of Jesus to Peter, "If you love me, feed my sheep." Be alert for opportunities to minister to others, conscious you are consecrated to this by Baptism.

As King: Each time you see something in the city that does not reflect the reign of Christ—substandard housing, derelicts camped out at bus stops, run-down neighborhoods, pretentious affluence in homes and office buildings, degrading advertisements—accept corporate responsibility with the rest of the Church for not having transformed the world yet. Ask God humbly to teach you how to be a faithful steward until Christ comes again.

Thirty-First Sunday of the Year

"Today Salvation Has Come to This House"

Luke 19:1-10; Wisdom 11:22 to 12:1; 2 Thessalonians 1:11 to 2:2

D id anyone ever ask you, "Are you saved?" What did you answer?

For Catholics, who tend to think in terms of theology, to be "saved" means to be in the state of grace. It means that one has heard the Good News, believed, and been baptized "into Christ," so that now one is incorporated into the Body of Christ as a live member, a sharer in the divine life of Jesus, a true child of the Father through identification with Jesus, the "only Son of the Father," and therefore an "heir to heaven"—one who looks forward to sharing in the everlasting glory which Jesus won for himself and for his Body on the cross.

For Catholics, to be "saved" simply means to be alive with divine life, the life of grace. Therefore, to be "saved" allows for degrees: one can be more or less alive. People in a coma are alive, but just barely. A fetus in the womb is alive but not fully developed—as is an adolescent. People crippled by accidents are alive but wounded. And people can be in perfect physical condition but only more or less aware of what it means to be a human being. To be "alive" means something very definite—one either is alive or one isn't—but it admits of degrees. So does the life of grace. One can be "saved" but just barely; saved and undeveloped as a Christian; saved and crippled or unaware of what it really means to be a sharer in the life of grace.

And one can have life and lose it. One can be "saved" and later lose salvation (divine life) by abandoning the life of grace.

Members of the more fundamentalist religions tend to think in terms of experience rather than of theology. For them, to be "saved" means to be aware of having consciously and deliberately decided to believe in Jesus in a moment of deep psychological awareness. A fundamentalist who asks, "Are you saved?" is not really asking whether you have the life of grace, but whether you are aware of it. (Many fundamentalists also believe that "once saved, always saved"—once you receive the life of grace you cannot lose it forever. In practice, however, this doesn't mean much, because if you continue to sin after being "saved," they say you were probably never saved in the first place but only thought you were. So they try just as hard to keep out of sin as we Catholics do!)

There is one point on which Catholics and fundamentalists agree: salvation is not what it should be until we are able to rejoice in it in an act of conscious and deliberate response to Jesus Christ. Jesus did not say to Zaccheus, "Salvation has entered this house" when he first walked through the door. He didn't say it until Zaccheus had responded to him.

Jesus didn't say Zaccheus was "saved" until Zaccheus had caught on and appreciated who Jesus was. Then Zaccheus responded to Jesus, not only with faith, but with enthusiasm. And he showed it by generosity. He showed his appreciation of Jesus, and of who Jesus was, by declaring that half of everything he owned would be given to the poor, and that anyone he had ever cheated would be paid back four times as much. He showed his appreciation in deeds, not just in words.

If we have really been "saved"—that is, if we have been evangelized, if we have truly heard the Good News, then this should be obvious through our enthusiasm and our generosity. If we really are aware of the gift we received at Baptism, we should be generously trying to extend this same gift to others in every way we can. We should be sharing our faith, our light, with everyone who is open to it or who might be open. We should be using actively and consciously all the gifts for ministry that God has given us. And we should use our material resources also to help extend the life of grace to others and to nurture it in those who already believe. The real sign that we have been evangelized is that we have become evangelizers.

Reflecting on This Week's Gospels

Thirty-First Week of the Year

> **Pray daily:** *Lord, you said, "This is eternal life, to know you, the only true God, and him whom you have sent, Jesus Christ." Teach me to respond to you so radically that I will know that I know you. Amen.*

Monday: Luke 14:12-14: "When you hold a banquet, invite the poor, the crippled, the lame, the blind." What do you do that is so different from what is taken for granted that you experience it as the grace of Christ in you?

Tuesday: Luke 14:15-24: "A man gave a great dinner to which he invited many... But one by one, they all began to excuse themselves." How much of Jesus' invitation have you accepted? What have you declined?

Wednesday: Luke 14:25-33: "Any one of you who does not renounce all your possessions cannot be my disciple." How does the proverb, "You get what you pay for" apply here?

Thursday: Luke 15:1-10: "There will be more joy in heaven over one sinner who repents than over ninety-nine righteous people who have no need of repentance." Why do converts often seem to appreciate the faith more than those baptized as infants? When did you discover your faith anew, or begin to live it on a deeper, higher level?

Friday: Luke 16:1-8: "The children of this world are more prudent in dealing with their own generation than are the children of light." What do businesses and advertisers do to keep people aware of how good their products are? What do you do to keep yourself aware of the Good News?

Saturday: Luke 16:9-15: "The person who is trustworthy in very small matters is also trustworthy in great ones." How much use do you make of what is available in the Church to help you grow in knowledge and love of God—Scripture, sacraments, daily Mass, talks, retreats? What more might God give you if you used these more?

Living This Week's Gospels

As Christian: Tell one person how you encountered or discovered Jesus Christ.

As Disciple: Write down the verse of Scripture that means the most to you.

As Prophet: Choose, find or make one symbol which to you expresses your own particular way of appreciating or living the Gospel (what could they use to identify your statue if you were declared a saint?).

As Priest: Each day consciously offer up one action, person, prayer, or intention to God as sharing in the priesthood of Jesus.

As King: If you were told to mark with a cross everything you have brought under the reign of Christ, what could you mark? (For example, a recovering alcoholic could mark a cross on a bottle.)

Thirty-Second Sunday of the Year

Faith Is Sharing in
God's Act of Knowing

Luke 20:27-38; 1 Kings 17:10-16; Hebrews 9:24-28

O ur Lord's answer to the Sadducees in this Gospel
brings out the difference between human knowledge
and faith.

The Sadducees had a question that was quite legitimate
from their point of view. They didn't believe in bodily
resurrection, and to support their position they wanted to
show how complicated things could become if everyone rose
from the dead. If a woman had married seven times, they
asked, which man would be her husband in heaven?

Jesus' answer amounts to saying that they just don't know
what they are talking about—literally. Life in heaven is so
different from life on earth that the human mind cannot even
begin to imagine it. And so, to understand the answer to their
problem, they would have to be raised to a whole new level
of understanding: God's level.

What we want to focus on is the fact that there is a level
of understanding higher than the human. The Sadducees'
mistake was to assume that what didn't—or couldn't—make
sense to them didn't make sense, period.

This is pride. Pride means to make yourself the criterion.
It is not pride just to think you are better than you are: That is
"conceit" or "vanity," and it is not a very serious fault. Pride
means to think that what you are, or do, or know, is the standard
to which everything else should conform. This amounts to
making oneself God, and it is the most deadly of all sins.

Victor Frankl once asked in a psychology seminar
whether a chimpanzee being used in painful experiments to
discover a cure for poliomyelitis could possibly find meaning
or value in its pain. He then asked, "Could it be that on a

plane of understanding higher than our own, human suffering has a meaning and value also?" Just to admit that possibility is to reject pride and be open to faith.

Christian faith, graced faith, is more than just the human act of choosing to believe something, the way one might choose to believe the weather report. Graced faith is a gift. It is a light enkindled within us by God, a power given to us, symbolized by the lit candle we are given at Baptism. Faith is a divine gift, and what it really is, is a sharing in God's own act of knowing. By faith we share in what God knows, because we share in his act of knowing.

Faith is an element of grace, and grace is a sharing in God's own divine life. If we share in God's life, then we share in what God does. And what God does, essentially, is know and love. So to share in God's life by grace is to share in his knowing by the gift of divine faith and in his loving by the gift of divine love.

The gift of faith is given to us for the same reason that the gift of grace is given to us: and that is not only so that we can enjoy divine life with God forever in heaven. It is also so that Jesus Christ can continue to live his divine life in us on earth, and continue in us the divine work of his redemptive ministry. Grace is not just a gift; it is a mission. To have grace is to be sent, as the Body of Christ on earth, to bring his divine life to the world.

In the same way, faith is not just a gift. It is a mission. The light given to us is a light given to be shared. To believe is not just to affirm a certain number of truths that make up Catholic doctrine, Christian revelation. To believe is to be in possession of God's own divine light; to share in the knowledge God has of himself and of Jesus Christ. It is to know God's divine plan for the redemption and fulfillment of the world. It is to have knowledge on a higher level than all human knowledge. It is to be in possession of the light needed to transform the darkness of this world. Anyone with a gift like this needs to share it, and that is our mission as Christians.

Reflecting on This Week's Gospels

Thirty-Second Week of the Year

Pray daily: Lord, you are the light of the world. And you have kindled your light within my heart. I want to see with your eyes, know with your mind, respond with your heart, and live your life to the full. Enlighten me, and act in me without reserve. Amen.

Monday: Luke 17:1-6: The Lord said, "If you have faith the size of a mustard seed, you would say to this mulberry tree, 'Be uprooted and planted in the sea,' and it would obey you." Is your faith just the static fact of believing a certain number of things, or is it a dynamic, active power working in you? How have you experienced your faith as a power?

Tuesday: Luke 17:7-10: Jesus said, "When you have done all you have been commanded, say, 'We are unprofitable servants; we have done what we were obliged to do.'" Does your faith make you the "light of the world" when you just keep the laws accepted by Christians, or when it lets you see things differently in the light of Christ? Do you consciously try to do this?

Wednesday: Luke 17:11-19: Jesus said to the leper who was cured, "Stand up and go; your faith has saved you." In practice, what experiences have you had of your faith saving you from something? Has it saved you from making mistakes? From continuing in a destructive or distorted path? From mediocrity? From experiencing meaninglessness in life?

Thursday: Luke 17:20-25: Once Jesus was asked by the Pharisees when the kingdom of God was coming, and he answered, "The kingdom of God is not coming with things that can be observed; nor will they say, 'Look, here it is!' or 'There it is!' For, in fact, the kingdom of God is among you." Do you get more excited by new private revelations than by reading the revelation always available to you in Scripture? Do you run to the newest devotions instead of seeking Christ in a steady use of Mass and the other sacraments?

Friday: Luke 17:26-37: Jesus said, "Just as it was in the days of Lot: they were eating, drinking, buying, selling, planting and building, but on the day that Lot left Sodom, it rained fire and sulfur from heaven and destroyed all of them—it will be like that on the day that the Son of Man is revealed." If Jesus came today, would he find you doing just what he described? If you knew he were coming, not today, but some time this year, what more would you be doing? When is he, in fact, coming for you personally?

Saturday: Luke 18:1-8: Jesus exclaimed, "But when the Son of Man comes, will he find faith on earth?" What about your faith? Is it a consolation to Jesus? Is it bearing the fruits he desires? Is it an active force in your life leading you to know him more deeply and serve him more constantly?

Living This Week's Gospels

As Christian: Write three adjectives that best describe to you the Jesus you have experienced in faith.

As Disciple: Discipleship (theology) is "faith seeking understanding." Make a list of what is available to help you understand better what you believe. Which means promises to be most helpful?

As Prophet: Consciously choose each day to do one thing which simply doesn't make sense without faith.

As Priest: Participate in the Mass one day this week and in faith offer up with Jesus on the cross the needs of your friends, your times, your world. Do this as sharing consciously in his priesthood.

As King: Express in action your faith that Jesus has "overcome the world" by trying to change one thing that needs to be changed at home, at work, or in your social life.

Thirty-Third Sunday of the Year

"I Will Give You Words and Wisdom"

Luke 21:5-19; Malachi 3:19-20; 2 Thessalonians 3:7-12

It may seem strange that out of a Gospel that speaks of wars, earthquakes, famine, plague, and persecution, the phrase we focus on is, "I will give you words and wisdom." But this is the point of the whole Gospel.

The point is that, even in the midst of the greatest catastrophes, our first focus should be, not on the catastrophes themselves, or on what is happening, but on how we can respond. How can we, "in good times and in bad," bear witness to Jesus Christ in action and in word?

When we watch the news, we should be aware during every minute of it that God is giving us "words and wisdom" to respond to what we see and hear. From the very first word that arises as a thought or feeling still unspoken within our hearts, to the words we may speak in commentary to anyone watching the news with us, to the "word" of action we speak through our attitudes and behavior as we go about our daily business influenced by our awareness of world events, our response should be a gifted response. "I will give you words and wisdom"—words and wisdom to respond to everything that is happening to you or around you in this world, words and wisdom to bear witness to me "in good times and in bad."

This is what Christian life is: responding with the words and wisdom of Jesus Christ to every human event, initiative and accident that comes within our consciousness; responding, not just with our own wisdom, but with his; responding, not with human words and actions only, but with divine words, divine wisdom, divine love. And the key to doing this is an awareness that we are gifted to respond. "I will give you (I have already given you) words and wisdom."

A key element, a necessary element, in our shared mission as Church is this awareness that we are gifted. We have accepted *koinonia*, oneness, with Jesus Christ and with each other in the mission of bringing God's life to the world. As individuals and as a parish, we have embraced a task to fulfill; we have accepted the responsibility of carrying on the mission and ministry of Jesus Christ in our time, in our particular place. Without constant awareness of the gifts we have been given, this task and this responsibility would be crushing.

But every single one of us is gifted, and as a community we are gifted, not only with "words and wisdom," but also in a variety, a multiplicity of ways. "To each person the manifestation of the Spirit is given for the common good" (1 Corinthians 12:7). "As each has received a gift, employ it for one another, as good stewards of god's varied graces" (1 Peter 4:10). We are gifted, not only adequately, but overabundantly. As Saint John tells us, God "does not ration his gift of the Spirit" (John 3:34).

We need to recognize these gifts—positively identify them and call them by name, "own" them. We also need to appreciate our gifts: to appreciate what our gifts say to us about God's love for us, his appreciation of us. We have to accept ourselves as gifted people, with everything this implies. And the first proof of our appreciation is gratitude.

If we are truly grateful for God's gifts, we will value them and use them. We will want to decide on particular, concrete ways to use our gifts to bring about the reign of God on earth. That is what our shared mission as Church is all about.

What are your own special gifts of ministry? Through Baptism and Confirmation you were consecrated and empowered to minister, both within the Church and to those outside the Church. And for this you received gifts that come directly from the Holy Spirit. What are they, and how will you use them? (For starters, read 1 Corinthians, chapter 12; and Romans, chapter 12, but these are just examples.)

Reflecting on This Week's Gospels

Thirty-Third Week of the Year

Pray daily: Lord, I believe you have given me special gifts to use in ministry to others. Help me to identify them, to accept them, and to use them for others as generously as you gave them to me. Amen.

Monday: Luke 18:35-43: Jesus asked the blind man, "What do you want me to do for you?" He replied, "Lord, please let me see." If you changed the question and asked, "Lord, what do you want me to do for you," what do you think he would answer?

Tuesday: Luke 19:1-10: Zacchaeus stood there and said to the Lord, "Behold, half of your possessions, Lord, I shall give to the poor, and if I have extorted anything from anyone I shall repay it four times over." Zacchaeus was so impressed with Jesus' acceptance of him that he gave half of his wealth to the poor. What do you have to give that is perhaps even better than wealth?

Wednesday: Luke 19:11-28: Jesus said, "A nobleman went off to a distant country to obtain the kingship for himself and then to return. He called ten of his servants and gave them ten gold coins and told them, 'Engage in trade with these until I return.'" What has Jesus entrusted to you to use in continuing his mission until he returns? How have you invested your gifts? What results can you show?

Thursday: Luke 19:41-44: As Jesus drew near Jerusalem, he saw the city and wept over it, saying, "If this day you only knew what makes for peace...." Have you ever felt like weeping for the same reason over your city? Your country? Your parish? Family? School? The place where you work? What gift or talent do you have for showing people the way to peace? How are you using it?

Friday: Luke 19:45-48: Jesus entered the temple area and proceeded to drive out those who were selling things, saying to them, "It is written, 'My house shall be a house of prayer, but you have made it a den of thieves.'" What do you see that should be and could be changed in your parish? Do you recognize it as a gift just to see this? How have you used that gift for the Church?

Saturday: Luke 20:27-40: Some of the scribes said to Jesus in reply, "Teacher, you have answered well." Has anyone ever said this to you when you answered questions about the faith? How have you used the gifts of intelligence and education to learn more about the faith so that you can share it with others?

Living This Week's Gospels

As Christian: Find, choose or create a symbol you can put where you will see it at work which expresses to you what is different about a Christian's basic attitude on the job.

As Disciple: Think of a situation that bothers you at home, at work, in your social or civic life. Try to find some words of Scripture that give you a new slant on it.

As Prophet: Think of something you believe God wants of you, but which you don't do because you "couldn't explain it" to your friends or co-workers. Do it and let God provide the "words and wisdom" to explain.

As Priest: "Deliver yourself up" to the risk of ridicule or disapproval for the sake of defending or helping someone else.

As King: Imagine Jesus is coming in triumph this week. What would you want to change in your environment at home, at work, in your social or civic life?

Thirty-Fourth Sunday of the Year

"This Is the King!"

Luke 23:35-43; 2 Samuel 5:1-3; Colossians 1:12-20

We celebrate the feast of Christ the King, oddly enough, by looking at Jesus hanging in apparent defeat on the cross. But if we understand what we are seeing, we will understand what we are celebrating. The image of Jesus as crucified King says it all.

This image tells us, first of all, that Jesus has triumphed; he is King. He has conquered sin and all the power and consequences of sin.

The very fact that he needed to triumph—and triumph in this way—tells us something else: Jesus is a King who is not acceptable to everyone. He is a contradiction and a threat to the attitudes and values of this world—and especially of those who have the most power and influence in the world. Jesus was not crucified by the weak, but by the strong.

This calls on us to ask where we stand: are we on the side of Jesus or on the side of his enemies? Or do we, at different times and in different ways, unconsciously support both sides?

Divided loyalty is the common human condition. It is the source of all sin and the very definition of idolatry. When we serve "two masters" (Matthew 6:24), letting Christ reign over some areas of our lives and something else reign over other areas, we break the First Commandment: "You shall not have other gods beside me." Divided loyalty led Pilate to hand Jesus over to death: "If you free this man you are no friend of Caesar" (John 19:12). We cannot serve Jesus Christ with undivided hearts and at the same time cling to money and power, or the approval of those who have both.

Christians do not believe that money and power are evil in themselves. We do not believe that Jesus rules over the "good" things of creation, while the devil rules over the "bad" things. We believe that Jesus is King over everything that is, money and power included. Everything that is, everything that is done, must be subjected to his wisdom, his teaching, his rule of love.

And so we consecrate ourselves to serving Jesus with everything we are and everything we have. Our every act should bear witness to him. Every word we speak, every choice we make, should extend the reign of his love.

This includes the choices we make in our use of material things. How much of the evil done in this world involves the use of material things? The use of drugs, the use of alcohol, the use of guns? Every time we drive a car we are using one of our material resources well or dangerously. Every time we spend money we are doing good or doing evil. Every dollar bill is a "vote": What we spend it on speaks of what we stand for, what we believe in, what we want to support on this earth.

It is in this context that we look at the mission we share as Church to establish the reign of Christ on earth. We want to use everything we have—our faith, our gifts of ministry, and our material resources also—to express our priorities, to say what we believe in. We have a very small voice in determining the national budget, or the priorities our country expresses as a nation. But many small voices become one large voice when they are all saying the same thing. There is a cynical expression, "Money talks." We believe that. And we believe that our own use of money can say whatever we want it to say—and can express our belief as a parish in the kingship of Christ.

What actually determines your use of material things? What has the most influence on your choice to buy or not to buy? To use something or not to use it? To use it in this way or some other way? Is it whim? What you feel like at the moment? The persuasion of an ad or a very effective store display? Is it an unrecognized acceptance of the values promoted in the media? Or is it a conscious desire to use what you have received from God to do the work of God?

Reflecting on This Week's Gospels

Thirty-Fourth Week of the Year

Pray daily: Jesus, you are Lord. You came to bring everything in heaven and on earth together into unity under your headship. I acknowledge your rule; I offer to you and surrender all I own, all my gifts and talents, all my time on earth, to be used in your service, to extend your reign. Amen.

Monday: Luke 21:1-4: Jesus noticed a poor widow putting in two small coins. He said, "I tell you truly, this poor widow put in more than all the rest...." Who are the biggest benefactors of the parish: those who give the most, or those who give the most that they can afford?

Tuesday: Luke 21:5-11: While some people were speaking about how the temple was adorned with costly stones and votive offerings, Jesus said, "All that you see here—the days will come when there will not be left a stone upon another stone that will not be thrown down." If everything you build up is going to be torn down, and all you acquire is going to be lost or destroyed eventually, what is the best use you can make of your possessions? Is it a waste to hold on to them until you die?

Wednesday: Luke 21:12-19: When he predicted persecution to his disciples Jesus said, "Remember, you are not to prepare your defense beforehand, for I myself shall give you a wisdom in speaking that all your adversaries will be powerless to resist or refute." How much do your fears for the future keep you from using what you have to do the work of God today? How much of this is prudence and how much just failure to trust in God?

Thursday: Luke 21:21, 24-27: Jesus said, "But when these signs begin to happen, stand erect and raise your heads because your redemption is at hand." What do you fear? Poverty? Sickness? Death? Are you free of fear because none of these things are threatening you right now, or because you know that none of them can harm you?

Friday: Luke 21:29-33: Jesus said, "Heaven and earth will pass away, but my words will not pass away." Are you more concerned about making money or about learning seriously the word of God? How much time and energy do you spend on each? Which will last you longer?

Saturday: Luke 21:34-36: Jesus said, "Beware that your hearts do not become drowsy from carousing and drunkenness and the anxieties of daily life, and that day catch you by surprise like a trap." Every night, when you go to bed, can you say that you have spent that day preparing for the coming of Christ? Do you say it?

Living This Week's Gospels

As Christian: As an expression of your acceptance of Jesus as Lord, decide to tithe: that is, to offer at Mass each week some percentage of your income "off the top."

As Disciple: Take some time away from one thing you do each day or week and dedicate it to learning more about Jesus and his words.

As Prophet: Give away or get rid of one thing you own as a sign that Jesus is worth more than all your possessions.

As Priest: Use something you own to help or minister to others: drive someone somewhere, give someone temporary shelter in your house, lend someone a tool or utensil.

As King: Examine your spending to see if you are "voting" with dollar bills for anything you really do not believe in. Decide what you want to vote for by your spending.

SOLEMNITIES
OF THE LORD

During the
Season of the Year

Trinity Sunday (Sunday After Pentecost)

"In the Image of God"

John 16:12-15; Proverbs 8:22-31; Romans 5:1-5

To say human nature was created "in the image of God" means that, basically, humans were designed to do what God does. And what God does is be, know and love. To be human is to be designed for a trinity of being, knowing and loving.

We know, not in the act of taking in sense impressions, but in the act of expressing a judgment about them. How many times have we stared blankly at a hodgepodge of shapes and colors, then suddenly perceived a pattern in them and said (in a judgment), "It's a _____!" The word that fills in the blank is the "word" of decision in which we "know" a being.

The "word" of knowledge is a word we actively "utter" or "breathe out." When we "give existence" to this word in our minds by saying, "It is!" we imitate the act by which God gives existence to a being by saying, "Let it be!" In this act we know what a being is by "recreating" it in our minds in a way that conforms to what it really is in existence.

From all eternity God the Father has been seeing and knowing himself. He knows himself in the act of uttering a "word of knowledge"—"God!" This "Word" which is the expression of what God is, is the Second Person of the Blessed Trinity, God the Son. This is the Word that was made flesh in Jesus.

As the Father knows the Son, and the Son knows the Father, the love they have for each other is the Holy Spirit. The mystery of the Trinity is that Being, Truth and Goodness exist in God as three distinct Persons. What "God" means is a Person who is, God the Father, knowing the truth of what he is and uttering this truth in a Word of knowledge, which is the Person of God the Son, the "Word," and loving the goodness of what he is in an act of love which is the Person of the Holy

Spirit. Three Persons who exist as one Divine Nature, one God: that is the Blessed Trinity.

When we see intelligibility in something—that is, see that something "would make sense" if understood to be put together the way it is for some purpose which would explain all the different parts, we can see that the thing really was designed precisely for this purpose, and was given being for that reason. Then we can give the thing a name, which is to know it as a being.

The key to it all is purpose. A bunch of stuff that just happens to fall together or get stuck together in a particular way, but without any intention or purpose in anyone's mind, is not anything—and we don't give it a name. It's just a pile of stuff. But if we judge that something was put together for a purpose which, to somebody at least, seemed good, then we can decide it actually is something and give it a name. To know something as a being, then, means that we see it as intelligible and as good, and make the judgment that it is actually being given existence as a single whole (a being) for the sake of functioning in the way which explains the presence and pattern of all its parts. Everything we judge to be a being has unity, intelligibility (truth) and purpose (goodness).

We are like God because we can perceive the truth of beings and "breathe out" that truth in a "word" of knowledge, as the Father utters his Word, the Son. And we can perceive the goodness of beings which comes from their purpose, from what they are able to do, and echo the creative act which brought them into being by giving them a name. We know God and ourselves in his image by doing what God does: being, knowing and loving.

By grace we know God through faith, accept him through hope as the purpose and goal of our lives, and affirm his goodness through love. By this we share in God's own life, which is to know and love himself as he is.

Reflecting on This Week's Gospels

Pray daily: Come, Holy Spirit, enlighten our minds and move our hearts, that we might all be one with each other, as you are with the Father and the Son, and Jesus prayed we would be. Amen.

Body and Blood of Christ (Corpus Christi)

Body, Heart of Christ

Luke 9:10-17; Genesis 14:18-20; 1 Corinthians 11:23-26

Jesus multiplied the loaves in the desert. God gave manna from heaven in the desert. What is the difference between the two events?

First, the multiplication of the loaves was a preview of the cross and the Mass. Saint Luke makes the connection clear by quoting the familiar words of the eucharistic liturgy: "Taking the five loaves, Jesus raised his eyes to heaven, pronounced a blessing, broke them, and gave them to his disciples...." The bread Jesus gives us is his own Body and Blood (compare with John 6:1-59), and he gives himself to us as nourishment in every eucharistic celebration (see Luke 24:30-35).

Second, the loaves Jesus multiplies don't just come down from heaven; they come from community sharing. Jesus came down from heaven to be the Bread of Life, but he comes to us now in a community celebration. And the full nourishing effect of that celebration depends on two things: the contribution made by each person there, and the multiplication of each person's gift by the grace of God acting through it. Jesus gives himself to us in the Mass in many ways: in the words of Scripture proclaimed; in the visible faith-expression of each one's presence and participation in the singing and prayer; in the making present of the Sacrifice of Calvary; in the gift of Communion. But by the time we receive the Body of Christ in Communion, we have already been prepared through an experience of communion with the Body of Christ celebrating in the rest of the Mass. The Bread Jesus gives us is his real presence, both in the bread that becomes his Body during the celebration and in the people who became his Body at Baptism. Both are the Body of Christ. We need communion with both to be fed in the desert.

If we celebrate this feast of Corpus Christi as we should, it should focus our attention on the love of Christ expressed in three ways: in the giving of his Body for us on the cross; in the giving of his Body to us in sacramental communion, and in the communion we have with each other in the Church as his real Body on earth. For that communion the expression of our love for each other is required.

This explains why our Lord asked that the feast of his Sacred Heart be celebrated on the Friday after Corpus Christi. The heart of Jesus shows us God loving us, not just from heaven, but on earth, in the flesh, in a visibly expressed human way. It reemphasizes the closeness and intimacy with God made possible through the Incarnation. It encourages us to think of Jesus as a human being, to reflect on what it means for him to love us in a human way as well as divinely. And it calls us to respond to his love as we would respond to another human person's love: by recognizing it, acknowledging it, returning it and expressing our response in physical, human ways.

Devotion to the Sacred Heart calls us to physical acts such as receiving communion, visiting our Lord in the Blessed Sacrament, spending time with him in the place where he expresses his love for us through his physical presence in the Eucharist. It calls on us to recognize that to ignore his presence on the altar is in fact an expression of ingratitude, whether it is intended as such or not. Devotion to the Sacred Heart, by focusing our attention on the human embodiment of Jesus' love for us, calls us to be aware of how important the human expression of our love is to him.

A "devotion" in the Church is simply a focus. Devotion to the Sacred Heart means a special focus on the heart of Christ in order to comprehend and respond to its meaning. If we look at the symbol of our Lord's heart—pierced and open on the cross or revealed to Saint Margaret Mary aflame with love for us and pierced with thorns of human ingratitude and sin—it leads us to physical acts of adoration and thanksgiving, to reparation for sin and to loving one another as he has loved us.

Reflecting on This Week's Gospels

Pray daily: Lord, you gave us the gift of your body
and blood to nourish our love. Give me hunger and
thirst for the fullness of love that is life. Draw me to
you in Eucharist. Amen.

Friday of Second Sunday After Pentecost
Sacred Heart of Jesus

Luke 15:3-7

"Who among you having a hundred sheep and losing one
of them would not leave the ninety-nine in the desert and go
after the lost one until you find it?" How has Jesus sought
you out? Has he only tried to save you from sin? To what
more has he invited you? How?

OTHER SOLEMNITIES and FEASTS

Which Replace Sunday

February 2 • Presentation of the Lord

Presenting Jesus and Ourselves

Luke 2:22-40 or 1:22-32; Malachi 3:1-4; Hebrews 2:14-18

We celebrate the Presentation of Jesus in the temple, not just on February 2, but every time we celebrate Mass together. At the Presentation of the Gifts, when the bread and wine are brought up and placed on the altar, we are being brought up. We are placing ourselves on the altar. It is the Catholic "altar call."

In some Protestant churches, especially during revivals, the preacher invites people to come forward after the preaching and "accept Jesus as their Savior," or "give themselves to Jesus." It is a moment of choice in response to the word of God. And it is an adult choice: all who come up are declaring their faith personally and choosing as adults to live in relationship with Jesus Christ.

In this custom the Protestants have kept—and changed in some ways—that moment of the Mass which we call the Offertory, which begins with the Presentation of Gifts, when the bread and wine are brought up and placed on the altar. Like the Catholic Offertory, the Protestant "altar call" takes place after the Scripture readings and preaching. And like the Offertory it expresses a personal, adult response. But there are some differences.

In the Catholic celebration, it is taken for granted that everyone who is present, participating in the Eucharistic celebration, has already been consecrated and made one with Jesus Christ by Baptism—and is, in fact, a priest, offering Jesus to the Father and offering himself or herself "in Christ" for the life of the world. Just to remind ourselves of this, we have restored an ancient custom: during one phase of the Rite of Christian Initiation of Adults, we ask all those who are preparing for Baptism to leave Mass before the Presentation of Gifts. This is to make the point that, in order to really participate in what takes place from the Offertory on, one has to be, not just in intention, but in fact, a "priest in the Priest," made one with Jesus—Prophet, Priest and King—by Baptism.

That is why we don't invite just a few people, those who choose, to "come up and accept Jesus." The whole congregation has already done that by Baptism. And so we invite all present instead to reaffirm their Baptism, to recommit themselves by sending up a host, a piece of bread, and wine to be placed on the altar and changed into the Body and Blood of Christ. In that act they express their participation in everything that will be expressed in the offering of the bread and wine during the rest of the eucharistic sacrifice. "Pray, brothers and sisters in Christ, that our sacrifice will be acceptable..." And the people answer, "May the Lord accept the sacrifice at your hands..." the sacrifice we make of ourselves in union with Jesus Christ. We offer ourselves with him and in him, as his real Body on earth.

The offering we make of ourselves by placing ourselves on the altar under the form of bread and wine has a very precise meaning. It is not just an act of "accepting Jesus" in general as our Savior, or of "giving ourselves to Jesus" in some vague way. In the Offertory we join ourselves to Jesus precisely and explicitly to be offered with him as "Lamb of God." As members of his Body on earth we declare ourselves included in his body on the cross. By identifying ourselves with Jesus offered in the Mass, we identify ourselves with everything he did and expressed on the cross.

We die to ourselves and to sin to live in Christ. We go down into the grave with Christ as we went down into the waters of Baptism, and we rise with him, leaving all our sins behind, to live a new life on earth. In Paul's words (see Romans 12:1-2), we "offer our bodies as living sacrifices to God." This means that wherever our live bodies are, we are sacrificed, offered, committed, to doing whatever Christ wants to do through us. We live now, no longer for ourselves, but that Christ might live through us. We live for his mission.

June 24 • Birth of John the Baptist

Luke 1:57-66, 80

"Then fear came upon all their neighbors, and all these matters were discussed throughout the hill country of Judea." How, as a community, do we nurture in each other awe at God's working in each person and in the Church?

June 29 • Peter and Paul, Apostles

Matthew 16:13-19

He said to them, "But who do you say that I am?" What do your actions say Jesus is for you?

August 6 • Feast of the Transfiguration

Transfiguration Into Jesus Christ

Luke 9:28-36

The Transfiguration was necessary because the apostles, dealing with Jesus in daily life, naturally tended to look on him as just a human being—an extraordinary man, the Messiah chosen by God, but still just a human being. In fact, Peter thought he was paying Jesus a wild compliment when he suggested putting up three shrines on the mountain to honor Jesus as an equal of Moses and Elijah. God the Father thundered from heaven in response to that idea! "This," he said, "is my Son!" Jesus is not on a plane with any other human being. He is divine.

And so are we by Baptism. Jesus said that the least one "born into the kingdom of God" is greater than John the Baptizer (Matthew 11:11), more a "brother and sister and mother" to him than his blood relations on earth (Matthew 12:50), and more blessed by Baptism than his own mother was just by giving him birth (Luke 11:28). Anyone baptized "into Christ" is a "son in the Son," able to call God "Father" as only a true child can do (Matthew 11:27 and Romans 8:14-17), and able to do what Jesus alone has power to do (Matthew 10:1, 20; John 14:12; 20: 21-23). By Baptism we are not just forgiven or made acceptable to God; we are transformed. We are made one with Christ, members of his Body, true children of the Father, sharers in divine life. We are a "new creation" (2 Corinthians 5:16-17; Galatians 3:23 to 4:7; Ephesians 2:15-22; 4: 15-24; Colossians 2:9-19).

When Jesus was transfigured, "his face changed in appearance and his clothes became dazzlingly white." When we were baptized, our "face"—our person, our identity— changed: we received a new name, a name given by God. And our clothes changed: we received the white robe of

Baptism, the "wedding garment," sign of our espousal to Jesus Christ (see Matthew 22:11; Ephesians 5: 22-33; Revelation 21:2) and of the risen life (Romans 6: 3-11; Colossians 2: 9-12; 3: 1-4; 1 Peter 1: 3-5). No one should ever again look upon us just as ordinary human beings. We are the Body of Christ, children of God the Father, temples of the Holy Spirit, the embodied presence of Jesus Christ on earth. Baptism was our transformation, and the various symbols of Baptism are our transfiguration: they are that which expresses and reveals this transformation to the world.

Because we live with ourselves in daily life we tend to forget this. We fall into the habit of seeing ourselves—and others—as just people, just human beings, just ordinary men and women, children and adults. This is to forget our Baptism. It is to be unaware of the transformation Baptism accomplishes.

To forget what we are is to forget how we should act. To forget what others are is to forget how we should deal with them. That is the source of all Christian sin. We do not act as the Body of Christ because we forget that is what we are. We do not treat others as the Body of Christ because we forget that is what they are. We need to work against this.

One way to do this is to make a deliberate effort to avoid those small, daily sins that implicitly deny it. An example is bad language: the reason it is "bad" is because of the disrespect it shows for our own dignity—for the human body in particular—and for the presence of God. Few people cuss in church because they are aware of God's presence there. To cuss anywhere is implicitly to deny God's presence in that place—and in our own hearts. To "cuss out" other people is to deny God's presence in them.

Another way is to deliberately build reminders into our day. Set your watch alarm to buzz every hour and recall then the presence of God. Put a holy water font by a door you use frequently and bless yourself each time you go through it. Form the habit of putting your hand on your heart (unnoticeably) frequently during the day, remembering who dwells there. Say a prayer before every action of the day. Wear a medal or crucifix. Be creative and stay aware.

August 15 • Assumption of the Blessed Virgin

A Prophetic Sign for Our Times

Luke 1:39-56; Revelation 11:19, 12:1-6, 10;
1 Corinthians 15:20-26

During the Vietnam conflict, a young marine named Philip Caputo saw bodies disintegrated by death. "These bodies will not rise again," he said, and lost his faith in God.

Caputo's book, *A Rumor of War*, is more than a reaction to the disintegration of the human body in death. It is also a cry of disillusionment over the disintegration of human society caused—whether Caputo would use the word or not—by sin. Caputo lost faith in the power of God himself to renew a society corrupted by sin. If God cannot renew society, then God cannot renew the human hearts whose blindness and selfishness are corrupting that society. Then there is no Savior and no God.

Caputo lost his faith because he saw one side of the picture, the dark side, more clearly than most people see it. He experienced the reality both of death and of disillusionment with the society he believed in. His faith, had he given it time, and the doctrine of the Assumption, had he understood it, would have shown him the other side of the picture.

The "Assumption" or "taking up" of Mary, body and soul, into heaven, is not something God did just to honor Mary. Everything the Church teaches about Mary has as its goal to teach us something about Jesus Christ. What the Assumption proclaims is Christ's triumph, not only over sin, but over all the consequences of sin, beginning with death. And the Assumption tells us that his triumph is not only for himself but for us. By preserving his mother's body from disintegration, Jesus gave us a sign of his power to raise our own bodies from the grave and restore them to perfect wholeness. The Resurrection of Jesus is the sign of his victory over sin and death. The Assumption of Mary is a sign that his victory is also our victory "in him." The Assumption tells us that the body of Jesus which rose from the dead included all those who would become members of that body by Baptism, and so the triumph of Jesus extends to all who are his Body on earth.

If we have triumphed over sin and death "in Christ," then Jesus is able to triumph over sin and death in us today. In us, and through our actions, he can triumph over all the consequences of sin in our world, both in individuals and in society as a whole. The same Jesus who can restore bodies disintegrated by death can also restore societies disintegrated by sin.

The Assumption of Mary, then, is a special sign for our times. It is a summons to hope, and a call to show hope in action by making efforts to renew society, to transform the social structures, the business policies, the cultural patterns of behavior, that are corrupting family and social life, business and government. The Assumption calls us to believe that Jesus can triumph over sin and all its consequences, not only in his own individual body, but also in and through all the members of his Body on earth. He can renew and restore society through our efforts. He can triumph through us.

Through the definition of this doctrine by Pope Pius XII in 1950, God made the Assumption a particular sign and message for our times. The Assumption is a sign of God's love for the body, for human flesh. God did not treat Mary's body as if it were just the "wrapper" of her soul—something to throw away when he took her soul into heaven. Through the Assumption God proclaims that all human flesh is sacred to him. Our age, on the other hand, is an age of contempt for the human body, shown in nuclear devastation, violence, war, oppression, torture, pornography, abortion, the death penalty and easy sex. So ours is the age to which God has given the sign of the Assumption: a prophetic sign summoning us to recall society to respect for human flesh: calling us to dedicate ourselves to bringing about peace, justice and reverence for everything that touches human life. If we believe in the Assumption, we will work with courage to renew our disintegrated world.

September 14 • Exaltation of the Cross

John 3:13-17

Indeed, God did not send the Son into the world to condemn the world, but in order that the world might be saved through him. How can you respond to people who annoy you in a way that saves and does not condemn?

All Who Have This Hope

Matthew 5:1-12; Revelation 7:2-4, 9-14; Psalm 24:1-6;
1 John 3:1-3

E ach of us at Baptism was dressed in a white robe and
heard the words, "You have been transformed into a
new creature and have put on Christ. May this white
garment be for you a sign of your new dignity as a Christian....
Keep it unstained for eternal life."

The book of Revelation describes "a huge crowd from
every nation, race, people and tongue" standing before the
throne of the Lamb "dressed in long white robes and holding
palm branches in their hands." And John, who saw the vision,
was told: "These are the ones who have survived the great
period of trial; they have washed their robes and made them
white in the blood of the Lamb" (see Revelation 7:9-14).

The letter of John tells us that the white garment is a sign
of hope. Because we have "put on Christ"—that is, become
members of his Body through Baptism, sharing in his divine
life—we are not only called, but we are "children of God."
We are, in Christ, not only human but divine. This is our
"new dignity" as Christians. But even we cannot grasp or
appreciate the full reality of what this is. We live in hope of
experiencing completely what it means to be united with
Christ in one ecstatic sharing of his life and ours. The "white
garment" which each of us wears—invisibly but truly—is a
sign and reminder of that hope.

The white garment is also a bridal dress (see Revelation
19:7-8; 21:2). And this explains how we will enter into the
full experience of what it means to be one with Christ. A
wedding dress is a pledge of nakedness. And John says that
we will know what we have become through Baptism, what it
means to be one with Christ, when we "see him as he is."
When all the barriers are dropped, and all the veils are

removed, then we "shall know even as we are known" (see 1 Corinthians 13:12). When we see Jesus as he is, in all his truth and majesty as God and man, and experience our own being through union with his, we will "know as we are known." And "we shall be like him"—totally given over, surrendered to all that he is and wants to be in us, to all that he gives and takes from us in passionate union with him— "for we shall see him as he is." We will "know" him in the Scriptural sense of experiencing the reality of another in a mutual self-giving without reserves (see the literal translation of Genesis 4:1; Luke 1:34).

All who "have this hope," says John, "keep themselves pure, as he is pure." To keep the white robe, the wedding garment, "unstained for eternal life" means to fix our hearts without mixture, purely, on Jesus Christ like the bride longing for the bridegroom (see Psalm 42:1-4; 63:1-9; 73:25-26; Matthew 9:15; 25:1-13). It is the awareness of being espoused to him, and the anticipation of total union with him in the consummation of the wedding feast (Revelation 19:7-9), which inspires and strengthens us to "keep ourselves pure" for him "as he is pure" and unmixed in his love for us.

We celebrate the victory and the holiness of the Saints as a way of reminding ourselves of what we are, are called to be, and will be. We recognize in the saints a goodness, a love, a strength, an enlightenment that is more than just human. The saints surrendered so passionately to God living within them that the effects and power of his grace, his life in them appeared in their actions to a striking degree. That is why they were declared saints.

Saints are not different from us except in degree. We share in the same divine life that enlightened, enflamed and empowered them. The grace that appeared in their actions also appears in ours, if less impressively. We wear the same white garment they wore and are destined for the same palm of victory, the same ecstatic union with God. We celebrate the Saints and remember their great deeds to remind us of the power of grace and the promise it holds out to us. They focus our desire and excite our hope.

November 2 • Commemoration of the Faithful Departed (All Souls)

John 6:37-40

"For this is the will of my Father, that all who see the Son and believe in him may have eternal life, and I shall raise them on the last day." Does God desire your salvation more than you do? Does Jesus? How do you know this?

November 9 • Dedication of the Lateran Basilica

John 2:13-22

Jesus made a whip out of cords and drove them all out of the temple area, with the sheep and oxen, and spilled the coins of the money-changers and overturned their tables, and to those who sold doves he said, "Take these out of here, and stop making my Father's house a marketplace." How much respect do you have for church buildings as such? Why? How do you personally show respect when you are in church?

FEASTS and
SAINTS' DAYS

January 25 • Conversion of Paul, Apostle

Mark 16:15-18

Jesus said, "Go into the whole world and proclaim the gospel to every creature." Why do these words call you into relationship with every other person on earth? How do you make that relationship real?

February 22 • Feast of the Chair of Peter

Matthew 16:13-19

When Jesus went into the region of Caesarea Philippi he asked his disciples, "Who do people say that the Son of Man is? Who do you say that I am?" How would you answer this question? What is Jesus for you? God? Friend? Teacher? Leader? Spouse? How do you relate to him mostly?

March 19 • Joseph, Husband of Mary

Matthew 1:16, 18-22, 24 (or Luke 2:41-51a)

"Now this is how the birth of Jesus Christ came about. When his mother Mary was betrothed to Joseph, but before they lived together, she was found with child through the Holy Spirit." Joseph accepted to live with Mary, his true wife, as her brother all their life together. It was his contribution to saving the world. Do you think it was worth it? How are the sacrifices in your life the price you pay for helping to save the world? Is it worth what it costs you?

March 25 • The Annunciation of the Lord

Luke 1:26-38

"Behold, you will conceive in your womb and bear a son, and you shall name him Jesus." Do you believe you are called as truly as Mary was to "conceive thoughts" in your head through the seed of Christ's word, and "bear fruit" by giving them flesh in action? How do you open yourself to his words?

April 25 • Mark, Evangelist

Mark 16:15-20

"But they went forth and preached everywhere, while the Lord worked with them and confirmed the word through accompanying signs." Is this a description of your life? How are you exercising priesthood?

May 3 • Philip and James, Apostles

John 14:6-14

"Amen, amen, I say to you, whoever believes in me will do the works that I do, and will do greater ones than these, because I am going to the Father." What are the "works of Jesus" that you do as his priest?

May 14 • Matthias, Apostle

John 15:9-7

"I have called you friends, because I have told you everything I have heard from my Father." How do you recognize someone's friends? Is it obvious you are Christ's friend?

May 31 • Visitation

Luke 1:38-56

"For at the moment the sound of your greeting reached my ears, the infant in my womb leaped for joy." Are you conscious of bearing the presence of Christ to others in all your encounters?

June 11 • Barnabas, Apostle

Matthew 10:7-13

"Go, make this proclamation: 'The kingdom of heaven is at hand.' Cure the sick, raise the dead, cleanse lepers, drive out demons." Who have you healed, raised up, purified, made free? Do you keep trying, conscious of what you are?

July 3 • Thomas, Apostle

John 20:24-29

Then Jesus said to Thomas, "Put your finger here and see my hands, and bring your hand and put it into my side, and do not be unbelieving, but believe." In how many ways has Jesus met you more than halfway?

July 22 • Mary Magdalene

John 20:1-2, 11-18

She ran to Simon Peter and to the other disciple, and told them, "They have taken the Lord from the tomb, and we don't know where they put him." When Jesus seems absent from your life, where, how can you find him?

July 25 • James, Apostle

Matthew 20:20-28

The mother of the sons of Zebedee approached him, wishing to ask him for something. He said to her, "What do you wish?" What do you ask Jesus for? For yourself? For those you love?

July 29 • Martha

John 11:19-27

Martha said to Jesus, "Lord, if you had been here, my brother would not have died." What idea of Jesus as Messiah did Martha have when she said this? Did it change as Jesus spoke?

August 10 • Lawrence, Deacon and Martyr

John 12:24-26

"Unless a grain of wheat falls to the ground and dies, it remains just a grain of wheat; but if it dies, it produces much fruit." How does the offering of myself with the bread and wine express a dying to self?

August 24 • Saint Bartholomew

John 1:46-51

"Do you believe...? Amen, I say to you, you will see the sky opened and the angels of God ascending and descending on the Son of Man." If you believe Jesus is the "ladder" between earth and an open heaven, how does that change your view of life?

September 8 • Birth of Mary

Matthew 1:1-16,18-23

"She will bear a son and you are to name him Jesus, because he will save his people from their sins." Do you believe that every time you listen and live Jesus' words you are giving him birth within you? Do you see his saving power at work in and through your words and actions?

September 15 • Our Lady of Sorrows

John 19:25-27

When Jesus saw his mother and the disciple there whom he loved, he said to his mother, "Woman, behold, your son." How did Jesus' death enable him to give you Mary as your mother? To what must you die to be "brother and sister and mother" to others?

September 21 • Matthew, Apostle and Evangelist

Matthew. 9:9-13

"I desire mercy, not sacrifice. I did not come to call the righteous but sinners." Why does God prefer having mercy to exacting justice? What is his goal? What did he want when he created us? How does he get it?

September 29 • Michael, Gabriel and Raphael, Archangels

John 1:47-51

"You will see the sky opened and the angels of God ascending and descending on the Son of Man." Do you believe that by "dying" to old attitudes and values in faith you will see marvelous things? Like what?

October 2 • Guardian Angels

Matthew 18:1-5, 10

Jesus said, "Whoever becomes humble like this child is the greatest in the kingdom of heaven." Do you believe you will be happier by becoming "humble" (having no more prestige than a little child) or by becoming "important"? Why?

October 18 • Luke, Evangelist

Luke 10:1-9

"The harvest is abundant but the laborers are few; so ask the master of the harvest to send out laborers for his harvest." What work or responsibilities are you most conscious of each day? Do you think of them as establishing the kingdom of God? Do you perform them as a laborer for Christ in his vineyard?

October 28 • Simon and Jude, Apostles

Luke 6:12-16

"He called his disciples to himself and chose Twelve, whom he also named apostles." To proclaim the truth you have to see the truth. Do you believe in Jesus enough to want to see and spread everything he teaches?

November 30 • Andrew, Apostle

Matthew 4:18-22

"At once they left their nets and followed him." How is "following" Jesus different from just keeping God's law? What are you willing to "leave" to follow him more closely?

December 12 • Our Lady of Guadalupe

Luke 1:39-47

Elizabeth cried out, "Most blessed are you among women, and blessed is the fruit of your womb." How is the fruit of your life blessed? How does your life bear divine fruit?